MOTOR CITY MUSIC

Motor City Music

A DETROITER LOOKS BACK

Mark Slobin

OXFORD
UNIVERSITY PRESS

OXFORD
UNIVERSITY PRESS

Oxford University Press is a department of the University of Oxford. It furthers
the University's objective of excellence in research, scholarship, and education
by publishing worldwide. Oxford is a registered trade mark of Oxford University
Press in the UK and certain other countries.

Published in the United States of America by Oxford University Press
198 Madison Avenue, New York, NY 10016, United States of America.

© Oxford University Press 2019

Library of Congress Cataloging-in-Publication Data
Names: Slobin, Mark, author.
Title: Motor City music : a Detroiter looks back / Mark Slobin.
Description: New York, NY : Oxford University Press, 2019. | Includes bibliographical references and index.
Identifiers: LCCN 2018011265 (print) | LCCN 2018013204 (ebook) | ISBN 9780190882099 (Updf) |
ISBN 9780190882105 (Epub) | ISBN 9780190882082 (cloth) | ISBN 9780190882112 (online component)
Subjects: LCSH: Music—Michigan—Detroit—History and criticism. |
Music—Social aspects—Michigan—Detroit—History.
Classification: LCC ML200.8.D3 (ebook) | LCC ML200.8.D3 S56 2018 (print) | DDC 780.9774/34—dc23
LC record available at https://lccn.loc.gov/2018011265

9 8 7 6 5 4 3 2 1

Printed by Sheridan Books, Inc., United States of America

For Dan, who was there first.
Played piano to my violin; my best friend today.

Contents

Acknowledgments

I BEGAN RESEARCH on Detroit's music a shade late—several friends and prominent people had already passed from the scene. Calling people I had not talked to in over fifty years was a great pleasure, as was getting to know the thoughtful and generous musicians and keepers of tradition who shared their memories and insights with me, including these: Judy Adams, Greg Adamus, Pheeroan akLaaf, Geri Allen, Darrel Barnes, Robert Barnes, Harriet Berg, Peter Bernard, Kenny Burrell, Herb Boyd, Regina Carter, Lydia Cleaver, Norm Diamond, Dwight Edwards, Jorja Fleezanis, Natasha Foreman, Paul Gifford, Rodney Glusac, Kenneth Goldsmith, Harold Hagopian, Judith Hamera, Chris Hinderaker, Sally Howell, Ralph M. Jones, Jeff Karoub, Kim Kashkashian, Ani Kavafian, Hachig Kazarian, Arnie Kessler, Irene Kytasty Kuzma, Julian Kytasty, Petro Kytasty, David Levine, Philip Levine, Bill and Yvonne Lockwood, Cary Loren, Gaelynn McKinney, Gordon Mumma, Robert Newkirk, Bruno Nettl, Karen Palmer, Leonard Pitt, Dan Pliskow, Anne Rasmussen, Paul Riser, Harvey Robb, Jerome Rosen, Adam Rudolph, Pete Rushefsky, Ann Saslav, Paul Schoenfield, Leah Shelleda, George Shirley, Joseph Silverstein, Donald Sinta, Rita Sloan, Oren Sushko, Neal Stulberg, Freddy Sweet, David Syme, Patricia Terry-Ross, Lily Tomlin, Blue Gene Tyranny, George Tysh, Don Was, Hayden White, and Crystal Williams. My Detroit-area cousins Ruth and Jim Grey and Barry Nemon and Barbara Stark-Nemon have been very supportive. Jim's archival contacts helped, as well as his reconnecting me with the Tigers. Art Lieb, David Goldberg, and Yossi Chajes supplied helpful source materials.

My brother Dan has been an invaluable advisor—being nearly four years older, he remembers things about family and community that stretch beyond my knowledge, and his photographic memory for detail makes him an expert witness. My parents, Judith and Norval Slobin, offered endless support and a storehouse of songs. My daughter Maya, an editor, is an always helpful interlocutor. After 53 years of publications, I finally need to thank my Detroit junior high- and high-school journalism teachers, Mrs. Browning and Mr. Gow, for strict training in the craft and discipline of writing. Al Young has been an inspiration through his creative work, the long insightful talks we had in Berkeley, and his response to the manuscript.

Kathy Makas at the Benson Ford Research Center, Christo Datini at the General Motors Archive, the staff of the Walter Reuther Archives of Labor History, and Marian Krzyzowski of the University of Michigan were extremely generous and helpful in supplying and recommending sources, as were Judith Gray and Nancy Groce at the Center for American Folklife. For material on the Jews, the staff of the Detroit Jewish Community Archives and the Michigan Jewish Historical Society are a boon to researchers. Grace Earl supplied newspaper data, Abigail Shneyder and Isadora Dannin did GIS maps, Jennifer Caputo helped with a translation, Ian MacMillen supplied background, and Jonathan Schwartz offered his father's poetry. For readings of chapter drafts, I'm grateful to Jim Leary, Deborah Dash Moore, and Lila Corwin Berman. As always, Jeff Titon and James Clifford offered insights, and Dick Spottswood his invaluable tips on performers and pieces. Dan Georgakas offered sources and a helpful reading. Carleton Gholz and Denise Dalphond, founders of the Detroit Sound Conservatory, offered my first forum for a talk, in 2013, and deserve great credit for their recuperation initiatives. Special thanks to the Society for Ethnomusicology for inviting me to deliver the Charles Seeger Distinguished Lecture for 2014, which pushed me to formulate my ideas at an early stage, and to Ellen Koskoff for publishing the resulting article in *Ethnomusicology*. The two anonymous readers from Oxford challenged my thinking constructively.

Wesleyan was extremely generous over my forty-five years of teaching, with frequent sabbaticals and stays at the Center for Humanities. The colleagues I talked to about diaspora and American music were invaluable for my work: David McAllester, Gage Averill, Su Zheng, Eric Charry, Neely Bruce, Jay Hoggard, Khachig Tölölyan, and Richard Slotkin. Semester by semester, my students, undergraduate and graduate, stimulated my thinking and offered a stable space for inquiry and creativity at the highest level. Many of their personal projects were inspiring.

MOTOR CITY MUSIC

1   A City in Motion

DETROIT IS HARD to figure. The earliest inhabitants, indigenous tribes, called it The Strait of the Coast. In 1701, an upstart French aristocrat settled a bunch of Norman farmers onto a strait—*détroit*—but that's called a river now. With their backs to Canada, they headed north, which seems odd. Even in French, switching from an island called Isle aux Cochons to one called Belle Isle seems willful—pigs to beauty. The local Red River (sounds western, right?) is called the Rouge River or River Rouge. A huge parkland, it lost ground to the largest factory ever built—a hundred thousand workers from all parts of America and the world.

This American city was always restless and very violent. Historian Tiya Miles's description of eighteenth-century Detroit rings true even today: "a place of overlapping borders—natural, cultural, and political—where peoples of various backgrounds struggled to make their lives in a context of growing economic disparity and political volatility." There's not much to read about the early musical life, though there's a grim anecdote from 1821 about two Indians, Kewabis and Ketauka, who were about to be hanged for killing a couple of white citizens. They called for a piece of rawhide and made a drum out of a pail. "One of them sat down on the floor and began beating the drum with his fingers. . . . The other, standing with his face to the sky before the open window, chanted his death song." A few years later, it was the turn of Stephen Simmons, a white man convicted of killing his wife. At his public execution, "in a strong baritone voice," he sang a familiar hymn, including these lines: "My crimes are great, but can't surpass / The power and glory of Thy grace." We don't have any accounts of music in the more communal moments of violence that marked early Detroit, but it is the only one occupied three times by federal troops—someone must have been singing. The city kept burning down, accidentally or deliberately. Famously, its motto offers the hope "that something better will rise from the ashes." After one fire, the city fathers voted for an urban design based on the rational French layout of Washington, D.C.: a small hub with three long avenues radiating diagonally and indefinitely into the flats of the Northwest Territory. One was named for a Frenchman—Gratiot, pronounced *grashit*; one for an Anglo judge, Woodward; and one just plain Michigan Avenue. They added Grand River, a road on the site of a no longer running river. None of these actually starts at the hub, and the town proceeded in all directions, on the usual grid, ballooning to the vast scale of 139 square miles.

But around 1900, Detroit was just a mildly prosperous, well-located city on a waterway, building ovens. Music was a significant industry in those small-scale days. There were a number of piano companies, and Jerome Remnick (1867–1931) was the largest sheet music publisher in the world and biggest music retailer in the United States. In 1914, a journalist compared Detroit to Buffalo and Cleveland. Among those three "sisters," Detroit was "the belle of the family," with a "sweet domestic kind of beauty, like that of a young wife."

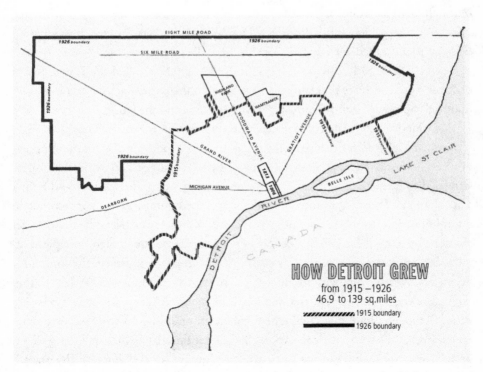

FIG. 1.1. Detroit's startling expansion as the auto industry exploded. Drawing: David Schorr

But even as this journalist was writing his squib, a handful of daring entrepreneurs decided this was exactly the place to create the latest advanced product in America's march to world industrial dominance: the automobile. The city rose by expanding the one industry that changed the American way of life the most. The population doubled from 1910 to 1920 and just kept doubling, as tens of thousands of immigrants piled in to take advantage of the vast new factories. They were mostly Europeans, but some came from Turkey and Afghanistan. Factories sprang up like giant mushrooms, on a scale never seen before. Detroit was an upstart city, not like Pittsburgh or Cleveland, which had nineteenth-century histories built on steel and oil. This had implications for cultural life. A Rockefeller could be the patron for the Cleveland Museum of Art, while Detroit had to wait decades for auto barons to catch on. Meanwhile, Chicago carried many industries on its legendary broad shoulders and grew to second-city size. There, a nationally important African American theater was up and running by 1906, and a growing black middle class enjoyed "race film," an exciting modern form of self-expression. All of this came before the massive tide

FIG. 1.2. Civic music and recreation in the "sweet domestic" city of 1903. Belle Isle, the working-class recreational refuge. Postcard courtesy Leonard Pitt.

of black workers flowing into Detroit's factories. It's surprising that a late-blooming, single-minded city could so quickly jump to fourth rank in population.

It changed its nature just as fast. A few years after that 1914 "young domestic wife" quote, here's how another journalist described the Detroit of the early 1920s:

In Detroit you find the consummation of the salesman's ideal. [The housing] is as alike, as cheap, as ephemeral, as quantitatively produced as the Ford to which they owe their presence. . . . In the spring, one sells one's house and buys another. These places are built not to be lived in, but to be sold. Detroit is coming to be a city sweet to the eye and satisfying to the intelligence of the salesmen and mechanics who inhabit it. One of the boosters selling you his city may ask you, after dinner, whether you like music . . . [but] the Orchestra has a deficit every year, and the public is asked to subscribe because as the jazz-adoring salesman tells you it will be a wonderful advertisement for the city.

Sunday afternoons Detroit gets in its car and goes riding. . . . On his Sabbath outings [the salesman] drives fast, taking the same straight, flat roads after work, the roads everybody else takes. When he gets home he squints at the speedometer to see if he has had a good time; how many miles has he traveled?

This account skips over the horrors of factory life, staying with the story of the rise of the salesman and managerial classes. At the peak of the industrial age, the great photographer Robert Frank launched the 1955 trip that would become his classic work, *The Americans*, and he saw—and heard—it differently: "I went to Detroit to photograph the Ford factories, and then it was clear to me I wanted to do this. It was summer and so loud. So much noise. So much heat. It was hell. So much screaming."

I was born in 1943, between the salesmen and the screaming, into a striving family, comfortable in its ethnic enclave and leaning toward professionals, not businessmen or workers. It was a crazy period for Detroit. Hundreds of thousands of white and black southerners made the journey on closely watched trains or just up the highway from Appalachia, the joke being that they taught the three Rs in Kentucky and Tennessee: "Readin', Ritin', and Route 23." These immigrants were working in the "arsenal of democracy," as the president called it, and were turning out one bomber plane every hour. But they were leading a miserable life around the huge Willow Run factory, as described graphically by the *Washington Post* in 1943 a few days before I was born:

Today I saw one of these houses in which the original family of five live on the first floor, five men sleep in the basement, four on the second floor, nine in the garage, while four crowded trailers are parked in the back yard. The ground is flat, badly drained, covered with refuse whose filth, mingled with stagnant water, seeps rapidly into the ground around the well.

Most of the African American population was crowded into a neighborhood near the river, where my father was teaching in the all-black high school, and if they tried to move out, they were under siege in the next neighborhood, often the target of violence. When I was three months old, Detroit was a pressure cooker with the heat turned on too high. It exploded in the great wartime race riot of 1943. I was with my family at the epicenter of the riot, the beautiful park of Belle Isle, designed by Olmsted of Central Park fame. We spent countless idyllic hours there in the canoe canals and listening to civic music at the bandshell. It is typical of Detroit that a place so lovingly planned for pleasure descended into chaos at a moment of wartime crisis, then bounced back to its placid peacefulness. Figure 1.3 shows me there with my parents and brother Dan.

No one was in Detroit more accidentally than I. It was only because my great-uncles succeeded in the city that my mother's family could find a home. They were living in Romania as refugees from troubled Ukraine when they got practically the last visas to the United States, in 1922. Otherwise, I would not have appeared at all, except in some incarnation in Buenos Aires. But my father jumped the gun—he was actually born in Detroit in 1911, and even his mother was New York born. This sense of staggered entrance on the social stage continued to mark the drama that was Detroit.

FIG. 1.3. The Slobins on Belle Isle on the day that the 1943 "race riot" started there. Author photo.

This was a chaotic scene, and everyone was improvising. Detroit has been called "the capital of the twentieth century" for aggressively defining modern industrial life, "being in a state of continuous flux, with as few stagnant moments and interruptions as possible." It changed the lives of the people we knew, helping to break up the old neighborhood. From 1910 on, corporations, city managers, and average citizens had to make things up as they went along, as the city limits kept pushing ever farther north, east, and west, and new neighborhoods sprang up with amazing speed. Unlike other industrial cities with older housing stock, Detroit could accommodate the American ideal of single-family houses, with lawns and garages, no matter how small the square footage. The rate of home ownership was double that of any other place, but it was all carefully segregated, supported by hardened, racially biased government-backed financing structures. This unevenness marked every facet of life, and it was policed with precise brutality. At the same time, the city drew people looking to have an impact, to be at the center of social, musical, and even religious change, like the Reverend C. L. Franklin, a dominant Detroiter (and father of Aretha) who left placid Buffalo in 1946 because, he said, "I wanted to be in a city where there were crossroads of transportation: trains, planes, where people were coming and going, conventions of all kinds, and migrations. A city that is not static in its growth."

As Reverend Franklin saw, transportation and rapid change were linked. Like every household, our family was shaped by the automobile, the machine that made the metropolis. The workers bought the product they constructed, and the automobile introduced its own logic, spawning the snaking of expressways to the new suburbs and the invention of America's first shopping center, Northland, in 1954, which opened the week I turned eleven. That marked the victory march for the car, which already by the 1920s "came to stand for the rights of private property and personal choice, getting the upper hand over the streetcar, a public service." My father knew how to take apart his first Model T back in the early 1930s. But in my early years, we still lived in both transport worlds, taking the streetcar and the bus. One of our home movies even captured a horse-propelled junkman in the alley out back. Foot traffic was still strong, up to your door—the milkman, the egg man, and a bit earlier, the iceman.

So I grew up with a sense of multiple mobilities, speeds, distances, and angles of vision that suits the story I aim to tell. It's about musics that came from far and wide, lived in sprung-up local centers, and traveled in a number of cultural conveyances along regular and irregular lines. To round out the metaphor, the city sported musical junctions, dead ends, limited-access highways, one-way streets, boulevards, and a lot of merging traffic. This was also the city with the first red-yellow-green stoplight, a suitable symbol for a place obsessed with color and marked by cycles of stoppage, caution, and progress. The white line dividing directions also started in Detroit, another stand-in for the channeling of cultural traffic. But not everything obeyed the rules. Music flowed like the stream of cars—around every obstacle, often through social amber or red lights, creating the city even as it navigated it. Other American cities produced strong sets of scenes and musicians, but with its jazz network, Motown magic, ethnic inventiveness, and classical talent, Detroit animated America with music that was propulsive, exciting, and influential. As funk pioneer George Clinton put it, "Detroit is the most important place for American music, hands down."

Detroit's music was not always so adventurous. Many American cities started their arts scenes with stolid nineteenth-century German openings. Early on, it was the Harmonie Club that laid the groundwork in 1849. Dance pioneer Harriet Berg still remembers the place: "They had a choral group, a Hamburg bar in the basement with a bowling alley and murals of Hamburg, a first-floor elegant dining room, a second-floor beer hall, and a third-floor auditorium with a ballroom, where they put on operas." The group was responsible for infiltrating classical music into the public schools, as we'll see, and for founding the nationally important Interlochen Arts Academy. Nearby lay the Michigan Conservatory of Music, at the hub of the street spokes.

Like the city, my early musical life radiated outward from a solid geographic center, along avenues of the classical, the subcultural (Jewish), and the countercultural. This book maps the music of my formation onto my hometown. I see the place through

FIG. 1.4. Grand Circus Park—hub of the city plan—with the Michigan Conservatory of Music. Undated postcard, courtesy Leonard Pitt.

my eyes, but also with the help of statistics, recordings, and the memories of fellow Detroiters. I arrived at the height of the city's power in the early 1940s and left the area when its decline could not be denied, in the late 1960s. It was when the older generation of jazz greats emerged from the hardscrabble start of the 1920s—Wardell Gray, Yusef Lateef, Thad and Elvin Jones, Barry Harris, Betty Carter—to the constellation from the 1930s: Kenny Burrell, Tommy Flanagan, Ron Carter, Sheila Jordan, Pepper Adams, and the younger guard—Donald Byrd, Paul Chambers, and the rest of the future stars. Rhythm and blues emerged out of older black southern roots, with arrivals such as John Lee Hooker finding an audience among fellow immigrants and adjusting to newer sounds.

Musically solid, the African American neighborhood was physically doomed. By the early 1950s, the Paradise Valley entertainment center was torn down, repaved as the Chrysler Freeway, just as taste was shifting to new forms of dance music. Motown provided a transition to pop dominance as rock edged into the traffic from suburban white on-ramps, with the MC5, Iggy Pop, and Bob Seger picking up on new possibilities. Meanwhile, the durable classical music scene produced a huge number of talented kids that went on to prominence on America's concert stages. All the while subcultural sounds echoed in the neighborhood hotspots and downtown venues. Radio offered a great range of sources that deeply influenced Detroit, a city that loved to listen.

I'm intrigued and unsettled by the gap between how I remember music in my ears and bones and what I've heard from other people or read in the remarkably few available sources on the local musical life. My family was musically oriented, with its own profile. In cities, experience can be shared or singular, local or mainstream, even house by house. Urban studies can help to think this through, but that work skips over music's odd mixture of the stable and the mobile. Throughout my long research and writing career, I've been fascinated by the way the fixed and the free, the likely and the unpredictable, the probable and the possible share space, in minds and memories, as well as acoustic territories. In a city as raw and rough, varied and volatile as Detroit, the ground kept shifting. A synagogue would change into a church, the symphony hall into a jazz site and then back to a home for the orchestra. Immigrants became musical emigrants from the city, to New York, Nashville, or Los Angeles. No one lived where their parents had settled down; everyone listened to all kinds of music. What looks solid came from a huge effort of the will to find footing on marshy ground that might turn to quicksand, as freeways swallowed neighborhoods and fields faded into suburbs. The all too familiar American cocktail of capitalist disinvestment, unrelenting racism, and misguided government policies left the city tentative and pushed its decline. Some of this story is shared by all the great northern industrial cities. Still, Detroit was a special space. Communities do have profiles. Corporations, city managers, and the public schools ignore them in their relentless quest for social order. But communal resistance doggedly challenges, and can undercut, the systems of aesthetic, economic, and political control.

To navigate Detroit's musical system in my day, my strategy is to blend facts, voices, and memories. I appear as a soloist in the chorus, particularly in the early chapters, at other times commenting on the unfolding scene, as in a Greek tragedy. Writing about my life is not the point of this book. The story starts with me and my family because getting to know one corner in the vast panorama of Detroit's music can be grounding. Intimacy offers insights into citywide patterns. The book then moves out from my personal hub along avenues that intersect with the lives of many others, some of whom I've been lucky to contact directly for their thoughts. I'll be describing only a few of the sectors of the city: the public schools; the music of neighborhoods; the activities of corporations, unions, and the counterculture; and the commercial drive of record companies, studios, and the media. Their intense interaction crosscuts the handy categories of music—ethnic, classical, popular, pedagogical. In any case, Detroit was too dynamic and desperately uncontrollable to summarize in a scheme.

This book offers a partial panorama, because I think that's how the place worked. People had limited visibility and high mobility. I don't have a handy street atlas for the city's music, or even a road map for research, because the history is so thin. Things are improving, thanks to the Detroit Sound Conservancy (begun in 2012). But at their first conference, in 2014, people were surprised that I was digging into the decades before techno, hip-hop, and late rock. It's not just music: even the very fabric of Detroit's social order—its constant weaving and tearing—has hardly been studied and written about. There's more journalism about the city's decline and recent rebound than real research on its gritty urban history. It's hard to believe a place this important to America and the world has such a scanty set of studies, presented at the end in a guide to sources. I have talked to some terrifically knowledgeable and cordial people, but alas, I started too late to catch many important old-timers.

Detroit has been on the international radar for some years now, first as a site of abandonment during "the ruin porn" years of picturesque photography in the late 1990s, then as the crisis city, until the bankruptcy agreement took hold in 2014, and more recently as the comeback city, with its trendy gentrification and grassroots grit. The past is increasingly emerging from this dense trafficking of Detroit images. But among these mostly journalistic exercises, rich sources of memory remain untapped, only some of which I can cover, given the vast scale of the city.

Throughout, I will offer traffic metaphors, suitable for a place that lived and died with locomotion. As the sociologist Ulf Hannerz once said, "If you ride on a metaphor, you have to know when to get off." This warning itself uses a traffic analogy, as

Hannerz does elsewhere: "Culture . . . is a matter of traffic in meanings. . . . It is immediately apparent that urban traffic patterns have some peculiarities, and that some vehicles may be better suited for them than others." In this book, I argue that music is a "vehicle" that's supremely suited to Detroit's diversity and volatility.

In cities, you see people you know or recognize here and there—on the bus, out of your car window as they walk, at a concert, at the office, or on the evening news. Some of the people I profile get a longer look, some just fleeting glances, as the chapters move through the life of a pulsating, pluralist city. As for myself, I appear as an individual in a family, a school kid, and a member of multiple musical circles.

In what follows, I begin with "The Construction Site," about the way personal musicality is assembled, move to "The Traffic Circle," the interchanges where public schools direct incoming traffic onto different avenues, then take up the "Local Traffic" of neighborhood subcultural sounds, consider the "Border Traffic" of the Jewish community, perched uneasily between larger black and white populations, and end with "Merging Traffic," the converging music flow designed by corporations, unions, the counterculture, the music industry, and the media (radio and newspapers, and later television). I round out the city tour with "The Rear-View Mirror," the backward glances of observers like me: writers, poets, and artists who have also been thinking about how Detroit shaped their creative lives, often coming up with traffic metaphors themselves.

Time to rev up the narrative engine and step on the gas.

2   The Construction Site

In the big city, each individual is a construction site, a cluttered set of cones and sig-
nals, detours, and pedestrian walkways. Behind the noise and grit, something is getting
built, often at intersections. The musicians I have talked with and cite below credit many
shaping forces. But there's a looseness in the design, just as things don't get built on time,
within budget, and by the blueprint. Materials get rethought, new solutions emerge,
funny things happen on the site.

Even people from very similar backgrounds start with drastically different musical
profiles, and then they move into new musical niches, learning from the media, their
peer group, and accidental encounters outside the cozy circle home, school, and place of
worship.

Later chapters will detail the influence of central planning—schools, the media,
industry—and the ways that local neighborhoods build their musical homes. Here the
story centers on the individual and the family circle, the spaces where people try to shut
the door on the traffic noise.

To visit this pulsating, dense city, for me the surest place to start is my family, the
richest source I have for how music built lives in Detroit. At home, on the road in the
car, or even abroad, songs and symphonies created my consciousness. It was all heavily
European, but also deeply American. It was far from typical—no family is—but
I shared a common experience in having a wide variety of sources and influences, many
from beyond Detroit.

FIG. 2.1. On dad's side: grandparents' honeymoon at frozen Niagara Falls, 1910. He is twenty-three, born in Ukraine she is nineteen. Author photo.

FOR STARTERS, A few family photos will show the pathway to America and assimilation that my people shared with a large percentage of Detroit's population, being of European background. The pictures show my mother as a small child with her family in Uman, Ukraine, 1912. They emigrated to Detroit in 1922, at the tag end of the era of mass immigration. Then we see my father's parents, Samuel K. and Miriam Greenberg Slobin, on their honeymoon in 1910. Apparently, Niagara Falls was the immigrants' romantic destination even in the dead of winter, and a backdrop of the Nabisco factory dramatically darkens of the air. The next photo presents my parents, Norval, born in Detroit in 1911, and Judith (originally Yokheved). They're in a properly patriotic setting—the Statue of Liberty, a landmark for happily Americanized eastern European Jews and many other groups.

My childhood avenue was marked with milestones of popular culture imagery: the cowboy-and-Indian motif, a comic-book costume for Halloween, and, on a family trip to Mexico, acting out the role of gringo tourist. A 1915 photo of my Detroiter father and his brother shows how far back these stereotypes go, particularly the Indian dress-up moment, with war whoops as accompaniment. Like me, Dad would have

FIG. 2.2. Mom and Dad, Norval and Judith Slobin, on their 1932 honeymoon. Author photo.

seen Hollywood Indians at his weekly pilgrimage to the movies. We Jewish kids were not the only outsiders playing at this game—Marvin Gaye's brother remembers, "We played all the shoot-'em-up games of children. Cowboys and Indians, cops and robbers. He was a better cowboy, but I was a pretty good Indian." Despite all this role-playing, I grew up never quite feeling like an "American." There was the strong effect of the Yiddish spoken at home, memories of "the Old Country," including much music, and the minority status of being Jewish, though other European immigrant kids felt the same way in that era. Congress stopped immigration, and the pressure to assimilate was at its highest.

After starting life at the time of the 1943 riot, I left the Detroit area from nearby Ann Arbor in 1967 to do my dissertation research in Afghanistan, just at the time of

FIG. 2.3. The author with a cowboy tie and his friend David as an Indian, 1947. Author photo.

FIG. 2.4. Dad and his brother Sidney as Indians, back in 1915. Author photo.

FIG. 2.5. The author as the recently minted superhero Superman, Halloween, 1946. Author photo.

the next riot, now called a rebellion or uprising. So my experience is framed by two social explosions. It was a time of generational shift and social dislocation, even as the city seemed so solid. Strong family ties, my parents' steady if underpaid work as public school and Hebrew school teachers, and the "progressive" educational system kept me upright against the winds of change that would lead to disastrous decline. I was a lucky boy in a tough city.

Two vignettes can suggest the wide range of my musical sources and experiences. My father being a teacher, we had months of summertime to take American road trips, to destinations from New England to Yellowstone to Mexico, site of the first musical moment. We passed the long hours in the car with games and songs. The second episode takes place in Vienna. My father had a Fulbright grant to teach there when I was ten years old. Learning German was easy. My early immersion in classical music let me savor the Viennese musical banquet, from violin lessons to operas and orchestras. I was bringing European culture back to Europe, and then reimporting it to Detroit when I was just eleven. The Yiddish I heard around me fell into place, as a kind of homey German. Being dipped into Europe repeatedly, like a tea bag

FIG. 2.6. The author as an American tourist in Mexico, 1951. Author photo.

in a mug, colored my life. For other kids, black and white, it might have been the summer trips back to Alabama or Pennsylvania, where they or their parents built musical memories that could be tapped back into.

Vanka on the Road

It's a dog-day dusk in the summer of 1951. A black Pontiac literally steams through the haze, approaching Texarkana in the dusk. Pontiac himself, the chrome Indian chief above the hood, carves the sultry air for a car without air-conditioning, in a land before interstates.

In the back seat, two plump boys aged eight and twelve—they will be called *gordito* (fatso) when the family gets to Mexico—brave another day of a weeks-long road trip from Detroit. We check the license plates of passing cars and note the states, trying for all forty-eight before the border. We wait for the gas breaks at stations with enticing coolers, where local soda pop stands patiently in cold coolers, ranked deep in flamboyant colors that shift from state to state. Up front, Mom and Dad sing their songs. At dusk, they harmonize for the timely "Just a Song at Twilight," an early twentieth-century pop classic that must remind them of their courting days of the late 1920s:

> Just a song at twilight, when the lights are low
> And the flick'ring shadows softly come and go
> Though the heart be weary, sad the day and long,
> Still to us at twilight comes love's old song,
> Comes love's old sweet song.

Everybody knew this Irish sentimental song of 1884. Filmmakers used its title for silent movies that came out when Mom and Dad were kids. James Joyce featured it prominently in *Ulysses*, no less. Nothing could be more clichéd and comforting in a roadside gloaming. Next the lovebirds turn to a song so different that it might startle anyone but the brothers, who are used to sudden switches of languages and customs, in the house or the car. For this one, they know the Russian words:

> Po naprasno, Van'ka, khodish;
> Po naprasno nozhki biosh.
> Nichevo ty ne poluchish,
> I durakom domoi poidesh.
>
> You're going there in vain, Vanka;
> You're wearing your feet out in vain.
> You won't get anything,
> And you'll come home like a fool.

Wait a minute. Isn't this an odd song for a family vacation? No matter. Dad clearly thought it was fun, since he always sang it jokingly. But why did he sing Russian songs anyway? He was born in Detroit (1911) and his mother in New York (1890), so even though his own dad was an immigrant from tsarist lands, he needn't have been interested. But he was, enough to marry an immigrant girl from Jewish Ukraine and to invest a huge amount of time and energy in getting a doctorate from the University of Chicago—in the depression, no less—on Soviet disarmament proposals. Lots of Russian there, and few fellowships.

But there's more. Tracing a song is like an archaeological dig. You pluck a scattered shard from the dust, brush off the dust, and hold it to the light. You need to imagine how it got where you found it. What layer was it in, who left it there, and how did they use it? Back in Russia, Vanka was a figure of fun, the fool, *durachok*, something like the Jewish *shlemiel* who never gets it right. He walks and wears out his boots. You could almost imagine him trudging wearily beside the plush Pontiac, our first post–World War II car.

Still, the Pontiac couldn't protect us from the rutted southern roads. Arriving in Texarkana, we hit a terrible bump and Mom flew to the ceiling—no safety belts then. No matter—nothing could squelch the staged good humor of our yearly road trips. One night in Mexico, Mom even had a sip of beer. Ours was a family that knew no alcohol beyond the sacramental sugar water called Manischewitz. So the Mexican brew went right to her head. In her peasanty blouse and full print skirt, she danced and trilled a homemade song: "I am tipsy because I had some beer." It's probably the only song in my whole childhood collection that came and went spontaneously, just as this was the one unscripted moment Mom allowed us and herself. Dad made sure we read our lines from her book and sang the right songs.

"Vanka" was a good road companion in childhood. But a dark side loomed as well in the 1950s. All things Russian were suspect in the American mind. I remember worrying whether people would notice our early 1940s album of Soviet Red Army songs, a souvenir from when the United States and the Soviet Union fought side by side against Hitler. But at the same time, my 1957 junior high school suddenly announced an after-school Russian language class. When the Russians launched Sputnik, the first-ever space satellite, we Americans had to play catch-up. I signed up for that class and found myself learning Russian songs as a patriotic gesture. Families and institutions can overlap in surprising ways in musical construction.

Songs are cultural currency—you never know when you'll earn them, save them, or spend them. Many years later, I bought goodwill with "Vanka" as the delegation head for a group of American ethnomusicologists visiting the Soviet Union. It happened as the climax of an elaborate toasting ritual, with musicians flown all the way up from Soviet Georgia. I had to offer the last toast after a series of colleagues came up with clever choices. Anxiously, I ransacked my mental storehouse and suddenly came up with "Vanka." "Ah," I said. "For some days we have been celebrating what you call *mudrost' naroda*, folk wisdom. But the folk are not always so wise." I could see some furrowed brows—what does he mean? "For example, I learned a Russian folk song as a child, and it was about a failed journey." Then I sang "Vanka." "But," I quickly added, "we have not worn out our boots, we have not come in vain; it's been a wonderful trip." Warmth spilled across the banquet table. They were surprised I knew such an odd, old folk song, and the sentiment rang true. This homecoming of a Russian song created musical fellowship. It was a far cry from Detroit, but it was part of European-American cultural traffic that I could navigate with confidence as a boy from a city on the move.

Brahms in Vienna

It's 1954. I'm sitting with my family in the Grosse Musikvereinssaal, the temple of Viennese classical music. It's even built like a sacred space. The whole place is in red velvet and gold. Lines of giant classical figures run along the seating space. The imposing organ backs the orchestra, heavily framed in wood, as are all the doors to the shallow balcony boxes, with everything topped by triangular porticos. Quite the combination of classicism and Christianity. They leave the lights on, as in a church or synagogue service. The conductor appears—a high priest, mediating between the faithful below and the officiants on high, an all-male group of temple musicians clad in immaculate black and white.

I know the music. Back home, we had neatly shelved albums, almost all of classic standards, from Mozart to Tchaikovsky—nothing from before or after, and only selected composers. Each item in our record collection, broad as books, contained several discs that rotated at high speed—seventy-eight revolutions per minute. You needed a stack of them for a whole symphony or concerto. As three absorbing minutes passed, the music stopped. Whir! The needle pulled back before a clunk! when the next disc fell on to the platter. Another whir was followed by a scrape— the needle found its groove, and the piece carried on. To this day, I know where some of those breaks fall in, say, the Tchaikovsky violin concerto played by my idol Jascha Heifetz. We wore those albums out, often as background to incessant reading. Brahms's Fourth Symphony still suggests Sherlock Holmes to me. I kept playing it as I followed through the London fog with the detective. So a live concert was magical, just because it was so seamless. Being at the mother church of this cult in Vienna was a very intense experience for a little boy who had already been playing the violin for six years.

You were supposed to listen actively, intensely, and go into a trance of transcend-ence. One such moment happened in the last movement of Brahms's first symphony. The composer had been blocked by the long shadow of Beethoven's revolutionary, domineering orchestral works. The astonishing last movement of the Beethoven Ninth, with its "ode to joy," Turkish march, operatic soloists, and massive chorus, stunned everyone for decades. How could you write a follow-up symphony? Brahms finally pulled himself together, and his First Symphony bows to Beethoven in the last movement. After some mournful skulking and manly questing, a mighty horn summons opens up a new sound space before the broad theme—rather similar to Beethoven's—moves everything into realms of grand humanity from the solitary splendor of the romantic composer's meditations. Somehow, I wasn't prepared for that moment, particularly in that storied space of perfect sonic splendor. It seemed to me that the walls fell back, opening up a radiant field of sound and light as a seraphic flute ushered in a horn chorale. Finally, the surging string theme returned me to an excited reality as I flowed along to the finish line, the whole crowd around me surging in their seats.

For me, this classical music connection came naturally, part of the construction of my Jewish community. The tradition condensed into a single object: the violin. The Jewish-violin connection is very old in Europe. It's been well described in fiction, memoir, and drama—that fiddler on the roof— as well as the long list of Jewish violin greats. My violinism ran in the family. My great-uncle Maurice (or Moishe) never found the time to play the instrument he loved, but he took me to concerts of artists like Mischa Elman and Jascha Heifetz. He also made me a lifelong baseball fan by taking me to Detroit Tigers games in fabled Briggs Stadium. The Jewish-baseball connection is all-American, celebrated in film and fiction (Chaim Potok's *The Chosen*). By combining the violin and Hank Greenberg, our local Jewish athlete-idol, Uncle Moishe fits right into the pattern of Europe plus America that so constructed my consciousness. There's also a snapshot of my father fooling around with a fiddle. He was handed a violin as part of the ethnic package but never picked up on it, though I inherited his student instrument.

My experience on the construction sites of family and school was shared by Detroit's huge population of European immigrant families: a layering of Old World and American sources, the influence of classroom and summer camp, the pop songs from the peer group, and local music that varied from house to house and block to block. My father, my aunt, and my brother will each serve as one local example of the depth and range of Detroit's musical construction potential. My father, Norval Slobin (1911–97), was a native Detroiter, and my mother's sister, Ann Liepah (1917–95), came as an immigrant from Ukraine at age six.

Ann Liepah: From Summer Camp to Refugee Camp

Ann arrived in 1922 as a child who had survived pogroms, a harrowing escape, life as a refugee in Romania, and a trip through Ellis Island to Detroit, where her family found kinfolk. She grew up as a dutiful but dubious daughter, eager to move beyond her *kleyn-shtetldik* (small-townish) neighborhood, craving the cosmopolitanism she eventually found abroad and in New York. But meanwhile she was off to a Jewish summer camp in 1937. Among her papers I found a sheaf of her favorite songs from Camp Mehia (Yiddish *mekhaye*, "pleasure"). Ann's construction site is typical and yet distinctive. Down to the present day, every immigrant stands at the intersection of two musical roads: the long pathway of homeland music and the shorter road of the rapidly evolving American soundscape. Here is what's on just one sheet of her camp songs: "Over Hill Over Dale," the 1908 anthem of the US field artillery, a gesture to patriotism' a pop song called "There's a Rainbow Round My Shoulder"; and a parody of another current tune, "Organ Grinder's Swing" with the text: "The blues oh yes the blues, we're the team that's hard to beat." The camp was split into rivals, "the blues" and "whites," using the Jewish colors. The blues got to sing a Yiddish taunt, "A rakhmones af di vayse" ("Too bad about the whites"), which is just one of a pageful of cheers and jeers, including "Let's give some cheers / Let's give some yells/ Let's show those boys / We're good old gals." No surprise that another page has the fight songs of a dozen American colleges. These chants sit next to "Ta-ra-ra Boom-de-ay," an 1891 pop song that had a long life, down to its use on *Howdy Doody*, the famous television puppet show of my childhood.

Camp Mehia rang with songs from all over the map. There's the American folk song "Erie Canal," next to a hoary vaudeville German shtick about twins called "Yacob and Hans" who are so alike that when one dies, the other doesn't know whether he's "Hans who is living or Yacob that's dead." It's a rather ominous song for the late 1930s. Next to this are Yiddish kids' songs and the sad tale of the smiling lady who blithely rides a crocodile on the Nile: "At the end of the ride, the lady was inside, and the smile on the crocodile"—also a bit grim.

Included are many classic Yiddish folk songs that somehow survived the loss of eastern European daily life, sung by lively Jewish American teenagers even as they knew Broadway hits, English folk songs ("The Raggle Taggle Gypsies"), a German band number, and American kids' verses. Ann passed on to me her favorites from those early days, songs still circulating today among American Jews that know the Yiddish tradition. "Arum dem fayer" (Around the campfire), was popular in both Poland and the United States in the 1930s. It's the perfect campfire song, since its own setting, and it creates instant nostalgia—even as you sing it, you imagine remembering the moment. What "the dreams" might be—personal or political—is left to the imagination. It's just a celebration of being romantically young and together:

> Arum dem fayer iz altsding liber,
> Di nakht iz tayer, lomir zingen lider
> Un zol dos fayer farloshn vern
> Shaynt oys der himel mit zayne shtern
> To kroynt di kep mit blumen-krantsn,
> Arum dem fayer mir veln tantsn
> Vayl tantsn, zingen iz undzer lebn
> Arum dem fayer khaloymes shvebn

Around the fire everything's nicer
The night is dear, let's sing songs.
And if the fire goes out
The sky shines, with its stars.
So crown our heads with garlands
Let's dance around the fire
Because singing and dancing is our life
Dreams hover around the fire.

Also in Ann's small stash is a songbook from the "Dormitory Summer Association" of the University of Wisconsin. Nothing Jewish here—it's classic Americana: *Community Songs—Let Us Have a Singing, Smiling, United People*, courtesy of the National Recreation Association. In those days, people sang around the piano at home and expected song sessions at places like college dorms. The huge range of songsters—personal, institutional—tended to offer the same basic groupings. Ann's includes Stephen Foster's "Old Folks at Home" and "Old Black Joe," both of which I sang in grade school, alongside "Water Boy (American Negro Song)." Race was never far from American singing, in commercial or community contexts, at home or in school. But it was all just called "folk song" in those days. Then there's the Anglo-Saxon section, which can be found across the generations, with Scottish items like "Loch Lomond," "Annie Laurie" and this comment on "Men of Harlech:" "The Welsh, famous in battle, are equally famous in singing." Ethnic origin includes "Spanish Melody," "Santa Lucia" (Italian), and "Juanita (Wa-nee-tah)." You could always find vintage pop standards: "Seeing Nellie Home," "When You and I Were Young, Maggie."

It's not much of a collection for romantic Jewish American youth. Ann preferred the deeply sentimental and philosophical songs of the modern Yiddish tradition, such as "Margaritkelekh," about a seduced and abandoned maiden, and the plaintive "Zol zayn," a "Let It Be" ballad that verges on the sunnier sentiments of *Fiddler on the Roof*:

Zol zayn, az ikh boy in der luft mayne shleser,
Zol zayn, az mayn glik iz in gantsn nito,
In troym iz mir heler, in troym iz mir beser
In kholem der himl iz bloyer vi bloy.

Zol zayn, az kh'vel keyn mol tsum tsil nit derlangen,
Zol zayn, az mayn shif vet nit kumen tsum breg,

Mir geyt nit in dem, ikh zol hobn dergangen,
Azoy lang az ikh gey oyf a zunikn veg.

Maybe I'm building castles in the air
Maybe my luck just isn't there.
In dreams, things are brighter, in dreams things are better
In dreams, the sky is bluer than blue.

Maybe I'll never reach my goal.
Maybe my ship will never come to harbor.
It doesn't matter what I've gone through,
As long as I travel a sunny road.

In Ann's song world, the personal and the political mixed freely. One of her favorites was this labor-union ditty: "Get up, get up, get up and exercise-you've got to have a healthy body to fight the finks [informers] and spies"

In 1945, still in her twenties, Ann was enlisted on one day's notice to board a ship for Germany and help organize the lives of Holocaust survivors—then called "displaced persons." She arrived at a scene of anarchy and neglect, and forcefully took charge, finding food and shelter for traumatized victims barely out of concentration camps. She wrote down songs, including the one that became the anthem of the Jewish wartime resistance struggle, the "Partisan Song," along with "Reyzele," a classic love song. Most poignantly, she kept a handwritten version of a rare item that speaks plainly to the hard-won realism of the survivors:

Di gantse velt iz mer nit
Vi a maysele, a maysele.
Di gantse velt iz mer nit vi a shpil.
Eyn balade fun hunger un noyt.
Eyn balade fun tserisene shikh
Eyn balade vos endikt zikh nit.

The whole world is no more than
A fairy tale, a fairy tale.
The whole world is no more than a game.
A ballad of hunger and need.
A ballad of torn shoes.
A ballad that never ends.

FIG. 2.7. My aunt Ann Liepah, as photographed by Aaron Siskind in 1942, when they had a fling. Author photo.

Ann's music world was even wider than this survey shows. As a good daughter, she learned to play piano, and her leftist peer-group musicking gave her an unrealized dream of mastering the mandolin. But the site of her construction offered rich resources of European and American genres, items, and attitudes that she never really added to. It was similar to my father's story.

American music offers everyone musical memories that blend selective family choices, collective recall of other places of origin—Europe, the American South, Mexico, Lebanon—and the all-purpose musics of state and commercial culture.

My dad's construction site was particularly dense with musical meaning.

Norval Slobin

Norval Slobin was born in the Polish enclave of Detroit, where his father had a store. He grew up around the Hastings Street neighborhood, which later became the pulsating center of African American music. Norval carried a name his mother Miriam took from an eighteenth-century Scottish play that begins this way: "My name is Norval; on the Grampian hills / My father feeds his flocks." The name moved

Miriam away from her early life among Jewish peddlers and tradesmen. Somewhere in the 1920s, his mother sent him to a YMCA camp, apparently not caring about its Christianity, so he was able to sing "What a Friend We Have in Jesus" and "He Walks with Me and He Talks with Me," two standards of that faith. He had a life-long fascination with languages and learned many, from Latin and Greek in school through the German he got by working his way to Europe on a freighter at nine-teen, in pre-Nazi times, and his college Russian. He knew some Ukrainian, from the land of his immigrant father. Yiddish was a household language, and he studied Hebrew deeply, even as part of courtship with my immigrant mother, whom he met in a classroom. Norval was hardly alone in taking multilingualism for granted. So did masses of other Detroiters from many lands of origin, from French Canada to Afghanistan.

My father's song knowledge went on and on. There are melancholy Ukrainian songs about being lonely as the winter winds blow, American pop songs of his childhood like "I Love a Sailor, a Sailor Loves Me" or "Come Ride with Me in My Airship," and "Barney Google." These were up in his brain alongside sentimental German ballads and Russian songs, ranging from children's street taunts through Red hymns preaching revolution. When he sang that last one on tape, my reticent immigrant grandmother sang along—she had heard that in her young people's circle back in Russia. Detroit only gets referenced in this kid's street song: "My father went to Germany, my mother went to France / My sister went to Hastings Street to buy a pair of pants."

Of the whole set, one of the most curious of them all is "O'Brien," written by someone like him—a Jewish American teacher, just for fun. It's trilingual—English, Yiddish, Hebrew—and kind of outrageous. It has lines like "*Adoshem* [the Lord] is a jolly good fellow, which nobody can deny," sung to that American tune, while other parts use a kind of Hebrew prayer, sing-song setting. Dad's generation got a huge kick out of playing with their linguistic and musical resources, and that song does it all. It's part of a penchant for parody that my parents shared with their peer group, who would sit around of an evening and translate Shakespeare or Gilbert and Sullivan into Yiddish as a way of showing their mastery of, as well as their distance from, the expressive culture they grew up with. To top it off, Dad sang the English words of "O'Brien" with a Yiddish accent for comic effect. It's an echo of the earlier "Jewface" period (1890s–1910s) of ridiculous songs by serious songwriters like Irving Berlin ("Cohen Owes Me Ninety-Seven Dollars") making fun of immigrants, largely for an audience of Jews out for an evening's laugh. You can find this kind of song straight across early American ethnic recording as part of a pattern of self-knowing parody that sold well. He liked to recite a Yiddish-accented version of Poe's classic poem "The Raven," starting "Once upon a midnight, deary" instead of "dreary." Then there was "Abie at the Opera," making fun of both a philistine Jewish listener and the opera he and his wife are attending.

To get closer to my own experience, I turn to my brother Dan's memoir. Being born four years earlier, in 1939, he has a longer view. He also happens to have a keener sense of the household atmosphere, from the emotional tone down to the placement of the furniture in the place we called home, in dead-center Detroit. Dan and I absorbed all the attitudes and many of the songs from both our cosmopolitan home and the Americanizing public school. People used to make homemade records on machines in the living room to send back home or to distant relatives. There's a disc from 1945, when I was only two, that we made while visiting family friends in Chicago. Dan sings the Thanksgiving standard "Over the River and through the Woods" and a Sabbath blessing in Hebrew, followed by squeaky me, producing the same, plus "Twinkle, Twinkle, Little Star." It was all just songs to me, and I was pushed to perform early. Later discs include such oddities as the German-parody vaudeville ditty "John Jacob Jingleheimer Schmidt," and the kids' version of the all-American "Stars and Stripes Forever," which starts this way: "Be kind to your web-footed friends / For a duck may be somebody's mother." Alongside "Home on the Range," that valentine to a mythic American West, we also recorded "The Anniversary Song," new at the time and always sung at my parents' anniversary, partly because the Jewish American star Al Jolson popularized it.

Not surprisingly, Dan's first musical memory is of the classics. In a later chapter, I will explore the Jewish community's love affair and strategic use of classical music; for now, here is Dan's version of our own family's obsession with the European concert repertoire. Some of my peers did not grow up with classical music, whereas for us it was almost a religion.

> Grandma took me to hear a matinee concert for children. She treated it as a sacred event and I felt very privileged. I must have been under five, because I was wearing dress shorts. It was the only experience I had like *shul* [synagogue] or church—it was sacred music. The only music that counted was classical music. Everything else was ethnic music. I didn't hear much ethnic Jewish music either; I hadn't gone to any weddings with Jewish music, we didn't have television, it wasn't on the radio.

This was hardly typical of all Detroit Jewish families. Dan did get to a service with our other grandmother: "The only time I was taken to hear religious music was from grandmother Slobin—she took me to hear a great *khazn* [cantor] sing 'Kol Nidre.' I was very proud, dressed neatly. I was stuffed in the balcony among all these heavily perfumed and powdered women." Kol Nidre, an opening prayer for Yom Kippur, the Day of Atonement, had a very strong magnetic pull, even for those who came to services just once a year. They were called "Kol Nidre Jews," showing just how powerful a spiritual musical experience can be.

In our home, on a daily basis, classical music was the most personal and physical, and its charge carried across generations. "Mom and [aunt] Ann had piano lessons, Grandma had a piano, I could go upstairs to practice. It's what the first kid does. Eddie Menczer [next door, from a Hungarian Jewish family] played the piano. Everybody knew this music." This immersion could bring on piercingly poignant moments, stories that speak volumes about how musical and personal construction cannot be separated.

The last time I saw grandmother [Dad's mother], I was ten and I was playing with a friend, we were wrestling on the floor, she looked in. She said "would you play the piano for me, 'Barcarolle' from *Tales of Hoffman*?" I told her go away, can't you see I'm playing. And then she died the next day and I felt really guilty. And that "Barcarolle" has that association for me. You knew who liked which piece. Mom always played the "Venetian Boat Song" from Mendelssohn's *Song without Words*. That was her piece, so I never played it.

Inside the classical picture, Mom and Dad painted a line of taste with the fine brush of their personal aesthetic. It's like the paint-by-numbers kits that Mom liked to do, where you get a set of colors and fill in the blanks to make a pleasing picture following the instructions, only here my parents had designed the whole box themselves.

The only real instruments were violins and pianos. We didn't know anyone who played wind instruments—they were lower. Music didn't involve the body. Ballet wasn't really music—we didn't go to ballet concerts. They had this very narrow musical range. Mozart was sort of OK, but not deeply beautiful. It went essentially from Beethoven and Schubert to Tchaikovsky. Everything from the twentieth century they found hard to listen to. They didn't listen to baroque music either. Dad said "it just sounds like a sewing machine."

Even old Grandma was a classical music aficionado, with a taste of her own. I would play her albums, and she would tell me which pianist she preferred, and she had her own favorite composers, such as Schumann and Chopin. Russian high-culture values had made it to her home, deep in southern Ukraine. But as she cleaned, she would sing the all-American "Oh, What a Beautiful Mornin'," from the recent hit musical *Oklahoma*, in a clear, Yiddish-tinged lilt. She stood comfortably at the crossroads of Europe and America.

Vocal music opened up a broader soundscape, but not if it was based on Christian texts. Again, early soundscapes can deeply etch later experience: "Mom had a negative response to religious music. She heard the great works in college and brought it home, but she couldn't listen to that music because it reminded her of the pogrom back in the Ukraine of her childhood. She'd be passing by the church hearing that music and people would come out and beat up Jews." Instead, they chose operas and musicals. "They loved Galli-Curci and Caruso records. Dad told me the whole story of the Nibelungen [from the Wagner *Ring Cycle*]," despite Jewish disapproval of the Nazi's love of Wagner. As for musicals, "*South Pacific* was the closest to exotic ethnic music." That's revealing—Dan heard the stereotyped Broadway "Bali Hai" sound, written by two Jewish American, as a kind of world music. Music for many Detroit families was still a social practice. We'd sing around the piano, with friends. There'd be the book of Russian songs, Gilbert and Sullivan, and the *Fireside Book of Folk Songs* and the Red Army Chorus, because they were involved in Russian war relief, for which Dan remembers gathering old clothes. "They had leftist sympathies and Russian nostalgia, so that worked fine."

This train of thought leads Dan to link family trends to those of his friends in a way that's deep Detroit and will return below, when the counterculture makes its appearance:

> When I was in high school, Bob Mates and Al Young would come with their guitars and we would sing union songs and labor protest songs and we sang Mexican folk songs, Spanish civil war songs, French folk songs. There were also communist and former communist friends and relatives.

Outside the house, institutional life offered abundant musical choices, in two kinds of schools, ethnic and mainstream. Our parents both taught part-time in religious schools, and sometimes sent us to Sunday school. Dan remembers not just boring Bible lessons but Zionist songs: "We learned *Hatikvah* [the future Israeli national anthem] and other Hebrew songs even before the State of Israel arrived in 1948." But mostly it was public school music that set the tone:

> There was the glee club at Roosevelt [Elementary School]. Everybody sang. It was American folksongs and Christmas carols. We weren't allowed to sing any Chanukah songs. We went caroling in the neighborhood. The head of the glee club was a Jewish woman. We all went out with red hoods and capes singing Christmas carols because that's what the Board of Education said we should

do. And we stopped at houses and the parents and grandparents would come out to the front porch and they would *kvell* [beam] to see their little boy or girl in the choir, even though everybody was Jewish—the director, the kids, the neighborhood—but everybody thought it was good to sing Christmas carols. That's when we would substitute words.

The Jewish kids' problems with Christian lyrics were already generations old in our day. Even though Jewish Americans had made their peace with Christmas long ago, we were still reluctant to extend the truce to singing about Jesus. We had not had my father's experience of getting cozy with Christ at the YMCA camp. We were far more likely to sing the secular seasonal hits, many written by Jewish songwriters, like "A Marshmallow World," one of our sheet music purchases. The exclusion of Chanukah is striking, given the many later court cases and community decisions that have put its emblem, the menorah, in American public spaces.

The media infiltrated the home back in the 1920s with the parlor radio, later privatized in small sets like the red Zenith in my bedroom and, eventually, the portable transistor set. I've already mentioned sheet music and phonograph albums. Older patterns persisted, even as television arrived, rather late in our case (1951). "There were those programs with Heifetz, Rubinstein & Piatigorsky and Leonard Bernstein." Even the old folks began to watch, but they turned intuitively to familiar faces: "Grandma and Grandpa would come down and watch *Your Show of Shows* with us. There was also Eddie Cantor and Milton Berle and that Jewish vaudeville stuff." Us kids waded more boldly into mainstream currents: "We watched *Your Hit Parade* every week. And I would go out and buy some of the sheet music." The show was shot live, with second-rate sets and costumes and a hokey format spotlighting clean-cut singers with names like Snooky Lanson and Dorothy Collins, who had a quick wardrobe change for each number. The show was driven out by rock 'n' roll, but had a steady presence in our living room on Saturday evenings. Music that came from subcultural systems got bleached out in those days, like Hank Williams's "Jambalaya," set in bayous far from Ukraine or the Detroit River but not too exotic.

When rock 'n' roll did arrive in the house, it was in another format and context: "We had those little 45 rpms—we had 'Sixteen Tons,' and then there was 'Rock around the Clock,' and there were parties where we would do the twist, in the late fifties." Dan remembers "Sixteen Tons" as 1950s rock, when it's a 1946 country-based miner's lament whose only pop feature is a back-beat finger-snap. We had Tennessee Ernie Ford's hit version of 1955, now in the National Recording Registry, but for us it was a bit foreign. It was only when we worked out the meaning of "I owe my soul to the company store" that we recognized the critique of industrial life that was all around us in Detroit. It was our only connection with the music of the white southerners. Our distance from the pervasive Detroit country sound was extreme, but neither did the jazz wave from the black community lap at our doors, even at its height in popular culture. "There was never a moment of jazz in the house. Dad scorned jazz—they were all drug addicts and used marijuana." But this was not a racist remark—Dad was proud to be a member of the NAACP and, as we'll see below, spent the days of my early childhood encouraging inner-city African American students at Miller High. "Marian Anderson was fine because she sang the right kind of music and Paul Robeson because he had such a beautiful voice."

But Dan dabbled in jazz anyway, since even the cautious public school system ceded space to the Detroit sound: "I did play the piano in an eighth-grade jazz band. I remember playing "Blue Moon" and people danced to it." Still, such jazz as there was got watered down by other dance forms, some domestic, others imported: "In junior high school, dance was an obligatory physical education course. It was the one time we had coed mixing in the gymnasium. We did square dance—the teacher was a very good caller—and all the dances, fox trot but also cha-cha, tango, samba, and boogie-woogie. It was the one time you could get close to a girl and hold her, for ballroom dancing."

Just as *Your Hit Parade* tamed outside sounds, the gym class provided a safe space for the erotic pull of Latin dances They were wildly popular among almost all layers of society, partly because Hollywood injected them into film after film. Our Jewish community was strongly drawn to these domesticated Caribbean and Brazilian styles—they pushed out traditional Jewish dances at weddings. In the safety of the school, budding girls and boys could get intimate with each other to the beat of exotic sounds. The Henry Ford–inspired square dance, which we will return to, provided an all-American grounding for these flights of fancy footwork. There was not much choreographic inspiration in the house: "Dad couldn't dance, or thought he couldn't, but they had friends who did ballroom dancing. Mom loved the polka and tried to teach him, but he kept getting confused about the steps."

The polka returns to the family story to the European construction materials that popped up at many intersections of private and public space. The tendency toward Old World songs was reinforced by the visits from an irrepressible friend from Cincinnati, Zolly, who arrived with his mandolin and his songs, in Yiddish, Polish, and Russian. He was a tale spinner, provoking hysterical laughter with his tales of the stupid Austro-Hungarian army and his parody of Yiddish grammar. Outside, we went to visit other European-heritage people in a safe space, the International Institute downtown, a place where immigrant cultures converged. "At one of those international things there was a bandura—something about that music resonated with me. And some kind of balalaika group. And I liked bouzouki music."

Dan's account confirms a loose pattern of contact and affinity that opens up a space of intersection that leaves the family hearth and travels into the city's vast and varied soundscape. This book will keep returning to the way that music built its own lanes of sensibility that crisscrossed the city's traffic and demographic grids. It's a story of dense construction: fathers and mothers with different song stocks, kids picking up music here and there, strong influences from "back home" spaces, whether in Europe, the South, or elsewhere. Nearly everyone was a recent arrival with long musical memories. And, arching over all experience, the American song world loomed, always eclectic in a settler country, and asserting dominance through the commercial items that became common cultural currency: "Oh Susannah" from the minstrel show, "Yankee Doodle Dandy" from an Irish Broadway star, "White Christmas" from a Russian-born Jew. Popular culture is the umbrella over a vast continental country, covering the classroom, the jukebox in the corner drug store, and the record player in the rec room.

It's impossible to map so many musical construction sites, though they have a lot in common. To extend my family's testimony, I've assembled a short set of quotes from other personal accounts I've gathered. Some of these musicians' memories appear in later chapters, as part of the city survey that follows. The citations below are not chronological, and they come from interviews, unless a source is given. The dates approximate their childhood years. The idea is to get a view from streetcar level into the musical windows of the city. You see how different the living rooms are, but you can hear some of the same songs coming out to the street and on car radios. There are also subtle overlaps in the quotes, as the voices merge into a chorus of musical Detroiters: the influence of mom, dad, brother, music teacher, church, radio DJ, movies, and more.

This chapter closes with a meditation on the nature of individual musical development, where the personal and the social intersect. Then we can move on, from the private to the public spaces of the city's throbbing music traffic.

Selected Musical Memories

I'm from the musical womb of Detroit. If you were serious about the music, the older ones would spend the time.

Ralph M. Jones, 1940s–1950s

I was born in Mississippi. . . . My parents, they took me to Ecorse, Michigan, then we moved to inner-city Detroit. It was like a culture shock to me because where I was at, it was like semirural, and the people were like from the South.

VC Lamont Veasey, musician, 1950s–1960s

I was more in the jazz world. Dad was a jazz fan, but disapproving [of my] piano playing] at first. But my parents came around due to influence of friend, a basketball player—Lawrence—so Mom would take me to clubs and Dad would pick me up when I was too young. Then they handed me over to study with Marcus Belgrave.

Geri Allen, pianist, composer, band leader, 1960s–1970s

My parents came from Kentucky. I went to school, went home and practiced, and that was it. I only heard country music on visits to Kentucky; my uncles put the radio on to soothe the cows when milking—it was my only exposure.

Robert Newkirk, cellist

The house didn't have much music on the phonograph. The family would go to picnics once a month. I heard a sax player—they were socialist labor party picnics. Sax players—Tommy Dorsey, etc.—were my models.

Don Sinta, composer, performer, educator, 1940s–1950s

Nobody was a musician in the house. There was nothing but jazz and classical playing all the time. Father was draftsman for Army Corps / commercial artist, mother worked for Michigan Bell. I was always singing commercials, and I picked out tunes on a friend's baby grand.

Patricia Terry-Ross, harpist, composer, educator, 1950s–1960s

I went to Brady Elementary. The principal, a round Irish woman named Mary Sullivan, used to take me and my brother Sheldon to play for nuns at a parochial school.

Jerome Rosen, violinist, 1940s–1950s

When I was four or five, I wanted to be a violinist because my aunt had Gershwin recordings and the [Beethoven] Eroica Symphony with van Beinum. I was weaned on that and all the standard repertoire, and took to classical music like a duck to water. Mother played a recording of a string quartet playing Chopin transcriptions, and I play it often now. At home there was a running feud— Dad liked gospel and they fought all the time. I started on piano, paying for lessons with *Free Press* paper route money. I got to Interlochen [Arts Academy] on the basis of Kreisler's "Preludium and Allegro," and was concertmaster of the All-State Orchestra by 1961.

Darwyn Apple, violinist, 1950s–1960s

McKinney was inspired to study classical music as a child by his mother, Bessie Walton McKinney, an organist. He was converted into a jazzman when he walked into an ice cream shop and heard Charlie Parker on the jukebox playing bebop on the alto sax.

Harold McKinney, performer, band leader, 1930s–1940s

I followed my elder brother, who was a child prodigy, and I pretty much looked up to him as a musical genius. My mother listened to classical, my dad to jazz piano, but they didn't play instruments. They moved up from the South after the war. I listened to Kenny Constant's avant-garde jazz show on WDET, and also heard electronic music. There was a pretty wide base of education for me and other Detroiters. I went to Baker's Keyboard Lounge to hear Roberta Flack when I was fourteen or fifteen—painted a mustache on my face. When I was even younger, I'd go downtown with a friend to concerts at Masonic Temple—Horace Silver, Alice Coltrane, all the jazz concerts, as a kid.

Pheeroan akLaff, performer/composer/improviser, 1960s–70s

Mother gave piano lessons, and I was torn between piano and math—no one applauded me for mathematics. I was a snob about classical music, starting on piano at age seven.

Paul Schoenfield, composer, educator, 1940s–1950s

My mother also played in community orchestras. She gave up the Detroit Symphony Orchestra because of the twins [he and his musician brother Robert], when they were two or three. But she kept playing in shows like the ice shows, the Leonard Smith band at Belle Isle Park. I played due to my mother.

Darrel Barnes, violist, French hornist, 1950s

Mom was a piano major at the University of Michigan. Both of my older brothers played. I spent summers at Interlochen. I studied [piano] with Mischa Kottler from six to eighteen, with constant trips to Masonic Temple to hear everybody.

Neal Stulberg, conductor, 1960s

I started playing at three, by ear, till I was twelve—I could play anything I heard, and didn't want lessons, but my father got me to Mischa Kottler [the top piano teacher]. I didn't want to read music, so he would ask me to play and he would play it back until I caught on. I stayed home and practiced rather than join the

Music Study Club or play with friends. By 1967, I played the Rachmaninoff Two with the Detroit Symphony Orchestra.

David Syme, pianist, 1950s

I was not interested in any other kind of music than classical—not till being in the Boston Symphony did I realize that the Beatles were good.

Robert Barnes, violinist, 1940s–1950s

My parents joined the Tuesday Musicale, so I started studying with Regina Muscherbach of the Musicale. I became a string player because the school gave a $fifteen-dollar scholarship. I loved the violin because of my parents, who played in community symphonies. My sister Ida and I soloed with those groups to try out repertoire. When I visit Detroit, it feels like home. We belonged to an Armenian church and played at church, but there was no real music connection. I mainly heard Armenian music at weddings.

Ani Kavafian, violinist, 1950s–1960s

I began my musical training in fifth grade when my band director gave me a much-used Conn cornet and told me to clean it inside and out. I was inspired to make music my career by a Detroit Symphony's children's concert I attended while in junior high school. While in high school I organized the Dearborn Boy's Club Band, the experience that led to my decision to become a conductor.

Harry Begian, band leader, educator, 1920s–1930s

We had Armenian songs in the house, opera. My father sang at home; he was a child immigrant at twelve; my mother from Boston. I heard genocide stories repeatedly and the singing of the older generation, but didn't learn the language.

Kim Kashkashian, violist, 1950s–1960s

Coming from a Polish family, I started on accordion, playing professionally at Polish weddings at eleven. In junior high, Miss Miller gave me a tuba and the string bass, which no one else wanted to play then. That teacher had a huge impact on my life.

Art Lieb, music historian, administrator, 1940s–1950s

There were Greek dance records. At big family gatherings—twenty-five-plus—they would put on LP records and dance. Mostly from Samos. We did the roll call of all the island dances. So I was dancing a lot of 5/8 and 7/8 meters. I found out later that metric complexity spoke to me. I bought classical records, some violin, Fritz Kreisler. We couldn't afford concerts, though we went to one of Callas's last concerts, since she was Greek.

Jorja Fleezanis, violinist, 1950s–1960s

We had Serbian traditions at home—Serbian Christmas. I really didn't start into it till Cass Tech. I met a fellow I knew from church; he hustled me into the choir. We would sing church music—responses in church every week—Serbian composers' arrangements. They might throw in something strictly folk, but not much. My brother was starting an orchestra with two other fellows at home, but he got drafted to Korea. I started a Serbian band in high school that lasted over fifty years.

Rodney Glusac, 1930s–1940s

I paid no attention to pop music, even though in school they had kids playing air guitar to rock 'n' roll. I thought that was silly, since I was surrounded by real [Ukrainian] instruments. My mother was a huge Tom Lehrer fan. They listened to Red Army Chorus recordings because there was nothing else in that genre, but zero classical music. I went to public school with no English in a neighborhood with five other Ukrainian families, which I regarded as the known universe; Other houses didn't exist, they were blank spots.

Julian Kytasty, performer, composer, 1960s–1970s

Bennie Maupin's early sources were the church, the band shell in Belle Isle— Sousa. European immigrants—there were so many Polish—brought classical music, played in the Detroit Symphony Orchestra, "one generation after another, because the instruction was so good." Boarders from Alabama brought a player piano with them; he experimented as a small child. When the family moved, they took the piano, so he lost that. Then he saw jazz on Detroit television in one- or two-minute slots.

Bennie Maupin (from Oral History of American Music interview, Yale University), performer, composer, 1940s–1950s

The great pop song by Lou Christie, "Lightnin' Strikes," will forever be linked with my memories of circling the ice, trying to avoid the snarling [white] bullies spitting the N-word who loomed like monsters over us.

Marsha Music, historian of Detroit, daughter of a record producer

My mother didn't believe in barriers; she didn't let us use color as a barrier. We weren't allowed to use excuses. Some of my early teachers, although they weren't all African American, saw something in me. They said, "She'll have a difficult time if she wants to do European music, but she can do it."

My mother would take me to Ford Auditorium to hear the symphony, ballet, opera as part of the Suzuki program. Sitting up there I said I'm going to be part of this.

Hampton elementary was pretty mixed; I met people from other backgrounds. The church was quiet, not a Baptist one—Plymouth United Church of Christ, with low-key hymns. Grandmother was a pianist, she got her degree in 1915. We had a Greek neighbor. The father was choir director at a Greek church, so I heard some Greek music, and also heard Chaldean music. The Summer Festival of the world downtown featured another culture each week.

> Regina Carter, violinist, band leader, 1970s

We were called factory rats when I was growing up. . . . I put hubcaps on the DeSotos.

> Russ Gibb, musician, 1930s–1940s

My dad got me a job working in the factory before I started getting serious about music. . . . I was fifteen.

> Mitch Ryder, band leader, 1960s

I lived in an old apartment house with everybody in the world, a lot of southerners up from the South to work in factories, old teachers who couldn't move. I just embraced everybody, I was for everybody. There were people who would give me communist literature, others more conservative, but I would play the room. I liked R & B, didn't like Elvis or Pat Boone, even. I liked all the get-down funky dirty R & B and blues artists. So I liked different kinds of music, except I knew what was hip and what reflected well on you. I constantly played a role, and Detroit was an ideal place to be that way.

> Lily Tomlin, comedian, actor, 1940s–1950s

They would have gatherings all the time, also my mother's family, and when they did, people sang. Mostly Yiddish songs. There was a family friend, Russian, a violinist named Barsh (his father and brother went into the Toronto Symphony). He was possibly from a klezmer family, since a photo shows them all with instruments. He'd play fiddle at the party. He taught violin, filled in with the Detroit Symphony Orchestra, but his primary job was barbering. Even had a fiddle in his barber shop.

I must have taken some fiddle lessons with him and dropped it. I found a mandolin in my uncle's attic. The style of playing was pretty boring. I was starting to play folk music. I bought a gypsy mandolin for fifty dollars.

Harvey and George [high school friends] were into jazz; I wasn't into jazz.

Sid Brown's father had been a violinist who lost a finger being a printer but still somehow played. His sister was supposed to become a top-notch violinist, and she did end up in the Metropolitan Opera orchestra.

Arnie Kessler, amateur musician, 1940s–1950s

I took clarinet lessons. I didn't do much practicing. I had a lot of encouragement; my aunt and uncle went to Juilliard, but it had a negative effect on me. He trashed every concert he heard, so it gave me a bad sense. I wouldn't want to play anything when they were around—they didn't think [famous violinist] Oistrakh played in tune. Grandma, a Stalinist, was a piano teacher. I wasn't very attracted to folk, but friends dragged me along. I took some bass lessons to learn jazz standards, went to Greektown clubs, heard Hachig [Kazarian, an Armenian musician], and listened to an all-black radio station out of Inkster.

Harvey Robb, amateur musician, 1940s–1950s

As a small child, I went to movies on Hastings Street and watched a cowboy movie over and over until my sister dragged me home. My grandad in Port Huron had a cattle ranch, and I spent a lot of summers there. It was kind of living a dream when I made these pictures.

Herb Jeffries, singer-actor, 1920s–1930s, on making *The Bronze Buckaroo* (1936), the first feature-length all-black singing western.

As an impressionable fifteen-year-old music hound, I would frequently call and have lengthy conversations with the DJs while ostensibly doing homework.

Chris Morton, musician, 1960s

I played in a German lederhosen band because my junior high school teacher thought it was important for us to understand that music; we went around the neighborhood in a truck with lederhosen on. Everyone was so hungry to get the next experience.

I remember hearing Lateef, Burrell, as kids—they were playing local clubs at Sunday matinees. It gave me an appetite for all music. Later, my rock 'n' roll band rehearsed in a church basement, thanks to a minister who had worked in grassroots housing, urban renewal, so I got fascinated with the church at that level, not so much as a spiritual activity.

Dwight Andrews, musician, minister, educator, 1940s–1950s

There was a World of Music in Detroit in those days; I grew up with WJLB playing in the kitchen while my mother cooked knishes and kishkes after a day spent production sewing in a factory. . . . Each night you'd hear the Greek, Arabic, Polish, Ukrainian, and Yiddish "hours." Afternoons we heard Frantic Ernie's R & B show, and on Sundays black gospel music. This omnipresent matrix of diverse scales and rhythms affected the music we began playing.

Sid Brown, folk and rock musician, 1940s–1950s

My dad could never play it [trombone], so he took it to the pawn shop and traded it for a clarinet.

My parents took me to the Paradise Theater to hear Duke's band. . . . I knew then and there I wanted to be a musician.

Teddy Harris, musician, 1940s–1950s

My dad worked at the foundry at Ford but he played trios at night at the Famous Door. I grew up listening to jazz, mostly standards. They would cart me along to any joint they were in, and mom would give me a little wine and put me on the bench in the booth. Jazz was the melody of my life when I was young. I actually didn't like Motown very much.

Crystal Williams, poet, 1940s–1950s

Building Personal Music

What intrigues me about the lives of myself, my family, and the other people just quoted is the availability of musical sources and resources and how that shaped their construction and development. Some musical materials come with your territory. They are *inherently* there, built in at home, in church (or synagogue), in the classroom, on the record player or radio. Other sounds are *nearby* in some sense, and some are *out of reach*, beyond your soundscape. The urban theorist Henri Lefebvre says city life is about "plurality, coexistence, and simultaneity." But even that vision of variety is limited when it comes to music, a particularly slippery social operator. Many sounds and musical moments were accessible in ways that other political, residential, or economic materials could never be in a vast industrial city like Detroit.

To spin out "availability," I'll start with the figure of Yusef Lateef. His name loomed large in many conversations with musicians. In the mid-1950s, Lateef was drawn to Islam. He was also actively looking to expand the range of instruments familiar to his circle. He picked up the rabat, a North African fiddle, and used it on early recording dates. Lateef did not find the instrument through black Muslim connections or Folkways Records, but rather through an Arab American coworker at the Chrysler factory. This is a Detroit story, speaking to the camaraderie of the polyglot workforce of the auto industry. For Lateef, the rabat was different from the *inherently* available resources he had from Miller High School and the African American music mecca Hastings Street. It was nearby, but not in the neighborhood. The factory allowed for the nearness of a music that might otherwise have been an *out of reach* resource. This kind of instrument transfer via the factory can take place even at the top of the industrial pyramid. Later, I'll explain how Henry Ford himself adopted an odd instrument, the Hungarian cymbalom, into his old-timey American folk band. There again, a seemingly remote resource could be made available by the city's rich musical storehouse and openness to influence, one of the main themes of this book.

This industrial example reminds me of a passage in a poem by Philip Levine, the eminent Detroit poet. It offers another angle the Lateef story. Jews tended to stay off the assembly line, being suppliers and managers, but poor young Levine was forced to work in a tool and die shop. He writes about his "friend Marion, the ex-junkie and novice drop-forge worker, off by himself humming 'Body and Soul.' . . . He played with [Coleman] Hawkins before his troubles and now has four ten-inch Bluebirds left to prove it," Bluebird being a jazz record label. Here the workplace gave Levine access nearby to the inside story of a jazz musician like Lateef.

Another Lateef vignette comes from my own experience. At the end of the 1950s, I used to clutch my violin case at 6:45 AM on a cold corner to catch the Dexter bus down to the orchestra rehearsal at my high school, Cass Tech, with its celebrated music programs After white flight, I lived in a neighborhood that by then held only 7 percent of Detroit's Jews. I peered into a glass-fronted club by the bus stop. It was called the Minor Key. There would be hand-lettered signs in the window advertising, for example, Yusef Lateef, Miles Davis. Indeed, the book *Before Motown* says that Lateef played the Minor Key in the late 1950s when I would have been standing on Dexter. But though very much nearby physically, the Minor Key was not available to me *conceptually*. As detailed earlier, I had a very wide range of inherently available music. A song in Russian about stupid Vanka, a Brahms symphony, or a chorus from Gilbert and Sullivan—these culturally distant items were way closer than the space of a jazz club that was just a few feet away. It never occurred to me to step inside to hear the music, so I missed the golden age of late fifties jazz. I was on the classical track. It wasn't even an ethnic matter—Jewish kids I knew went to the Minor Key all the time. One of their classmates was the manager's son, who let the underage kids in free. Harvey Robb surprised me by saying he and his buddy Sid, who played guitar and banjo in my folk revival crowd, would visit southern white bluegrass clubs. They wanted to see how much better people could play those instruments. That's a much more aggressive notion of "nearby" than I could muster. Fortunately, some of those friends introduced me to jazz when I couldn't understand why someone had written "Bird Lives" on the wall at Cass Tech after Charlie Parker died. My *conceptual* space shifted, even as I ignored the nearby physicality of the music.

This is not to say that Lateef and I were not somehow adjacent. The jazz musician's teacher from Miller High, the renowned Louis Cabrera, appeared on the same program as me, as documented by the program of my first concert. Lateef and I overlapped in the designed arena of public music training and performance, but not in our personal spaces.

Let me take my Dexter Avenue moment one step—or two blocks—further than the Minor Key. At an early Society for Ethnomusicology convention, I met a young African American ethnomusicologist named Sylvia Kinney. It turned out she was a fellow Detroiter, and she lived two streets away from me and the Minor Key. She was enthusiastic about Detroit's music, especially the terrific Emancipation Day concerts, which I had never heard of. This is what I'd call an *out of reach* resource, located in a space not just conceptually unavailable to me, like the jazz club, but actually inaccessible.

As we'll see, African American Detroiters had daily and difficult experiences with inaccessibility, even in the musical realm, when trying to get a job as a music teacher in the public schools or as a member of the Detroit Symphony Orchestra, until well into the 1950s. They became unavailable as musical mentors. White bassist Dan Pliskow says it was the other way around for him. He was excluded from the black jazz scene, which was always nearby for listening but unavailable for hiring, since contractors picked up players on a racial basis.

All through this book, I suggest that the musical traffic of Detroit, like so much of city life, brought people of different backgrounds together in unexpected ways, even as its highways and byways tried to channel the traffic flow. It's an approach that matches the ways that urban theorists talk about the complex design of industrial cities. As Fran Tonkiss puts it, "If the official order of the city is *written down* as so many rules, codes, maps and plans, the individual's version is a spatial story told as if out loud in the streets of the city, leaving no trace other than a movement in the air." Music is a special case of "movement in the air." Its story is not just told but sung, played, and recalled, by both individuals and collectives, who might not agree on the

FIG. 2.8. The author and Sylvia Kinney, two young ethnomusicologists and Detroit neighbors, 1971. Author photo.

narrative. Major thinkers like Walter Benjamin and Michel Foucault also thought that spatial stories could be written in many versions. Ulf Hannerz says that the individual even "comes to accept instability and insecurity as normal. . . . The circles in which he participates cannot be arranged hierarchically or concentrically but touch or intersect in a variety of ways." The mobile citizen can never see the whole picture, so "collective behavior in the city tends to become unpredictable." That gives the urban space real mind-opening potential.

In the case of Detroit, volatility could be socially dangerous but culturally enriching. Music is a force that not only supports the special spaces of family and subcultural solidarity but also opens people up to sonic instability and chance encounters. Theorists of sound are fond of saying that we can close our eyes and noses more easily than our ears. The generous spread of sound and its attractive power make it a dynamic shaper of both personality and identity within the changeable city. Black or white, lower or middle class, we could all converge in an urban imaginary built from shared cultural experiences, like the visits to the art museum, accessible on foot or streetcar from core neighborhoods, that jazz musicians describe as so influential to their creativity. Across the street from the endless galleries of artworks lay the roomfuls of music you could check out free from the main library. Even the hellish sonic space of the factories could musically inspire a poor white boy who lived in a trailer: the rock star Iggy Pop pays tribute to the huge metal clank of the steel press at the River Rouge plant, a literal construction site, when his family took visitors on a tour, as he says in the 2016 film *Gimme Danger*. That's a core memory for many of us proud Detroiters showing off our city.

In the next chapters, I turn from the individual to the collective in the structured sites of the school system, the neighborhood, entertainment hubs, industrial spaces, and the media.

The boy who blows a horn will not blow a safe.

—1941 EDUCATIONAL BOOK

I once heard it said that Detroit produced musicians like it produced automobiles.

—ART LIEB

3 The Traffic Circle

In 1949, I appeared at the Olympia Stadium at the tender age of six. It was a hallowed haunt of hockey, just as the Red Wings were at their height, led by the immortal Gordie Howe. They had won the Stanley Cup the year I was born, and would win again in 1950. Jake LaMotta (of "Raging Bull" fame) beat Sugar Ray Robinson, Elvis sang, and the Beatles appeared twice at the Olympia. At the opening, in 1927, there was a boy scout parade and a rodeo. But my debut was different, being shared by dozens of pint-sized violinists, winds, and brass players and scores of little pianists, spread out across the vast arena. My little subgroup, the All-City Junior Orchestra, only played three pieces, right at the beginning, and then it was the other units' turn, scraping and blowing their way through a selected set of "light classical" arrangements. As we waited for the signal to descend, we horsed around in the stands. My tiny fiddle came with a metal bow, not the usual wood. It made a great sword, since it was unbreakable, so I did some fencing at the Olympia before going down to play "The Happy Farmer."

What was I doing in this storied space? It lay at the intersection of two of my avenues, one European—classical music—and one American—public school music. A new metaphor comes to mind. Detroit is a city without traffic circles, rotaries, roundabouts— whatever you call them—those devices that force cars to merge for a moment before sending them whizzing off in some direction. "Rotary," the New England term, even suggests the wheels of industry, drivers as cogs in a machine—highly fitting for the Motor City. It's true that Detroit's grid, with its long-lined avenues and diagonals, left traffic circles out of the design, but they're suggestive anyway. Think about how they work: from the daredevil spirals of Tehran and the urbane flow of Columbus Circle to the stately Place Concorde in Paris, traffic circles are built to slow down the stream, make drivers think, and offer them a choice of exits from a shared space. These are demanding devices. You'd rather just drive on through, but the traffic circle sorts and processes you. You might have an idea of destination, but this regulatory device might have its own rules. There could be construction or no-entry signs blocking an exit route, so detours can loom as you round the bend, looking warily for competing cars. You might just spin around for a long time until you dare to forge ahead. Though Detroit ignored the physical traffic circle, as a metaphor, it works for the social engineering of the school system.

EMERGING OUT OF tree-shaded streets in their neighborhood, teenage students trying to drive into their future hit a rotary, dominated by a controlled educational system. Some had to yield. Others didn't get to choose their exit avenue, being channeled onto side streets that might lead them right back to their neighborhood. As we'll see, the Board of Education rigged the traffic circle. Still, music could change the flow. The American public school system made a huge ideological, and sometimes economic, investment in the idea of music as a social good. It worked for some students, in some places, particularly Detroit. Everyone concedes that music helped to soften the blow of racism and to create career tracks for black and white, southerner and European. This surprising success evokes a different traffic metaphor: the progressive light. When I first saw New York as a child, I was enchanted by the long vista down the avenues of light after light turning green. It seemed like rational magic. The public school music system could also work that way, from kindergarten through high school graduation. "Progressive" needs some unpacking, so let's start with the ideology.

Arlene Law points out that for the first long stretch of Detroit's history, Protestant-tinged choral singing dominated the classroom. All nine teachers hired for the schools from 1849 to 1933 were either choir directors, church organists, or church pianists. Also serving were music teachers who had run their own private schools and members of voluntary associations such as the Germanic Harmonie Society. Most were published composers. They were "musicians in need of jobs" as part of a "music subculture" that was heavily collective: "Virtually all the religious denominations valued choral music and nobody loved it more than the large German population. Musical events jammed the calendars of churches, concert halls, opera houses, and meeting halls. . . . Touring professional musical troupes and solo acts, largely American, included stops in Detroit. At one time or another, thirty-two musical societies performed around town." It was "a mecca for music lovers." The takeaway is that the schools mirrored mainstream society. Popular culture blended the classical with pop songs, patriotic hymns, and sentimental songs, and the whole stew had a German flavor for a long time.

After the horrors of the Civil War, healing a splintered society shifted the stress on religion towards national identity through music. Emma Thomas took over teacher training in 1888 and became a star, sending pupils across America to preach the gospel of music's power to change society by "building character, improving physical well-being, improving aesthetic enjoyment, encouraging patriotism, improving home life, [and] assimilating the population" of immigrants and internal migrants. Music, she said, "reaches the realm of the child's highest feeling and trains the heart and mind in the ways of virtue and right." It would "discipline the mind, improve the physique, and elevate the morals." And the result would be patriotic unity, as in the chorus of two thousand voices she produced for a visit to Detroit by Admiral Dewey. "There will be no room for anarchy where children learn to sing of the glories and achievements of their country."

Emma Thomas was very specific about the need to integrate newcomers by means of music: "We must instill into these aliens the essence of our free institutions. . . . It is almost always the case if I ask, even the babies, what song they would like to sing to me, that they respond 'My Country.'" How satisfying for her, since "the nation's strength is reflected in the nation's hymns." Her work directly parallels the Ford Motor rituals for foreign-born workers. Children in "native" dress walked up some steps, disappeared behind a melting pot, and emerged looking like "regular" American kids. This hand-in-glove pairing of education and enterprise is very American, particularly so in Detroit, dominated by a meteoric, massive industry and a quickly improvised blueprint for social engineering. But it was an uneasy partnership, as a 1939 book explains: "The "function of music in life [is] to provide nurture for the spirit of man, which the ravages of the machine age are inexorably starving." How can social control and uplift coexist on the avenue of education? It's one of those long-running American paradoxes.

Detroit was a particularly pressured example of national trends, strikingly summarized in a series of books, just before World War II. Emma Thomas had preached the gospel of songs, but nationally, instrumental music was equally valued. By 1930, there were thirty thousand school orchestras:

> Nothing is more significant of the increasing socialization of education than the rapid extension of instrumental study in connection with schools. . . . Playing upon an instrument is not merely a personal accomplishment with individual benefits, but is also a social power which affects many persons in addition to the performer. . . . The individual and the collective both need recognition for society to progress.

Yet not all small citizens were equal. Thomas did not include African Americans or Jews in her list of children to be musically motivated. And the national mission recognizes the need for coddling an elite: "It is the duty of the public-school system to do its assigned part in producing diverse but happy, devoted, and efficient citizens." So there should be some kind of music for everyone, but space for more talented ones. They designed "All-City" and "All-State" groups for selected students like me but submerged us into the greater ensemble, machining little Americans into a unified whole of talented cogs. It's not that minorities were left out. They were carefully integrated in stereotyped or caricatured in songs, dances, games, and pageants. Illustrations from the 1941 book *School Music* surveys the scene visually in a set of arresting photographs of children's music and dance. Some images come straight from commercial culture, always the trendsetter in the United States: cowboys, Indians, grass-skirted Hawaiians. Americans were going to the movies more than once a week and soaking up those images. Kids were encouraged to dress up, sing, and dance out stereotypes of peoples from around the world, an educational approach that goes way back into the nineteenth century. Northern Europeans get pride of place, being so much like the white American majority—Swedes, Norwegians, Dutch—but parts of Asia and Latin America also get the dress-up treatment. Square dancing was a special case, with local resonance in Detroit. Henry Ford's virulent anti-Semitism, racism, and fear of cultural pollution from degenerate urban forms like jazz led him to champion older American good, clean fun. I remember square dancing well, putting on my cowboy or flannel shirt and jeans. In those days, it made a "healthy" substitute for sexier dancing. Once I was even invited to a square dance by a girl at Liggett, the ritzy prep school, and felt awfully out of place in terms of both class and ethnicity.

But it's time to move to a main focus of music education, instrumental music. The little girls with their violins are my female counterparts. Detroiters who went on to successful careers in classical, jazz, and subcultural music scenes universally credit elementary school teachers and programs for their generous access to instruments, the switch-on for a progressive-light avenue. As Regina Carter recalls: "When we were coming up, we all had access to instruments, in elementary school, and we had a chance to determine which instruments appealed to us. We could take home a clarinet or violin and try it out for a couple of days." The violin captured me early. Already by age four, I told Mom and Dad I wanted to play, having already been to numerous concerts. Even with their classical values, they couldn't quite imagine someone so small actually taking on the violin. There was no Suzuki method then. They turned to their friend Ben Silverstein, a gifted public school music teacher. After all, he had trained his own son, Joey, who, as Joseph Silverstein, later became the concertmaster of the Boston Symphony. Joey had just left home as a preteen for the prestigious Curtis Institute in Philadelphia. Maybe Ben liked the idea of transferring his attention to a new little boy. Soon, I was off and running, squeaking and squawking on the one-eighth-size fiddle I took to the Olympia.

My teacher Ben was one star in a bright constellation of teachers who launched careers. Among the most notable was Ara Zerounian (1926–2012). It's worth quoting his obituary to see how he profited from the system that he returned to, after advanced degrees and wartime service:

> Zerounian was born in Detroit and showed musical talent at an early age. After training in Detroit, where he attended Cass Technical High School, he went to Northwestern University in Chicago for his undergraduate studies, followed by the Eastman School of Music in Rochester, NY for his Masters. After serving in the US army in World War II, he returned to Detroit and immediately began a long and storied career teaching music in the public schools as well as privately, where he began the studies of some of the top string players in the world, including his stepdaughters, the violinists Ani and Ida Kavafian. Zerounian was the first teacher of many other renowned string players including the former Concertmaster of the Minnesota Orchestra and present Professor of Music at Indiana University, Violinist Jorja Fleezanis: Principal Violist of the Cleveland Orchestra and Professor at the Juilliard School and Cleveland Institute, Robert Vernon: Principal Violist of the Metropolitan Opera Orchestra, Michael Ouzounian: concertmaster of the Utah Symphony, Ralph Matson: Amalia Joanu of the Toronto Symphony, Carolyn Edwards of the Pittsburgh Symphony, Catherine Compton of the Detroit Symphony as well as many others. Mr. "Z", as he was affectionately called by his students, had one secret to being a great teacher that he followed faithfully, which was to "love your students". Zerounian also had a long affiliation with the Interlochen Center for the Arts, where he taught for many summers. He received many honors for his teaching, including the ASTA Teacher of the Year Award in 1977.

My interviews with Ani Kavafian, Jorja Fleezanis, and Michael Ouzounian support their early mentor's star status. When Ouzounian was small, Zerounian happened to be his string teacher at Burns Elementary School. He auditioned the kids and helped them to choose an instrument, supplied by the school. Jorja Fleezanis agrees that Zerounian "would simply decide which instrument you would play in public school." "He drove to every student's house for lessons, organized string quartets, and coached us on rotation in the four houses," Ouzounian recalls, and he states that he wouldn't have gone on to a career in music without motivation from "Mr. Z." The teacher had a "pipeline" to the Interlochen Arts Academy, a major national hub for training classical kids. His students had automatic entry, with scholarships, as soon as they were ready, "basically when they could vibrate" the notes. At age eleven, Ouzounian was the first all-state violist at Interlochen, joined by another Zerounian student, renowned violist Kim Kashkashian. "You knew that if you worked and progressed, then *this* would happen, then *that* would happen," says Ouzounian. It's the perfect description of progressive lights on the road to a career, once you get past the traffic circle of the school system. But "when he was nearing retirement age, they abolished the music program, so he ended his career teaching math. A kick in the rear."

Pianist Geri Allen agrees about what happened later to elementary school music: "Taking that away might have been a place where things started to change." Detroit switched on the red light, ending the period of signals that speeded kids down Music Avenue. These metaphors are pretty down to earth. Access meant a lot for kids trying to break into what was a thriving industry. In 1950, at the height of the Motor City's power, there were 938 symphony orchestras in the United States. Music in general (teaching, performance, instrument manufacture) was the sixth largest American industry, after automobiles but before steel. For Detroit, then, music was both ideology and a commercially competitive business, almost as valuable nationally as cars. "In the first half of the twentieth century, the auto barons produced cars and culture, but in the second half, the city manufactured musicians." The kids themselves wanted to move into the fast lane and enjoyed every experience their pushy teachers offered, as Dwight Andrews remembers from his grade-school days in the early 1960s: "I played in a German lederhosen band because my junior high school teacher thought it was important for us to understand that music; we went around the neighborhood in a truck with lederhosen on. Everyone was so hungry to get the next experience."

In that golden age of public school music, what started in grade school continued into junior high. Mine, Durfee, had a lively musical life. The photo below from my 1957 yearbook drives home the point, with its doggerel tribute to music. That picture could be out of the 1941 guides to school music, except that the kids are refreshingly multiracial. That was the Durfee demographics of my day, not the top-down national image of whiteness.

The orchestra, which included me and my buddies, was even more diverse, with my Armenian friend Hachig (who will figure later as an Armenian American musician), all led by a Polish conductor, Mr. Klocko. He was a music union member, and probably played gigs on weekends like music teachers across America. I wonder if he was in polka bands. I was totally smitten with Rhonda Rubinoff, the dark, glamorous concertmistress who reeled off the famous *Czardas* at her senior concert. She wowed me not just with her looks but with her fiddle. Her uncle, Max Rubinoff,

FIG. 3.1. Durfee Junior High, 1956. Bonding through music in a changing neighborhood. Source: Durfee yearbook.

had a radio program—*Rubinoff and His Singing Violin*—and sometimes he loaned her his Stradivarius. So yes, not all public school musicians were equal, even if the opportunity they got was. Green lights flashed for some of us.

Durfee Junior High offers a fine survey of mid-1950s music attitudes and activities, courtesy of the *Durfee Review*, for which I was an editor. The selection and some of the prose might actually be mine. Journalism class brought me to interview Charlton Heston at a posh downtown hotel when *The Ten Commandments* came to Detroit, and I won an American Legion essay contest on "what democracy means to me." Ideology was fully in place, backed by America's assertion of authority. I was also a Roman consul elect in the Latin Club, with the power to turn my classmates into Roman citizens, while dressed in a toga. Christianity came along with the mix; the junior chorus sang "Bless This House," "Thanks Be to God," and "Thanksgiving Prayer." As mentioned earlier, we Jewish kids faced a dilemma when the Holy Child turned up in the Christmas carols. We would mutter or substitute words under our breath, even as we walked around our largely Jewish neighborhood under the leadership of Miss Belkin (herself Jewish) to carol for enthralled parents in the snowy streets of Detroit. It was just blocks from where Berry Gordy would soon establish his Motown headquarters.

Americana pervaded the performances, from the minstrel-era "Sleep Kentucky Babe," the African American spirituals "Joshua Fit the Battle of Jericho" and "Rock-a-My Soul in the Bosom of Abraham" through the Better Schools Association Family Night, which combined Henry Ford's beloved square dancing with a DJ spinning "popular platters." In 1954, the list of favorites ran from the conservative Eddie Fisher's "I Need You Now" to the insurgent rock 'n' roll of "Shake, Rattle and Roll." As the *Durfee Review* put it, "This record is real jive (jump-gone-crazy)." The hip jive continues in 1955: "Dig this crazy column and see what you Durfee hepcats think of the latest hit records." Eddie Fisher hangs in there with the Mills Brothers and the Drifters. Home Room 315, under the watchful eye of Ms. Hempleman, picked its own pop culture epithets.

9A 315's Jive Corner

Don Ahrens - Speed-o.
Joan Albert - Eloise.
Linda Bernstein - Juke Box Baby.
Merry Helen Bolden - Devil or Angel.
Steve Brooks - Tutti Fruitti.
Janice Buchanan - Maybelline.
Carl Bullion - Davy Crockett.
Gerald Chaben - Blue Suede Shoes.
Michael Chudler - Hot Diggity.
James Cornelius - Please, Please, Please.
Steven Ellis - Poor People of Paris.
Arlene Frank - Teen-age Prayer.
Erica Gelberman - Why do Fools Fall in Love?
Cindy Gittleman - Going Steady.
Beverly Haugabook - Great Pretender.

Raymond Hawkins - Daddy Rockin' Strong.
Joe Hill - The Happy Whistler.
Clifton Hoke - When the Saints Come Marching In.
Marcia Kanarek - Angels in the Sky.
Hachig Kazarian - Hajji Baba.
Don Mendelson - Red Convertible.
Robert Nelson - Rock and Roll Waltz.
Emma Nixon - Little Girl of Mine.
Myron Morrison - See You Later, Alligator.
Rosa Powe - Dungaree Doll.
Emmett Robinson - Good Rockin' Daddy.
Elliot Weinhaus - The Lord Has Time.
Edsel Walimaa - The Love of Bridie Murphy.
Miss Hempleman - Moments to Remember.

37

FIG. 3.2. Home Room 315's self-identification through pop culture, Durfee Junior High, 1957. Source: Durfee yearbook.

In addition to the classical, patriotic, ritualistic, and pop music that Durfee enabled, the school made sure to speak the emerging language of ethnicity, which conveniently avoided race. We were told that Detroit had a "cosmopolitan nature" and carried "indebtedness to the cultures which meet and merge here," though it was about "the worth of the citizenry who trace their descent from European sources." These people blend "the rich old cultures of many other countries" with "American ways and customs," giving "a special sparkle to our language, a special character to our art." The civil rights movement had not yet shifted the rhetoric, and the exploding black music scene did not count as "art" or offer a "special sparkle." Gender roles stayed stodgy too. The year 1957 saw a new ensemble, the Modern Dance Club, where "the girls develop poise, leadership, and personality."

The progressive lighting of elementary and junior high hit the traffic circle of high school. While some serious strivers were channeled onto broad musical avenues that led to New York's big bands, college campuses, and concert halls, many took the exits that led back to neighborhoods, where high school grads like my Durfee conductor Mr. Klocko settled into music teaching jobs, local club gigs, or both. For African American teenagers, constant policing and the eventual teardown of their neighborhood literally produced roadblocks and side streets that led to housing projects. Their musical development depended heavily on the positive pedagogy of dedicated teachers. It's a story repeated in other American cities, but it is particularly important in Detroit. I'll single out Miller High, where my father got his start as a social science teacher in 1937, taking care of a stellar group of future jazz greats, such as Yusef Lateef and Kenny Burrell, and Cass Tech, my alma mater and that of countless important musicians, from Gerald Wilson and Wardell Gray in the 1930s to Ron Carter and Diana Ross in the 1950s and 1960s to Geri Allen, Regina Carter, and Jack White in the 1980s and 1990s. The overlaps and contrast between the two schools speak eloquently to both the control and the cracks in the system.

At Miller High, there were speed bumps and barriers. Miller was elevated to senior high status in 1933 to accommodate the huge influx of African Americans who poured into the city in unheard-of numbers in the 1930s and early 1940s, growing from 40,000 in 1920 to 150,000 in 1940 and zooming to 300,000 strong by 1950. White parents were told that they could move their kids out of the district, so the school quickly became all-black. This impacted the music. According to Vivian Dolman, a music teacher, by 1940 the board had removed all the classical instruments, sending them "to other schools whose students' background and breeding would lend themselves better to 'cultured' 'classical' music." Here's social engineering at work, redirecting musical resources, in synch with the relentless white dominance and policing, even in a city known specifically for high school orchestras. Dolman's eyewitness account here and below comes from a remarkable

1970 dissertation about Miller High by Clozelle Jones that focuses on the dedication of the teachers as a key to black students' success, despite all odds. The eminent Metropolitan Opera tenor George Shirley taught briefly at Miller and remembers Dolman as "sweet, pleasant," involved with the women's glee club. She is less known than Miller's main music teacher, the great Louis Cabrera, recognized by Yusuf Lateef and Kenny Burrell as an influence. When I asked jazz great Barry Harris about his Detroit training, suggesting that he must have had a good teacher at his school, Northeastern, he replied, "Not like the ones at Miller." Cabrera and Dolman struggled and succeeded in supporting an amazing array of topnotch musicians. The national establishment said this: "The aim of instrumental study in the schools is principally cultural and social, and only incidentally and remotely vocational." But Dolman makes a contrary claim: "Music classes were 'business classes' for our kids. [They] practiced long and hard to develop their skills, and that's why Kenneth Burrell and William Evans [later Yusef Lateef], Milton Jackson and several others are recognized as being the best at their instruments." I can't help mentioning that my father taught American history to Kenny Burrell and probably many other future jazz greats. Jones quotes Milt Jackson as saying that had he not dropped out of high school, he probably would have gotten a college music scholarship, like other classmates. The picture below shows my dad and Ms. Dolman on the same page of the 1945 Miller yearbook.

The book *High School Music* insists that "America does not have that racial solidarity which favors the development of peculiar musical idioms. . . . While we have discovered interesting folk music among the Indians and Negroes, and make use of it and enjoy it, yet it cannot be said that it is typical of the American people at any period." Dolman's response to this erasure of subcultural tradition was to build a model for success in establishment music. She tells us that African American students couldn't get buses to get to competitions, but they went anyway, and the kids would win the All-City Band contests. "They could read and play all types of music . . . even the Mozart that the big shots 'downtown' felt was not akin to their heritage." Dolman also made use of black resources right in the building in an egalitarian fashion, inviting a (presumably black) janitor to help train her women's chorus. Maybe he was a leader in the city's many strong church choirs. Louis Cabrera operated more on the citywide scale. When I discovered the program of my concert debut at the Olympia Stadium, I was delighted to see that I had shared the stage with Cabrera, credited as arranger along with my violin teacher Ben Silverstein. All of us, at different ages, driving on our separate avenues, merged at the public school music traffic circle for a moment.

Fine Arts

What the English Department seeks to accomplish with the word, the Fine Arts Department strives to accomplish through all the artistic media. These teachers help the student learn to appreciate the work of others and to express himself in music, painting, or sculpture.

Seated: V. Dolman, F. Wagstaff, R. Spencer. Standing: G. Engel, S. Alvey, L. Cabrera.

Vocational

All students are given the opportunity to learn how to use their hands. Drafting, mechanics, cooking, sewing, or similar course, the students can choose and take as much as they wish, enough to make it their life work, or just enough to come in handy around the house.

Seated: M. Henkel, E. Kopera, I. Kenny, G. Kantz (Department Head), H. O'Reagan, E. Bogan. Standing: J. Dodd, J. Reinel, C. Campbell, L. Bell, H. McKinnon, J. Sharpe (Not in picture.)

Social Studies

Man in relation with his fellowman, that is the subject matter with which the Social Studies Department deals. The student learns from history how man has gone through various stages of exploitation and cooperation in the past. In the civics class he learns the principles of our present government and the ideals toward which we are all working.

Seated: H. Becker, E. Primrose, C. Dacey (Department Head), M. McGuinness, M. Ross. Standing: A. Gornbein, N. Slobin, L. Cofer, J. Bosco.

5

FIG. 3.3. Teachers at Miller High School, 1945. Music teacher Vivian Dolman is under "Fine Arts"; the author's father, Norval Slobin, under "Social Studies." Photo: University of Michigan Chene Street History Project, Courtesy of Thomas & Vastene Woodhouse.

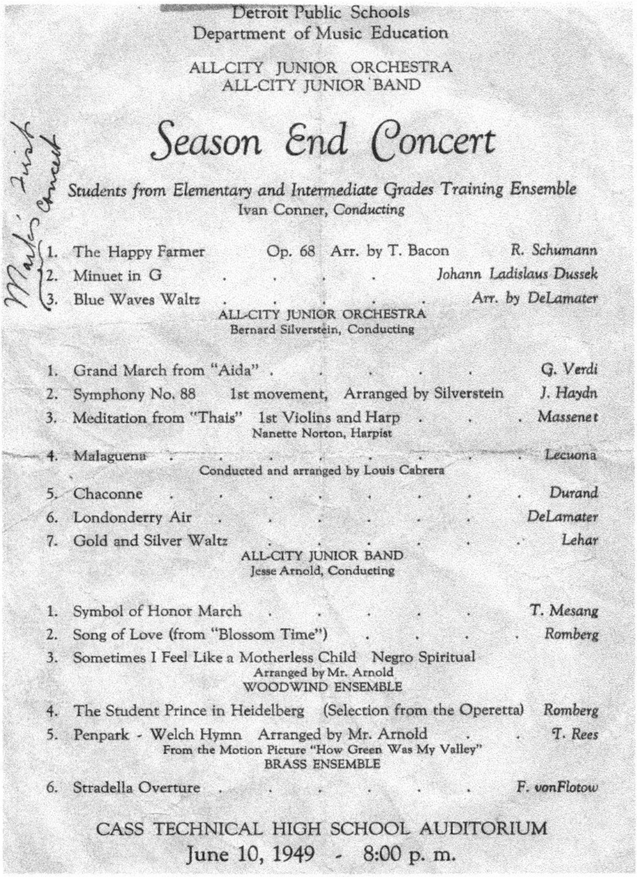

Detroit Public Schools
Department of Music Education

ALL-CITY JUNIOR ORCHESTRA
ALL-CITY JUNIOR BAND

Season End Concert

Students from Elementary and Intermediate Grades Training Ensemble
Ivan Conner, Conducting

1.	The Happy Farmer	Op. 68 Arr. by T. Bacon	R. Schumann
2.	Minuet in G		Johann Ladislaus Dussek
3.	Blue Waves Waltz		Arr. by DeLamater

ALL-CITY JUNIOR ORCHESTRA
Bernard Silverstein, Conducting

1.	Grand March from "Aida"		G. Verdi
2.	Symphony No. 88 1st movement, Arranged by Silverstein		J. Haydn
3.	Meditation from "Thais" 1st Violins and Harp		Massenet
	Nanette Norton, Harpist		
4.	Malaguena		Lecuona
	Conducted and arranged by Louis Cabrera		
5.	Chaconne		Durand
6.	Londonderry Air		DeLamater
7.	Gold and Silver Waltz		Lehar

ALL-CITY JUNIOR BAND
Jesse Arnold, Conducting

1.	Symbol of Honor March		T. Mesang
2.	Song of Love (from "Blossom Time")		Romberg
3.	Sometimes I Feel Like a Motherless Child Negro Spiritual		
	Arranged by Mr. Arnold		
	WOODWIND ENSEMBLE		
4.	The Student Prince in Heidelberg (Selection from the Operetta)		Romberg
5.	Penpark - Welch Hymn Arranged by Mr. Arnold		T. Rees
	From the Motion Picture "How Green Was My Valley"		
	BRASS ENSEMBLE		
6.	Stradella Overture		F. vonFlotow

CASS TECHNICAL HIGH SCHOOL AUDITORIUM
June 10, 1949 - 8:00 p. m.

FIG. 3.4. The great teacher Louis Cabrera and I share a school music program in 1949. Author's collection.

The struggle over the soul of Detroit school music at Miller contrasts sharply with the excellence and ease of Cass Technical High School's program, which deserves a close look.

Cass brought a varied group of people together. Cass was pretty central to the sense of a shared community.

Arnold Kessler

If Detroit was modeled on a French urban design, then educationally Cass Technical High School would be the Arc de Triomphe, a distant monument for those endlessly revolving around the traffic circle of Place de l'Etoile in search of an escape avenue. From 1922 on, this was *the* magnet school of the entire vast city, eight stories high, four thousand students strong, covering a huge block, strategically placed between the university and the downtown. You had to have good grades to get in and to select from the dozens of "curricula," specialized tracks ranging from Air Conditioning & Refrigeration and Automotive to the pre-med Chem-Bio, Art, and Music. You had to be recommended by your junior high to get in, and when you got out, you were likely to be at a good college or on the job. This was the place where Diana Ross became attracted to fashion and Lily Tomlin was the head cheerleader, where rocker Jack White chose business as his major and played trombone and drums in the band.

Cass represented Detroit's attempt to advance kids from every subculture simultaneously. As Don Sinta, who started a distinguished career at the school, puts it, "there is a Cass Tech tribe. There was no feeling about ethnicity." That was exactly my experience as well, and it ran counter to the city's nagging sense of categories. The place was supposed to be, in the words of 1926 businessmen, "a monumental achievement of education and architecture of which any city would be proud" This included its music programs, begun in 1919 and cited in the book *High School Music* as a national model. Unlike Miller, where a career track was hard-fought, the Cass program had a decidedly vocational goal, aiming, and succeeding, at placing students in "enviable positions in symphony orchestras, concert bands, radio, and dance bands," with fourteen alumni in the Detroit Symphony Orchestra alone by 1954. Still, none of them were African American—that had to wait for the 1960s. Many of the entertainment positions dried up in the postwar period: "Sound movies and the coming of age of radio and the recording industry eliminated many of the musical job opportunities," so the curriculum shifted to preparing students to be public school and private music teachers, creating a constructive cycle of educational continuity.

Starting in the 1930s, the streets and highways that led students to Cass's traffic circle spread across America, as in the case of the major jazz arranger and composer Gerald Wilson. Born in Mississippi in 1918 and starting on a Sears Roebuck trumpet, he had no local road forward. Somehow, he got up to Cass Tech, getting skills that moved him into bandstand work, and then arranging for Duke Ellington and Billie Holiday, as well as writing symphonic works. Wilson's generation was the first to map out the many career avenues that kids could follow. They were recruited straight out of the classroom to prominent jazz bands. Bobby, the son of Clarence Byrne, founder of the school's music programs, went from Cass to work with the Dorsey brothers, fronting his own bands, and ending up in the New York record business. Apparently, the Cass students would skip school to hear visiting bands at the nearby showcase, the Fox Theatre. The music teachers would also turn up there, take attendance, and stay to listen. Or they would all just hear the latest music on the jukebox in the nearby hamburger joint. Jazz singer and Cass student Sheila Jordan first heard

Charlie Parker that way, and it completely changed her life. Lily Tomlin recalls going to all the music joints in the neighborhood, mixing with "guys on motorcycles" and socializing with her fellow cheerleaders, African American girls. She also took off on a road trip to Chicago with Kathy King, a violinist in the Cass orchestra, even while hanging out with the guys in the engineering curriculum. She was "hyper-mobile," and so were many others. The huge magnet school opened you up to all of Detroit's diversity and encouraged the line-crossing that the city offered creatively and is one of the main themes of this book.

With all this high-energy contact, career opportunities to exit the traffic circle could be very local. Kirk Spry dropped out of Cass to play at the downtown Gayety Burlesk, moved on to work in circus bands, and merged into the Detroit black jazz circuit, unusual for a white musician. Still other students from that early era went home to their own neighborhoods, particularly the many prominent polka band leaders of the 1940s, who trained in performance and arrangement. Stan Wisniach, a prominent Polish personality put it this way: "When I heard that concert band, tears just rolled down my eyes—Boy, I'm going to be a part of this—it just warmed my heart." Visual artists also flocked to Cass, such as renowned conceptualist Ray Johnson (1927–95), who moved directly from school to Black Mountain College's arts nexus and New York's postwar scene, or Harry Bertoia (1915–78), who immigrated from Italy as a teenager to take advantage of Detroit's art education. His chair design still graces American offices, and he also created sound art sculptures, blending Cass's many arts offerings.

African Americans benefited from this rigorous yet open-minded curriculum but were not always able to move down the musical highway of their choice. Charlie Burrell, who eventually helped to break the symphony orchestra color bar, offers telling details. In his frank 2014 memoir, Burrell (no relation to guitarist Kenny Burrell) first expresses his gratitude at being allowed to take Cass's road to success, coming as he did from what he calls the "quasi-ghetto:" "I was on the bottom rung of the ladder because most of the young musicians there had had two to three to five to seven years of some piano or violin or something musical . . . but they accepted me. They realized that some kids were disadvantaged. . . . I was 15. There were maybe 10–12 Black students, and no Black faculty. . . . Cass Tech taught me more in music than I have since learned. It had a program which was designed to make you a good, professional musician." Burrell particularly enjoyed the Saturday sessions of the All-City High School Orchestra at Cass, which saw 150 kids gather from nine to four for coaching by Detroit Symphony musicians. But he was disappointed by the roadblocks ahead after graduation, seeing white students get onto the express lane: "By the time you came out of Cass Tech you could play professionally. . . . Most of the kids, they were all White, and they went to studios like WWJ and WXYZ.

In those days, they had orchestras with the radio stations. Of course, I didn't go anyplace but to the joints, the corner joints. That's as far as I could go, but I was happy because it all tied together and started my life as a musician."

Burrell even sees the success of 1940s classmate Bobby Byrne through a black lens: "My friend Billy Horner was the only Black dude that ever played [with Bobby's band], and the reason he did was because he was a little lighter than most of them." Burrell was a bass player, the first of a trio of major African American orchestra members out of Cass. Paul Chambers's groundbreaking solo bass compositions show the strong imprint of his classical training, on an early album suitably titled *Chambers' Music* (Blue Note, 1955). The great Ronald—later Ron—Carter could play in a string quartet, unavailable at Miller, and he credits his training there in interviews: "Cass was like a junior college for high school kids. To see [renowned band conductor Harry] Begian conduct rehearsals, to make them productive, to see something important about it. We had a full college load as a sixteen- to seventeen-year-old." Carter was so inspired by classical music that when asked what the "defining moment" was that made him decide to be a musician, he said, "After hearing the Detroit Symphony Orchestra play a concert." But he quickly saw that elite music was a dead end out of the traffic circle: "They were really not ready to add an African American to the rank of the solo cellos. I was playing in jazz gigs to make money to stay in college," so he took that exit instead. Accounts of the extent to which Cass Tech's vaunted programs could advance African American students remain very mixed. Ralph M. Jones, a musician and jazz educator, stresses the positive, pointing out that all the sax players studied privately with Don Sinta, an alum who became a reigning presence in the world of jazz saxophone, or local teaching legend Larry Teal. James Tensley, a trumpeter, went to the Curtis Institute of Music and joined the Boston Pops as a black classical trumpet player. Another black student became an oboist with the Guanajuato Symphony in Mexico. "There was an acceptance—it was just about playing the music. Made me work hard. Cass Tech spoils you in a lot of ways. You had great teachers, which made me reluctant to go into education, because how could you measure up? But later the idea took." My orchestra standmate, Darwyn Apple, was temporarily recruited to the Detroit Symphony Orchestra as part of their soul-searching about having no African American members, and he went on to posts in major cities. After Darwyn, Joe Striplin went on from Cass to decades in the DSO. He is very explicit about the opportunity the school offered:

> I felt I was very lucky to be in Detroit at that time. I came along when the public-school system was excellent, when there was genuine racial and ethnic diversity and therefore more resources in school, intellectually, financially and in every way you can think of.

Even as a teenager I could tell that the situation for me was right. The issue of blacks being denied entry into the professions was being discussed. If I had come along 20 years before I wouldn't have had a shot at it. If I had come along some decades later, Cass Tech and the public schools wouldn't have been what they had been and I wouldn't have gotten the necessary boost.

Another avenue off the circle was into education. Many Cass alums went on to academic training and even professorial careers, locally at Wayne State University or at the nearby University of Michigan. But that's not how Charlie Burrell saw it in 1949, according to his dramatic account of an interview with the head of music for the Detroit public schools. After congratulating Burrell on his upcoming graduation from Wayne State University as one of those successful Cass alums, the man that said that "as long as he was head of music in Detroit, there'd never be a black teacher. . . . The very next day I got on the bus and left for Denver. Thirty years of that was enough. That was what really opened my eyes. . . . As a musician, there was no way I could make it work there . . . maybe as a janitor. . . . I couldn't even teach in Detroit, because they were not gonna have it, why fight it?" In Denver, he realized his dream of winning a position in a symphony orchestra.

Cass kept trying to advance African American students through the late 1970s, when black students became the majority. They hired Marcus Belgrave, not a Detroiter, who came off the road after many years in Ray Charles's touring band. He taught the pianist Geri Allen, whose 2013 album *Grand River Crossing* highlights her Detroit heritage. She says, "At Cass Tech, we didn't just have a few music classes, we had three years of intensive training by master teachers and Detroit artists in residence . . . for the fields of the classics—old and modern—jazz, spirituals and the blues." It is striking that she particularly recalls the blending of mainstream and black resources within the training system. Another Belgrave student, violinist Regina Carter, supports this memory of Cass's approach, as do drummer Marion Hayden and bassist Gaelynn McKinney, who continue the mentoring tradition down to the present.

For other types of subcultural students who qualified for entry to Cass Tech in my day—the white southerners, Jews, Italians, Armenians, Ukrainians, Greeks, Serbs, and others—the grounding in theory and ensembles led to varied careers. They kept in touch with their neighborhood even as they commuted downtown to school. My orchestra mate, clarinetist Hachig Kazarian, says that he learned more about mainstream music at Cass than at Juilliard, but that's probably not how he became an icon of Armenian American music for fifty years. He got on that parallel track by going directly from school to a job at an ethnic bar. Another Cass musician, Rodney Glusac, told me that he started a Serbian band with two classmates in 1951 that played in Detroit and nationally for fifty-eight solid years. So music survives dislocation and suburbanization when a subculture knows what it wants from its school-trained musicians. Education moved these teenagers off a path to the assembly line, even though some still had to log time at factories to get by when music work dried up. Art Lieb says that Cass saved him "from the Detroit industrial ghetto."

Cass was very demanding, and most kids stayed strictly within their curriculum. Isidor Saslav was one of my role models. He lived on my block, was slightly older, and won every local prize and appearance before leaving town for classical music success. Loyal, like everyone, to the school, he said, "In all my years at Cass I never set foot on any other floor but the seventh where the music department resided, other than to visit the library on the third floor or the music library on the sixth." Michael Ouzounian relates how he and his buddies would come early so they could talk over fine points of classical music and play pieces straight off the shelves at the school's ample music library. Art Lieb, the librarian, would pick up arrangements of Stan Kenton's big band music, and the kids would play the charts after school. In the open-minded approach to education that Cass supported, bandleader Begian gave Lieb twenty dollars to buy more music, and the group was asked to play jazz for an all-school assembly despite the school not officially endorsing jazz. Kenton himself would raid the school's talent in the early 1940s when touring in Detroit, taking (white) kids directly from the classroom to the touring bus, so his work was a known quantity in the corridors of the music department.

As for me, with a strong interest in a liberal arts education, I went for the Avocational Music curriculum, which allowed you to be in the orchestra, but sample widely in other disciplines. I missed the brilliant music theory training and had to scramble for my qualifying examinations in graduate school. Many gifted students did not choose to exit Cass on to the music avenue. Rudolf Efram, from the 1940s, played with the Jewish Community Center Orchestra, then invented a punch card device and worked all his life for IBM while playing in the Hudson Valley Philharmonic.

Three Cass Classics

Looking at the work of three of Cass Tech's stellar teachers spotlights the teaching that built strong musical lives. Harry Begian, Michael Bistritzky, and Velma Froude were pillars of pedagogy. Each in a different way produced lineages that resonate today. Harry Begian (1921–2010) was the only one of the trio to move on to a major national career, using the school as a springboard. A Detroit-area native with Armenian immigrant parents, Begian had to struggle for his music

FIG. 3.5. The great Stan Kenton, right, cozying up to Polish bandleaders Svoboda and Safranski at the Warsaw Bar. He hired Polish American kids straight out of Cass Tech when he visited Detroit. Photo: University of Michigan Chene Street Project, courtesy Stan Svoboda.

education in the Depression era, ushering at a movie palace to pay for lessons. A music education degree was the green light to move into the schools, bringing him to Cass in 1947. The band he created was so celebrated that they didn't have to compete at festivals, just appear at national conventions to give clinics, as in 1954 and 1961. The recordings of his group, housed at the Library of Congress, are judged by one prominent bandleader to be "the finest high school band ever developed in the nation." Begian moved on to graduate work that led to directorship at the University of Michigan and wound up as the long-term leader at the University of Illinois. Begian cared only about his students' drive to succeed, not their origin: "People ask me stupid questions like, how many blacks did you have in your band at Cass? Hell, I don't know. I never counted. All I know is that they were the greatest kids in the world and they played like hell—because they were fearless and committed to do what they were doing and they were hungry to play music." But Begian concedes that his bandleader's color-blindness was not necessarily shared by the higher-ups, showing the ambivalence that so marked even Detroit's most idealistic handling of black talent. "Cass was often asked to send its best students to teacher conventions, PTA meetings and socials. Ron [Carter] rarely got the call."

Begian is just one of the many children of immigrants who slipped into the music stream and made careers possible for dozens of others. As a kid from no-where (Dearborn being the seat of Ford Motor, but not a musical center), he could draw on peers and older mentors in the city's music scene. Don Sinta, an important mentor even when very young, went on from Cass to the University of Michigan, like Begian, and stayed on as a faculty member. This closeness of major universities—Wayne State locally, Ann Arbor nearby—provided easy-access avenues for youngsters greenlighted by the school system. Education was a third avenue off Cass's traffic circle, along with the highway to national careers in jazz and the clover-leaf back to neighborhood music work. Sinta and Begian both drew on the immense talent and influence of Larry Teal (1905–84), a key player in Detroit's musical rise. A foundational figure in the advance of the saxophone into classical music territory, Teal mentored both future jazz musicians (Bennie Maupin, Joe Henderson) and students like Sinta and Begian. Begian called him his "friend and musical father." Only scattered writing is out there on the impact of great directors of private music studios in America. In Detroit, some of those appeared even back in the nineteenth century. 75% of Begian's band members took lessons outside school. It's the synergy of schools, outside teachers, and clusters of "conservatories," "institutes," and "academies" that allowed a city's scene to emerge and resonate over time and across genre lines—jazz and classical, academic and commercial. But there's also community. To get the band to its national workshop appearance in Chicago, the list of sponsors includes Baker Shoe Stores, Detroit Italian Bakery, Morris Kosher Meat Market, Kubiak Jeweler, and Malecki's Market. These stores were doubtless run by proud parents, and the listing gives a good indication of the non-elite background of the supported students. Even the harsh Detroit law enforcement system could be humanized by Begian's band in the early 1950s: "Khachaturian's Concerto for Piano and orchestra has been transcribed for performance by a full band by Patrolman Wilfred W. Berg, conductor of the Male Chorus of the Detroit Police Officers Association."

Begian's groups relied on a whole set of collaborators, from home to precinct, and drew on all the demographic diversity of the city. He himself did not stress his Armenian ancestry, but he did ask the composer Alfred Reed to produce a set of band pieces called "Armenian Dances." Similarly, the Cass Tech violist Kim Kashkashian, who grew up in an only modestly Armenian household, commissioned roots-themed music later in life, as a prominent concert artist. Displaying ethnic solidarity was not Cass Tech's way. It was as close to an ideal American meritocracy as one can find. Hachig Kazarian kept in touch with fellow-Armenian Begian, but the bandleader told the clarinetist that he was not going to show any favoritism based on their common ethnic background.

The same held true for Michael Bistritzky, the long-lived, presiding genius of the Cass Tech Orchestra (1898–2000). Though he never lost his accent and often connected with the Detroit Jewish community, what he transmitted to his mixed-ethnic trainees was simply immersion in the European classical tradition, offered with memorable flair and dedication. Art Lieb remembers "Mr. B." in the early 1950s this way: "Tall, elegant, with a shock of jet-black hair, and overflowing with Russian charm." This foreign aestheticism combined with serious discipline: "after four years of his tutelage, any student would have an astounding quantity of repertoire under his belt, ready to attack the world." In his richly accented English, Mr. B. would lecture us on how to take music seriously, personally, saying "back in Europe, we would stand in line for hours just for the chance to get standing room to see a great pianist, and you don't even practice." It was this appeal to us Detroit kids to feel capital-C Culture deeply that really resonated in later life, linking learning with an attitude of reverence for the classics and for artists who embodied emotion, not just technique. Indeed, Mr. B. was so overwrought by concert time that sometimes it was he who made the mistakes, muffing the downbeat. Bistritzky's enthusiasm allowed me to blend the European parts of my life, from family, with the American public school context, with its fixed class scheduling, in the vast space of Cass Tech, with all its demographic diversity. I learned about Europe, Detroit, and America in that vibrant, varied space. In a literally emblematic moment, I marketed "I Like Ludwig"

FIG. 3.6. Hipster irony of the 1950s: I sold Ludwig pins to my friends. Author photo.

pins to my classmates at the time of "I Like Ike" buttons for President Eisenhower's campaigns.

The orchestra drew a diverse crowd, but they all did well. I've mentioned my standmate Darwyn Apple, an African American and future orchestra professional. David Cerone, the concertmaster I looked up to, came from Syracuse and became the head of the Cleveland Institute of Music. Twin brothers Robert and Darrel Barnes found jobs in the Boston and Philadelphia Orchestras after starting off in the Detroit Symphony, straight out of Cass. Since Mr. B's life spanned three centuries, the memorial concert for this very nineteenth-century musician came only in 2002. The eminent roster of players for that event is a tribute to Detroit training. Instead of honoring their mentor with a couple of token pieces, these luminaries of American music played a full-length program featuring Shostakovich and Hindemith alongside Beethoven and Mendelssohn—because that's what Mr. B asked of them. They even included a work by Paul Schoenfeld, a Cass kid who became a well-known composer. Whole Detroit musical families grouped around Bistritzky: the Kavafians, Lubys, Barnes, Bagnolds, Cataneses, Levines, and Smiths. Neal Stulberg, conductor of the UCLA orchestras, gave me the phrase "affectionate and loyal" about how today's musicians relate to Detroit, that city of grit and turmoil, because of what the schools did to notice, foster, and polish their potential.

While having a nationally noticed band or orchestra for decades is remarkable, it was more surprising to float a distinctive harp and vocal ensemble for ninety years under the leadership of only three powerful women. It might have been the first school harp ensemble anywhere. The harp holds a special spot in Western music, from medieval images of King David through folk and baroque forms into an industrial-age instrument in the 1800s. It's been a women's instrument since then. In a 1980s study, the harp was rated the most feminine instrument of seventeen instruments among music students, when 90 percent of the harpists in American orchestras were female, even higher than the 80 percent figure of the 1940s. Some things never change. The first female member of the prestigious Vienna Philharmonic was the harpist.

It was in 1926 that the legendary Cass Tech music director Clarence Byrne picked a student, Velma Froude, to replace a teacher who had died. The Detroit approach of a decades-long harp and voice program seems unique, and apparently it was influential, as an undated 1950s blurb claims: "Year by year more and more leading schools, colleges, concert halls, homes and churches are using the harp regularly." Froude ran the Harp Ensemble and the Harp and Vocal group all the way to 2009, handing them over to her student Patricia Terry-Ross, who in turn promoted today's director, Lydia Cleaver. This was a transition from white to African American leadership, reflecting the school's changing population. Though the occasional boy has joined the groups, the signature of the ensembles has been girls in formal dresses. In my day, a racially integrated harp class of twenty musicians served as a pool from which Velma Froude chose a group of five harpists, with an elite pair of players moving up into Harp and Vocal to play alongside thirty-one singers, a string quartet, string bass, vibraphone, and chimes—all girls. They operated under the banner "The harp is to music what music is to life," a line coined by the great Carlos Salzedo, the path-breaking genius who was to the harp what Andres Segovia to the guitar or Pablo Casals to the cello: someone who knew how to take a marginal instrument into the limelight of the concert stage, just as Don Sinta of Cass did with the saxophone. Department head Byrne even sent Velma Froude on the train to study with Salzedo to strengthen the harp program. This broadening and democratization relied on a typically American, eclectic mix of music. In 1954, when the group made a star appearance at the convention of the Music Educators National Conference, they program included "Greensleeves," "Brahms' Lullaby," "Carry Me Back to Old Virginia," and "The Lord's Prayer."

A few years later, the old minstrel-show tune and the religious number were retired by Patricia Terry-Ross in favor of more contemporary sounds. After all, she was moonlighting at Motown, appearing in the cover photo of one album. Her sponsor was Cass Tech alum Paul Riser, one of the great arrangers. So even the feminine harp could get a green light and move down the musical avenues of Detroit. Indeed, Pat almost left Detroit with Motown in 1972, but getting the Harp and Vocal assignment kept her happy at home. Looking at the careers of two earlier local African American women harpists widen the lens of what school training could do. Dorothy Ashby (1930–86) went down the road much further, into the heart of the jazz world in a series of stunning albums, collaborating with top musicians, if sometimes meeting resistance from the men's club of bebop. Ashby's precise melodic and solid chordal playing, with a flair for improvisation, combines school and street training in a Detroit 1950s way that's audible in the work of her male contemporaries like Paul Chambers and Ron Carter. As time went on, she branched out, using arranging skills for the radical African American theater work she developed with her husband, John Ashby. Unlike Terry-Ross, Dorothy Ashby did move to Los Angeles for studio work, where Bill Withers recommended her to Stevie Wonder. But her open ears went beyond commercialism towards the "eastern arts" sound Yusef Lateef began in the fifties, on a late album based on the *Rubaiyat*. Ashby has been sampled by hip hop artists looking for interesting sounds, and what could be more original than a female jazz harpist from Detroit?

Ashby's Cass Tech confidence and eclecticism spilled over to another Detroit African American artist, the somewhat younger Alice McLeod (1937–2007), who gravitated from a church background to the intense local jazz scene as a pianist. In 1962, New York–based Terry Gibbs offered her a spot in his group because "he preferred to work with musicians from Detroit who, he felt, possessed the necessary combination of dexterity, blues phrasing, and harmonic sophistication that his music required. Before hiring Alice, Gibbs had toured with a host of Detroit natives." Alice Coltrane began as a school, church, and street-trained local musician. But after meeting and marrying John Coltrane, things changed as she found a new musical voice, which brought her to the harp, still connecting to Detroit musical roots. In 1968, for *Monastic Trio*, she taught herself to explore the harp in ways that would resonate strongly later in life, as she developed into a spiritual leader of her personally designed community. "Alice Coltrane's unusual confidence in the harp's potential was most likely grounded in her exposure to Ashby," as well as her husband John Coltrane's interest in the instrument as part of the restless search for new sound vehicles that started back in Detroit with Lateef's experimentation. Alice Coltrane favors string sweeps, letting bassist Jimmy Garrison do much of the chordal and melodic work, moving beyond the school training and bebop improv of her Detroit base, drawing perhaps more on the spiritual exploration of her early church music immersion.

Public school music training greenlighted democratically in my day and beyond. You could see a Mexican American girl in Harp and Vocal, before the group came to an abrupt halt in the 1970s as funding was cut back. Lydia Cleaver remembers the moment when she was in junior high when the support stopped—"It was fairly traumatic. It had a lasting impact on Detroit music." George Shirley, the eminent opera singer who taught briefly at Cass Tech, agrees that "students [were] being robbed of the possibility of music literacy." Cleaver says that the music and the opportunities for harpists changed, with the commercial opportunities dwindling after the removal of Motown in 1972. Church music ebbed as more students grew up without the influence of powerful choirs. Cass was eventually abandoned, vandalized, and demolished, but the rebuilt school next door still has a Harp and Vocal Ensemble, with its third-generation leader.

School-trained women played a leading role in Detroit's music culture, supporting the private lessons and performance breaks that young people need so badly to get started. The ladies of the Tuesday Musicale created a Student League to give talented girls "an opportunity to develop musical talents." In 1885, twelve women pianists gathered to establish a music club in Detroit. "Their idea was to improve their musical performance skills and to promote good music in a city that, as of yet, had no symphony orchestra or concert management. In the early years, the club brought quite the array of domestic and imported composers and performers: Paderewski, MacDowell, Nevin, Damrosch, Schumann-Heink, Gabrilowitsch, Hofmann, Kreisler, Lhevinne, and Cadman." The idea of a Detroit Symphony Orchestra started at the home of a Tuesday Musicale member in 1914, and some of the women became music teachers, moving mentoring from the outside to the inside of the city's musical system. Once again, the primacy of teaching emerges as the engine of advancement. Inviting American composers alongside European performers underlines the seriousness of the project—it's not just stars but creators of repertoire that young people need to see and hear. By 1926, a group of Jewish women music lovers decided to start their own parallel outfit, the Music Study Club, supporting both girls and boys. I spent many hours as a junior member at those sponsored gatherings, playing with student colleagues in well-appointed living rooms with grand pianos. Many of the kids who received scholarships to study with top-tier teachers went on to major careers in classical music. This tendency of women to be not just cheerleaders but activists for creating ensembles and students is well documented across the United States, and permeates every level of its "serious music" culture. Without women, there would be no infrastructure of orchestras, conservatories, and scholarships to grow talent and send it down the progressive-light streets of cities to national visibility. Musician Bennie Maupin went to Northeastern High, not a music training school like Cass Tech, but was launched on a career anyway after bumping into a woman who turned out to be the school's accompanist:

> Little white woman from somewhere, you know, from the universe, just came and saw me, embraced me, set me down in her office, whipped out the manuscript paper, I mean, just started, "Hey, this is what it is, this is where the notes are, this is how we do this, and this is why certain things are the way they are," and I was in her office once a week for the entire time that I was in high school.

The public schools, then, could rely on strong, often female, personnel paired with intensive community involvement. Outflanking restrictive codes, families, patrons, and teachers could agree on a social contract about music, both as a civic good and a personal pathway. Such support has waxed and waned in America, but it had a heyday in my day in Detroit. These efforts interlaced with the leanings and likings of neighborhood musical life, the focus of the next chapter.

"By day I make the cars / By night I make the bars"
—BOBBY BARE, "Detroit City," written by Danny Dill and Mel Tillis

4 Local Traffic

Detroit spread across 139 square miles of seemingly shapeless spaces, once you got out of the business bustle and the cultural center. But before Northland sprang up in 1954 as America's first suburban shopping center, people had a smaller sense of circulation. You could walk to familiar stores and might hear a homeland language or American dialect. You could drive downtown quickly, but you might also get there on a streetcar or bus, after standing at the stop and chatting. My brother and I rented comic books to people like that.

A neighborhood is physical, but also imaginative. Distant places arrive on your street on avenues of sentiment. Immigrants, relatives, songs, and prayers form part of a local traffic flow. "The neighborhood" was going through a shift, from a wartime view of solidarity and community to a postwar period that sponsored suburban growth and racial segregation.

Music still supported a sense of the local, offering an emblem of identity and employment for performers, some in transition from earlier homes in Europe or the American South. Sonic traffic circulated from local clubs to recording and radio studios, from the old downtown heart of entertainment out into national touring networks. It all started in the neighborhood.

When you traveled through an American city of the 1940s or 1950s, you sensed constant border crossings, even if the street sign never changed. Off the main avenues, traffic cruised more calmly, through side streets in what we call "neighborhoods." The word is not neutral. The Chicago school of sociology needed it as an "imaginative construct, a constellation of natural areas," each with a special character and function. Which was it, "imaginative" or "natural?" Ernest Burgess identified and named seventy-five neighborhoods in Chicago. By 1947, city planners had divided up his turf markers into no fewer than 513 units.

"Neighborhood" has been a battleground of ideas. Is it a reservoir of positive community or a roadblock to social progress? When does a zone become a "ghetto," a site of deep separation and dystopia? Are neighborhoods irrelevant as cities change? Robert J. Sampson argues for "multiple scales of ecological influence" from blocks to neighborhood clusters to wider community areas to networks that connect far-flung areas of the city. He offers two metaphors. One sounds like my sense of music as fluid culture: "Spatial network flows among neighborhoods are like rivers, with strong currents and whirlpools of activity. . . . Like an undercurrent, they are out of sight and usually conscious awareness." More industrially, Sampson sees neighborhoods "like a cog," with "bottom-up and top-down mechanisms." These two metaphors are intriguing for thinking about music. Yes, music can have an unsensed flow within and around the zones people live in. But the "bottom-up, top-down" image of music as just a cog in the machinery of power makes some sense too, given unequal access to jobs and resources and the sway of the media.

Avenues of European Sentiment

In my day, most people in Detroit came from somewhere else. When I entered the city in 1943, 20 percent of my fellow citizens were foreign-born, and 350,000 southerners had streamed in, when World War II started. The newcomers were mostly white, while about 15 percent of them African Americans. These people, mainly Protestant, did not necessarily get along with each other or with the earlier mostly Catholic immigrants, but they all sang and played their music. They blended what they remembered or heard at home with what they heard in their communities, in churches and at weddings. People did pick up songs at school and from the fairly sparse media: radio, records, and sheet music, with mass-market television only slowly creeping in. Just as Detroit was connected by the Ambassador Bridge and the Windsor Tunnel to Canada, people were linked to other places through music and traveled extensively on sentimental highways. Sometimes songs really did bridge gaps of time and distance or allow for a tunneling through dark spaces of experience into the Michigan light.

In this chapter, I offer the words of a few Detroit musicians and researchers that listened with newcomers' ears. Their experience repeats today across America, with its habit of opening and closing doors to outsiders who try to make a home in patchwork urban spaces. The Europeans and southerners of my day often came piecemeal, men first, sending for families when they found steady work. They forgot a lot of the music they knew, saved some, and improvised American homes and lives while trying to figure out what the city offered and demanded. They built structures of feeling, physically put together brick by brick in church and community spaces, out in the open in parks, on porches, at home in living rooms and basements, and in local clubs. Today, in the new immigrant era, it's people like Zimbabweans, Chinese, Colombians, and Kurds that are undergoing transit and immersion, making aesthetic adjustments. Each group sets up a local base and works out of it. When they move out, they come back for neighborhood flavors—food and music. They have kids that listen and ignore but might remember later, when they have their own families, or if opportunities open up for musicians. Those crosstown and cross-country networks spring up. Each city has its own hotspots of sentiment, where familiar faces sing the right songs to make audiences feel at home across the vast stretches of North America. Heritage groups form alliances based on shared sensibilities and neighboring homelands. The private and the public, the amateur and the professional, the local, national, and transnational separate and blend unpredictably in this musical traffic pattern.

America also expects these settlers to display themselves at public events. This pushes people to find ways to show off who they are supposed to be. The idea of spotlighting immigrant musics goes back to the nineteenth century, and was alive and well in my childhood. From the earlier decades of dealing with the "difficulties" of immigrant presence, this practice turned into a showcase for "mothballed cultures . . . periodically pulled out of a trunk for display," where the neighborhood become "a sort of museum of ethnic cultures" as the melting pot morphed into the ethnic pluralism of the 1960s. But mostly, the music of the groups in my Detroit shared a fate of neglect with much of the heartland. For a hundred years, "American traditional music" has largely been defined as "white" and "black," with everyone else as onlookers, unless they're very colorful, such as the "Cajuns," or raise their popular music profile, like the lumped-together "Latinos" or "Hispanics." Folklorist James Leary has spent a lifetime listening to the Upper Midwest, surveying "a creolized culture" of mining and logging camps, small industrialized towns, and larger cities in a region overlooked by folklore scholars. Earlier, the legendary collector Alan Lomax exhausted himself and his car driving around Michigan in 1938 and found it was "the most richly varied area for folk music that [he] had ever visited." But Lomax neglected the area in favor of the southern heartland—blues and ballads— that he promoted so well. The tireless 1930s local music hunter Emelyn Gardner also overlooked everything but Anglo-Saxon ballads as she traveled about the state, and rejected criticism for her failure to include songs from the "non-English-speaking population." Somewhat defensively, folklorist Albert Friedman says that "no one, Miss Gardner maintains, can say she has no respect for the folklore of immigrant groups," and she urged her students to collect what they heard in the home. She just wasn't going to publish it in her 1939 inclusive-sounding *Ballads and Songs of Southern Michigan*.

Leary's sketch of how immigrant European musicians adapted to American life fits Detroit pretty well. When he says that "nearly every self-respecting veteran of home and hall parties acquired at least one tune that might appeal to each of the many different nationalities," it rings true. He tells us that in the 1920s and 1930s, performers relied increasingly on "radio, the telephone, better roads, reliable cars, and sound recordings" that let bands "reach listeners from afar, arrange for paying jobs, travel on a dance-hall circuit, and supplement their income by selling records."

Leary and others describe a slow-moving Midwestern process, and in Detroit small communities of immigrants did stake out musical campsites early. But the post-1910 population and media explosion meant that shifts in the American lifestyle came late and fast to a city on the move. The increase of half a million "white" people from 1920 to 1930 and the tripling of the African American population in the same decade, then growing another 250 percent by 1950—it all created a more intense dynamic for music than in earlier urbanizing Midwestern sites. Detroit's constant reinvention meant that even some old neighborhoods saw explosive musical expansion as late as the 1940s and 1950s, as history brought newcomers, like the postwar refugee resettlement moment among Ukrainians and Jews.

The city kept its links to more rural Michigan with family ties, creating a layering of regional musics enriched by the immigrant waves. As Lomax noted, Michigan—including sprawling Detroit—"combined as the lusty tradition of the Northern woods singer with an infinitely varied pattern of immigrant European, Indian, and even Appalachian and Southern Negro music." Lomax's surprise at how powerfully mountain music survived in the city shows how Detroit expanded the range of his southern-dominated thinking.

Studying Detroit's diversity requires a demographic anchor, and there is a benchmark date and document. In 1951, the 250th birthday of Detroit stimulated a serious survey of "nationalities," headed by Prof. Thelma James. She was my mother's master's thesis advisor in the 1930s, an early collector of urban folklore, and the person who gave the eminent ethnomusicologist Bruno Nettl his first job. James and Nettl got their Wayne State students to collect family songs, though tape recorders were scarce. Thelma James scouted out ethnic partners, producing a population scan that included listings of music ensembles, radio presence, and entertainment spaces. It's a goldmine for mapping the city I grew up in at its height.

Some groups were smaller than I might have thought, and others were larger. Knowing the "other" comes from personal experience, not facts. Because I went to a Greek Orthodox midnight service with a classmate, and "Greektown" became a colorful downtown stop, I would have thought the Greeks, at 35,000, were more than just 10 percent of the Polish population, or just one-third of the Ukrainian figure. Driving to somewhere and seeing Albanian churches made me think they had a large neighborhood, but there were apparently only 3,000, split between Christian and Muslim. I thought of the Jewish neighborhood as fairly small and bounded, but at 90,000, it was a substantial subculture. With my east European orientation, I vaguely knew about the mid-range groups, such as the Czechs, Russians, Bulgarians, and Serbs, but had no sense there was a small Belgian, Danish, Turkish, or Japanese presence. I knew there were Mexicans, because of my brother's friend Roland Navarro, but had no idea of what he represented. Then there were the huge populations largely invisible to me, such as the 65,000 Franco-Americans and the 150,000 Italian Americans, who had little citywide musical profile. The second-largest group, German Americans, were the earliest and most musically important immigrants, but their culture was forced underground, being the expression of two-time enemies of the United States. No matter how small, groups had some kind of performing arts of their own. Even though the 2,000 Austrians relied on German-language outlets, they still had their own Austrian Society Dancing Group. The same-sized Chinese population had an Amvets Post that sponsored a song and dance ensemble. Even the 200 Estonians managed to support a choral and dance organization.

Each neighborhood went through its own development stages, from early settlers who built a local center of gravity to later breakup, all in a couple of generations. The music settled into layers, with some surviving and other forms buried in the dust of dispersal. Arab Americans arrived early; Detroit and America's first, short-lived mosque dates back to the 1920s. Today's huge and vibrant multilingual, multidenominational Arab population bears little resemblance to the modest community of my youth. Sally Howell describes Detroit's "Old Islam" as a small group that tried to keep a low profile and develop interethnic alliances, with little musical activity that has been documented beyond prayer meetings and a fledgling theater troupe. But the city's Middle Eastern minority produced an ethnically unmarked Arab American music giant, Casey Kasem (1932–2014), the Druze-origin developer and long-running voice of top 40 on the radio. Known for his narrative magic, Kasem credited his community: "I was drawing on the Arabic tradition of storytelling one-upmanship," he said. "When I was a kid, men would gather in my parents' living room and tell tales and try to outdo each other. I couldn't understand the language, but I was fascinated." Kasem's case shows how it's helpful to dig for local ethnic roots even among America's most assimilated music figures.

It is impossible to sensibly survey all the local music traffic of Detroit in its heyday. There's some deep documentation for selected groups, which offers a few online sources, some interviews, and a bit of publication. But many neighborhoods led musical lives that remain unexplored, such as that Mexican district. I know they had a movie house showing their popular musicals, and a couple of band names surface, but not much more. In what follows, I'm interested in a few issues: the pulsating inner life of subcultures, their musically interactive pattern, and how their singing streets flowed into the broader avenues of municipal culture. I'm saving the Jews for later treatment, because that group occupied an intriguing position in the city's cultural life, on the border between its own neighborhood and the wider world of municipal music.

I'll start with George and Lillian Ruzich, born in the late 1920s, who have offered an insightful interview about their early musical life. George's parents came from a village near Rijeka, Croatia, and his dad followed the pattern of coming first, then sending for the family. Surviving the coal mines of Pennsylvania, they came to Detroit for better work, like so many others. "As for music, my mom used to sing old Croatian songs, and my brother John used to find these old Croatian records. Pop had a little concertina, one octave. I used to watch him fool around with that and make up his own melodies—waltzes, polkas—and I started doing the same thing. I played the violin in grade school." The house rang with a rich mix of the mother's folk songs, commercially recorded "national" music, and homemade improvisations on Croatian themes. The woman singing, the man playing the instrument—that continues European custom. Soon enough, ladies dropped the folk songs connected to work and family, though some of them picked up concertinas. Meanwhile, the boy had gotten the green light from the Detroit public schools, becoming a violinist who could easily switch to mandolin when he was in the army in Italy, near the family's song sources. "I lugged that thing everywhere! My buddies used to hide it from me so I couldn't drive them crazy playing it. They used to tie it up on top of the barracks' rafters. One time they even hauled it up on the flag pole." The mainstream taste of George's fellow soldiers made it hard for him to enjoy his subcultural sounds, and he got the message—back in Detroit, he didn't switch to roots. He "played American tunes—polkas, tangos, rumbas and fox trots, but none of our Croatian songs yet." Why did George see those Central European and Caribbean tunes as "American," especially since his father was making up polkas right at home? Mainstream music is omnivorous, swallowing and assimilating sounds from all the internal groups as well as many tasty musics from elsewhere. This drive to assimilate is often commercially driven. Songs from the old neighborhood begin to stand in for the emotionally and physically distanced "homeland," even if the sound had been Americanized. Poles in Poland have no affinity for the American polka.

Lillian Ruzich's story parallels George's, with some inflection: her father came from Pennsylvania to Detroit, but her mother was taken back to Croatia. Since she lived there until she was twelve, she picked up more European songs and stayed bilingual in Detroit. The transatlantic twist reminds me of my own family pattern, and it is much more prevalent than you might think. The image we have of immigrants "never looking back," to quote Neil Diamond's song "America," is wildly inaccurate. Lillian's parents would "take an English word and turn it into a Croatian word, such as *streetcara*." This tell-tale word recalls the age of early mass transit. Streetcar society might be a term for the early working-class, newcomer neighborhoods, which lasted until the 1950s, when the freeway definitively displaced it. Lillian's parents taught the kids Croatian songs, and Dad ran rehearsals for his combo in the basement on Friday nights until midnight or one in the morning: "So here we were upstairs listening to the music and enjoying it." Personal sentiment merges with marketing in this continuing travel on the highways from the homeland. Surrounded by many European Families—Serbian, Polish, Bulgarian, Macedonian, Italian, Slovenian—Lillian vividly remembers the struggling Croatian family next door, the Babiches, with a widowed father and ten kids. The neighbors turned to music to survive, forming a household tamburitza band: "They were an enterprising family because these were hard times," says Lillian matter-of-factly. She herself teamed up with her sister Violet during World War II as a duo who sang in Croatian at events like a big war bond rally in the heart of downtown Detroit. This type of event brought the neighborhood communities to a central space and landed the thirteen-year-old sisters in the *Detroit News*. Doubtless the article stressed the enthusiasm of foreign-origin citizens for this patriotic cause. It's a very different context for the same Croatian songs than when the sisters sang on the air, for WJBK's Croatian Radio Club. "We'd sing requests for special occasions—anniversaries, birthdays." Located downtown but reachable on any car radio, early ethnic-themed radio offered yet another avenue of sentiment.

The Ruziches remained remarkably faithful to their neighborhood sounds: "Our wedding in Detroit was at the VFW Hall. We had eight hundred people on two floors! Two orchestras, including a tamburitza orchestra, as well as a strolling violinist, Julius Peskan. People danced kolos, waltzes, polkas, fox trots, everything, all to tamburitza music." Following the low-income custom of the times, the couple, like my own mom and dad, lived for a while with the parents: "There was always music and singing . . . spontaneous like," and they learned to play in the family band. This kept their bridges to the homeland, to the point of organizing the Detroit Tamburitzan Orchestra in 1957, which is still going after decades, even though the Ruziches moved to the San Francisco area. By its twentieth anniversary, the DTO was exchanging visits with the Pittsburgh tamburitzans, and by 1984 they toured Croatia itself. After 9/11, the group played a benefit for victims as "A Tribute to America." So even today, you can always take the music exit back to the old neighborhood as a source of sustenance.

In the early years, Lillian Ruzich would sometimes model her performance on the striking Vinka Ellesin, a Serbian American singer known as "the queen of *sevdalinka*," a sentimental urban song style. Ellesin lived in Detroit in the formative wartime period, ending up in the Tamburitza Hall of Fame. This creation of shared spaces of sensibility runs straight through the story of Detroit music, as indeed it does everywhere that groups of newcomers found themselves living side by side in American cities. Like Vinka Ellesin, Rodney Glusac, mentioned previously as a Cass Tech alum, came from the Serbian side. While playing for fifty-eight years in the band he started at Cass Tech in 1951, he appeared constantly at the Croatian club, mixing with Romanians, Macedonians, Slovenians, and Roma as band and audience members and audience over a long career. As a working musician, he would do a job with a Syrian youth group, play for the bar mitzvah of an Egyptian Jew, or do an upscale gig in chic Grosse Pointe, where they limited ethnic music to 20 percent of the numbers. One steady band had members of Slovenian, Croatian, Czech, and Roma ("Gypsy") background. There were three local clubs, with music coming in from the big Chicago Serbian settlement, where the celebrated Popovich Brothers held sway for decades. All this steady inter-group colleagueship and conviviality ran into speed bumps as history intervened, with the Syrian priest not wanting "that Hava Nagila" stuff because of the 1967 Mideast war or the Croat and Serb singers separating out during the bitter post-Yugoslav conflict around 1990. The Armenians willingly played Turkish music in the earlier decades of inter-group sharing, but not in recent decades, as attitudes toward Turkey have hardened. But earlier, as part of Detroit's open-ears-and-hearts attitude, Rodney Glusac hired Hachig Kazarian to play for his son's wedding. Hachig, mentioned earlier as my Cass Tech orchestramate, graduated in 1960.

It was still the golden age of the Armenian/Mediterranean scene in Detroit, lovingly documented by Ara Toupouzian in his 2014 film *Guardians of the Music*. The epicenter of the music scene was the Stockade, a place named for its slaughterhouse setting on the southwest side. It was in Del Ray, a neighborhood famous for its mixture of groups and musicians, especially the Hungarians and Roma. It was close to the auto plants, the magnet that had drawn all these people to Detroit. Everyone—except Hachig—had a day job, on the line or in the many support industries, such as Hachig's teacher, Kerkorian, in the dry-cleaning business. The Stockade's owner was not Armenian, but he saw a good business opportunity. At the club, Armenians, Serbs, and Greeks would gather, getting along with their common rhythms and scales. Hachig stresses musical sharing, whether listening or gigging. He played mixed Armenian-Jewish weddings, with a musician for each side. But when "Hava Nagila" came out, everybody danced to it, Armenians dancing clockwise, the Jews counterclockwise, he says. The clarinetist also spent long nights listening to music in Greektown or after-hours sessions where Roma fiddlers would play for tips. Some of those violinists also subbed in the Detroit Symphony Orchestra, showing the cross-over strength that "Gypsy" musicians display everywhere they are found.

Hachig's intergroup listening habits started with his earliest musical experience. Music in the house was "all Armenian," and as a boy he learned clarinet by rote from an oldtimer. But his grandfather sang the Kurdish songs he had learned in Turkey in the old days and used Kurdish as a secret language. American subcultures are never monolithic. Within the Armenian community, like dialects, "every melody had a different dance step" depending on local traditions. Some people were against ever using Turkish music, due to the horror visited on the Armenians in 1915. Hachig grew up with many kids of massacre survivors. But others shrugged and said "Music is music." Sure, the community was internally fragmented along ideological lines, but you could walk into any wedding and just dance. The older styles of instrumental music, "Istanbul style," were not deeply rooted in Armenian Detroit, as compared to the church and group dance repertoire. People would play in pickup groups and have music at picnics, like so many other groups did. They didn't make recordings locally, learning from the major-label records that were easily available to all American ethnic communities, dating back to the dawn of the twentieth century. The recording industry started in New Jersey, and nearby urban minorities formed a huge natural market, twenty years before the companies discovered the blues and "old-time" music in the South. Live events would be headed by stars from New York. Hachig and Ara Toupouzian have seen three generations of musicians come and go, and the specialized music has slowly receded. Ara's meticulous restoration work and his appearances as a qanun zither player help to raise consciousness of the lesser-known instrumental tradition, but he admits that many of his appearances are at municipal showcases for diversity rather than for his community. I saw him in 2015 at a Wayne State University event commemorating the centennial of the Armenian genocide, co-sponsored by Jewish organizations.

The Armenians are not alone in this shift from in-house to public presentation. The music can even build an off-ramp for the musical traffic flow, bringing Detroiters into a neighborhood for cultural tourism. This is how one small locale became "Greektown." As happens in America, it started with the movies. Dan Georgakas says that when *Never on Sunday* came out in 1960, local businessmen noticed that people were enchanted by the glamorous, languorous hooker played by Melina Mercouri and wanted to get up and dance like the happy natives in the film. Hiring musicians for tourism, not weddings, began. The clubowners also profited from 1964's *Zorba the Greek*, which etched the image of fun-loving, philosophical Greeks further into the mind of Americans, and Greektown flourished. It started with musicians at the Dakota Inn on Woodward, second-generation Greeks, Armenians, and Arabs. The emcee, Herman Torigian, was a taxi driver who moved when the scene shifted to Sammy G's on Six Mile Road, which tried to create the tavern atmosphere of Greektown closer to the suburbs. Toupuzian also cites that club as an alternative space, far from the homeland neighborhoods in the south of the city. Detroit is always on the move, and even ethnic music cannot survive without adapting to the nonstop mobility of an endlessly expanding city.

In pre-suburban times, the Greek community, like mine, lived in two-family houses (I had my grandparents upstairs). There was not enough money or people to float an extensive entertainment circuit. Also like me, Dan Georgakas has fond memories of family singing in the car, with his father doing "harvest tunes that often had a peppy sexual innuendo." Only occasionally did full-throated music rock the room, when the Toledo Five would appear from Ohio. This group of factory workers moonlighted as musicians. The leader played clarinet, and the others were fiddlers, sometimes amplifying the sound with tambourines, flutes, and goat-hide bagpipes. "They produced a wild mountain sound that had a thrilling piercing quality." For New Year's Eve, men would sit in the living room singing, with their kids feeling slightly embarrassed, "fearful that the American neighbors might disapprove, but even with this discomfort, we felt in balance."

But it's not as if the Americans next door were of ancient local stock; there were "all the nations of Europe and a considerable number of Near Easterners, Latin Americans, and a sprinkling of Asian." The block had Belgian, French Canadian, Polish, Romanian German, Irish, Scottish, and Italian families along with a cluster of Appalachian whites, a single "genuine Connecticut Yankee," and nearby one Jewish family who had a dry-cleaning shop. In the 1940s and 1950s, with so many newcomers from so many places, why would there be any problem flying your in-group colors? It was possible to cook Greek all the time, except for Thanksgiving and Christmas, to spend time as a kid learning to be "American" from Hollywood movies in long double-feature sessions with added cliffhanger serials, newsreels, and cowboy featurettes. As Georgakas says, "There was never a hyphen in Greek American" since he was simultaneously both.

Georgakas tellingly observes that he viewed the world with "a disembodied ethnic third eye." I also grew up with this special vision, and it permeates the fine American fiction writing about immigrant life that has blossomed recently. But even as you are embedded in local traffic, you scan the world for possible speed bumps. I worried about our Red Army Chorus album in the McCarthy era, and my brother felt shy about asking for "Russian pumpernickel," even at our local Jewish bakery. Watching others' behavior and locating your neighborhood among the villages that dotted the huge landscape of Detroit was second nature. Trips to the International Institute downtown regularly brought all of us immigrant types to the center, where groups showcased their dances, swirling skirts and all. The popular governor G. Mennen "Soapy" Williams, heir to a cosmetics fortune, had a folksy style that matched his signature green and white polka-dot bowtie. He turned up to dance Greek, a pattern of ethnic patronage-hunting shared by every American politician for at least a century. Nineteenth-century settlement houses tried to make immigrants feel comfortable and safe, spreading seeds of awareness of ethnic dance and music forms into public school and college recreation, local music and dance studios, church and synagogue outreach, or even shopping malls looking for multicultural consumers. This urge for intersections survived the cutoff of mass migration in 1924 and the isolation, and even stigmatizing, of groups during wartimes. It lasted until the ideology of multiculturalism replaced assimilationism and the melting-pot metaphor, after the reopening of immigration in 1965 and the celebration of "diversity" for the bicentennial in 1976.

There were few neighborhood names, since in Detroit's huge territory, people tended to locate by the basics: East Side and West Side, on either side of the main drag, Woodward Avenue, or to name by streets, as part of their traffic mentality: Twelfth Street, Dexter-Davison, Joy Road, Michigan Avenue, the Cass Corridor—it's the roads that fronted your territory and led you out to the center that counted in people's minds. Greektown was an exception, as was Del Ray, with its Hungarians and Roma, and Paradise Valley as the old black center, but not that many other districts were origin-specific. For the Jews, constantly on the move between large black and white blocs, the "Jewish neighborhood" kept moving steadily northwest, eventually beyond the city limits.

Perhaps the most iconic neighborhood was Hamtramck, a municipality surrounded by Detroit that Henry Ford carved out back in 1915 as his own factory fiefdom. It held nearly 20 percent of Detroit's people, the Polish Americans. Carefully and deeply described in Laurie Gomulka Palazzolo's work, this community offers a major example of in-group musicality. Starting back with the first wave of immigration in the early 1900s, Poles developed a deep set of customary celebrations, gatherings, and venues that gave work for three generations of musicians: "Name Day, pre-Lenten dances, pre-Advent dances, Easter dances, christenings, and funeral masses and marches. . . . The biggest events . . . were all-day bridal showers . . . and, of course, the Polish wedding." There were special pieces for "*na porciu*, on the porch, when the bride emerged, including the [US] national anthem, which stopped traffic, when everyone would sing along," a custom that waned only in the 1960s.

FIG. 4.1. Christine Bielat's wedding at the Radio Café, with outdoor musicians. Photo: University of Michigan Chene Street Project, Courtesy of Marcia Kubacki & Christine Bielat.

This combination of the Polish and the patriotic marked much of the musicality of Detroit's Euro-Americans. Ernie Skuta, a Czech American who played with Poles, Slovenes, and many other groups, organized the ten-piece Spirit of America Band for that all-American venue, the park band shell. Palazzolo is assertive, if a shade defensive, about the patriotic strain in Detroit Polish culture, when describing the group's impressive cultural clubhouses, such as the Dom Polski at Forest and Chene: "In their time, the once-majestic, proud Dom Polski halls were deemed pretentious by those of other nationalities, who simply did not understand the Polish immigrants' compelling need to erect monuments representing both their culture and Americanism." But much small-scale musicianship was literally in-house. Musicians appeared at people's name days and performed for just a drink and a small fee. Families were tightly tied to music economics—the Grzesik Brothers would get bookings when people walked into their family grocery to set a date. In the 1930s–1950s, every bar had a band playing every night. Ballrooms had a polka night every week and threw in a polka every night alongside the "American" repertoire. Swing, ballroom dances, and eventually Latin numbers infiltrated the Polish American sound, just as they did in all the Euro-American and Jewish neighborhoods.

FIG. 4.2. Edmund Krzyk with the McGregor Band at a nightspot on Chene Street, playing Polish and light classical music. Photo: University of Michigan Chene Street Project, courtesy Edmund Krzyk.

Distinctive to Detroit, perhaps, is the combination of long-simmering ethnic expression with a late-boiling moment, during and just after World War II, when older communities heated up their music, fueled by demographic and economic pressures: "The mass return of soldiers from World War II ushered in an unprecedented surge of bridal showers, weddings, and christenings. . . . The formation of veterans' clubs and the erection of VFW, PLAV, and American Legion halls resulted in parties and dances being held all over town every weekend. . . . Not only were weddings very numerous in the 1950s but . . . the big Polish picnics were in vogue. . . . A single polka record could sell more than 5000 copies in one record shop alone." But already by 1950, weekend dances declined as the audience aged. American ethnic music is very generational. Outside influences—Li'l Wally and the Chicago Sound—began to dominate, dislocating a Polish Detroit sound that was distinctive, "primarily because of its East Coast influence." These conflicting sources and local adaptations were not limited to one group. For Euro-Americans as well as African Americans, Detroit was always perched between the musical powerhouse of Chicago to the west and the magnetism of New York to the east.

Media moved music around. Within a community as large as the Poles, bandleaders used recording to promote their names, trying to get on the air to reach a mass audience. Recently reissued tracks of the Detroit polka sound display a technical skill and canny selection of styles and genres, from the purely old-time Polish to the Americanized, and out to interethnic influences. Within their territory, musicians concentrated on conquering a market share through variations on local themes: "The Detroit bandleaders were not afraid to take risks, to diverge, and to formulate their own styles within the Detroit sound; [each one's style was] unique and distinguishable from each other's." These hardworking musicians searched every social space for an opening, not wanting to do the brutal factory work that their fathers had suffered and sometimes died from. Like all Detroit entertainers, including jazz musicians, country music stars, and the young rock 'n' rollers, the Poles and other ethnic musicians would go on and off the factory line when times were hard, or move away from the dance floor to an office, if they could work up to a white-collar job. Back in the 1930s, Alan Lomax noted this necessary connection between work and music: "A Serbian played his shepherd's flute for me—a virtuoso performance by a steel chipper who reads and writes little and still plays his pipe for his amusement in the shadow of the automobile work." Polka bandleader Eddie Hoyt was successful on the bandstand but didn't give up his day job at American Metal Products. Ted Gomulka's hectic life in the year 1953 offers a snapshot of this lifestyle: "He played 95 gigs, including twelve weddings, while working a full-time factory job and privately teaching as many as a dozen students a week."

Gomulka—Palazzolo's dad—recorded for the national label Decca in 1950. On one side, he chose to celebrate Hamtramck itself, with lyrics by his wife Ruth. It's a blend of boosterism and self-effacing humor that was common in ethnic recordings meant for a wider American audience. Advertising your girls as pretty and your food as tasty is a standard device for this genre. The tune is general Central European, precisely played, and the voices are very mainstream. The text teases, as local pride in progress mixes with an apology for the "confusing" names. Before multiculturalism, this was the normal ambivalence of ethnicity.

"A City Called Hamtramck," Ted Gomulka and His Band, 1950

There's a city called Hamtramck
That really is dynamic.
The people there have put it on the map.
The girls, to be specific, are really quite terrific
Just feel a kiss, you'll find it's worth the slap.

There's Jaworski! Kowalski! Chybinski!
You won't find a Mr. Smith or Mr. Brown there,
But you'll find they've really got a growing town there.

But if you're in the neighborhood, why not go down there.
Pierogi! Herbata! Kapusta! And a lot of other food you won't be used to.
If you tell me you're Stasz and you tell me you're Jasz up and down
　　Hamtramck way
Oh, the names that they use are enough to confuse in Hamtramck, USA.

Yes, the city named Hamtramck is really futuramic
And once you do the town you'll want to stay,
For the people there are cheerful, their music is an earful,
You'll realize it is hard to break away.
Polka! Oberek! Mazurka! You will never hear a samba or a rumba,
For the band will play your favorite Polish number
So you can dance all night, forget about your slumber.
You'll find Sophie and Wanda and Stella, they're that pretty girls that go
　　with every fella
Oh, the dance that they do, it should happen to you,
And we know that you will say
There's a city of sun, there's a barrel of fun in Hamtramck, USA

For these hard-working ethnic musicians, such as my junior high orchestra director, Mr. Klocko, one way to stop juggling their careers was to work for music education certification. This avoidance of the bandstand is critiqued by Greg Adamus, a musician from an eminent polka family:

> They most likely defaulted to "music educator" degrees because they couldn't hack it as music performance majors. They also probably skipped over the gigging life during their formative years (ages 18 to 30), because they were in college then, and went right into a school job upon graduation. My point here: the gigging musicians who are/were also band directors in the schools, more than likely, did NOT start out that way as adults. They lived the gigging life first, built their chops, and only after being on the road awhile, settled down, got married and went to night school to get their teaching degree.

Top-notch or not, these teachers needed to moonlight in clubs and at weddings, given the low salaries of Detroit public school teachers (like my father, who held down two after-hours jobs).

Polish musicians formed their own extended professional family, competing with, but supporting each other in public, emotional ways. Palazzolo describes "the time-honored custom the musicians had of forming long funeral processions and performing while marching en masse to the deceased musician's graveside," which went on until the 1980s. "People drove out of the cemetery smiling, not crying, with their windows rolled down, singing along." Anticipating this celebration of their lives, musicians stipulated the music for their funerals. But the polka bandleaders were hardly parochial. They reached out in every possible way to extend their musicianship, either among fellow ethnics or in mainstream spaces of entertainment. Connections with Ukrainians were particularly close: "The single most influential music instructor on the west side was Ukrainian clarinetist, educator and mentor John Kustodowich [d. 1964] who mentored Polish boys. . . . If the Polish-American bandleaders were the soul of the orchestras, the Ukrainians were the heart." This affinity got its start back in Europe: "People like Onachuk and Silven Koltyk, accordionist, were from Galicia's Ukrainian-Polish borderlands and played both." Czechs also chipped in to the sound. Conversely, the Polish bandleaders got hired for all the other Euro-American weddings, particularly the Italian events, but also for Hungarians, alongside Roma musicians, and for Jewish celebrations. It's the same story as that for the other communities—Greek, Armenian, and the rest. As the Euro-Americans increasingly intermarried in multiethnic Detroit, someone like Bob Lymperis, with a Greek father and Irish American mother, could play "for Polish, Romanian, Italian, and Greek weddings," though he admitted that "Greek music, with its Oriental aspects, is extremely difficult to play." He did record a track with Wally Gomulka doing "Misirlou" the all-purpose dance tune best known for its appearance in Quentino Tarantino's film *Pulp Fiction*, a popular melody less demanding than the modal Mediterraneanism of southeastern Europe, Armenia, and Turkey.

As fraternal as the music making might be within the ethnic world, outside, bandsmen tried hard to blend in, frequently changing their names to match the increasingly "American" sound of their bands—up to two-thirds of the tunes by the 1980s. They had to be "masters of marketing and flexibility," like Ted (Gorzcyka) Gordon, who rose to the post of Detroit Police Band head, which he held for twenty-six years, also playing with the seminal black jazz band McKinney's Cotton Pickers. John Gajec got his start running the Boys Club band and orchestra, then went on to the University of Michigan for graduate work, returning to town to run the university's Extension Orchestra and playing in the Hamtramck Philharmonic and organizing the Redford Symphony Orchestra in another neighborhood. As with the Jews, as we shall see, for the Poles, classical music was an important influence and arena. In 1965, the Metropolitan Opera recognized this passion by putting on two performances in Hamtramck. For the Poles, as for many of Detroit's European-origin communities, singing societies presented the polished presence of heritage, removed from the rough and tumble of dance halls and raucous celebrations. The

Lutnia Society filled this function. Photos show the two faces of genteel musician-ship in 1938: the ethnic costumes often worn by children's groups and the formal dress—gowns and tuxedos—for the adult ensemble. Their coach, Sam Weinfeld was a Hungarian Jew who hung out with Roma musicians, so even the most "national" of Detroit's ensembles could be tinged with interethnic shades.

FIGS. 4.3 AND 4.4. Lutnia Society ensembles, 1934, with two looks: European folk for children, formal dress for adults. Photos courtesy Alice Murz-Maternicki and Marian Krzyzowski, Chene Street History Study.

From the 1930s to 1970s, Detroit's Polish community epitomized the model of a long-standing, fully formed internal music culture that collaborated, reached out, and flourished as long as the old city system remained intact. It paralleled the tightly knit groups in Chicago and Buffalo that Charles and Angelika Keil surveyed in the 1970s. They point out that every "Polonia" in the "Polish-American polka belt . . . evolves a different music in response to local history, personalities, economic conditions, and the particular mosaic of ethnic working-class neighborhoods that promotes some kinds of cultural borrowings and antagonisms but not others." Detroit's Polonia shared many features with others: waves of immigration, generational taste shifts, internal variation, outreach to other ethnic and mainstream opportunities and styles. Though "each polka locality could be the subject of volumes of reporting and analysis," not many such studies appeared when the polka system was in full bloom. Writing around 1990, the Keils were elegiac and anxious about the survival of the music and its celebratory lifestyle: "Can the echo of that social coherence, the resonance with all eras of Polish-American history, be transmitted to youth raised on television?" was already a question by the 1970s, and the answer has been, Well . . . maybe. Scattered into the suburbs, the closely concentrated, economically stable situation faded with the decline of the industrial base, the ongoing assimilation to newer American musical patterns, and the aging of the polka audience. In the 1980s and 1990s, newer waves of immigration from Poland clashed and combined with older musical habits and structures, an ongoing process familiar to many American immigrant groups. Both the bands and the choruses have survived as expressions of heritage. Recently, newer blends have emerged, such as the Polish Muslims, whose name mirrors the shifting demographics of Hamtramck, a city where Muslims currently hold a majority on the town council and the call to prayer is part of the soundscape. This large, well-synchronized band parallels the rise of the more mainstream "Weird Al" Yankovic, the Grammy-winning, accordion-based parodist. The Detroit outfit specializes in parodies of well-known rock and pop songs, substituting local references and the working-class lifestyle celebrated by the Keils' book, such as "Bowling USA" for the Beach Boys' "Surfing USA," with frequent shout-outs to local eateries and dances. It's a long way from the passionate persistence of polka in the days of a dense Hamtramck Polish presence, but the theme of local pride in the face of Americanization never changes.

To round out this small survey of the huge traffic pattern of Detroit's Euro-American neighborhoods, the Ukrainians tell a distinctive, dynamic story of musical survival, jump-started by a late wave of immigrants. Like the Poles and others, the Ukrainians made their presence felt one hundred years ago, with churches and drama and music groups. But the community was jolted by the charge of a highly talented set of musicians who came in 1949 as "displaced persons"—refugees—with a special skill set. The Kytasty family—Petro and his uncle Hrigory—had survived some of the most challenging experiences any musicians could undergo. As narrated by Petro, the story begins in Soviet times, when top-down cultural policy opened up spaces for children and young people to enter organizations that offered official versions of "folk" music and dance. Stalin massacred older representatives of the wandering minstrel traditions, clearing the way for this modernized form of "national" identity within a socialist state. Petro and his peers learned enough to participate in huge concerts by 1939, with a star conductor brought from Leningrad (now St. Petersburg). The bandura (zither) band appeared alongside chorus, dancers, and gymnasts.

The arrival of the war in 1941 changed everything. Fourteen members of the bandura band ended up in German slave labor camps, where the Nazis saw they could raise morale among the suffering workers. They ended up in Soviet territory and finally, at war's end, made their way to the American occupation zone in Germany, where they also concertized for Ukrainian refugees in the British and French zones. Finally, they met a sponsor who brought them to Detroit in 1949. This epic tale is told in Oren Sushko's moving 2014 documentary *Music for Survival*. Like so many other musicians, Petro ended up on the Chrysler assembly line before he was drafted into the US Army as an intelligence officer. Petro stayed under the military umbrella, training as an engineer under the GI Bill and working for the Army Corps of Engineers. All the while, the Kytastys energized the Detroit Ukrainian community with their knowledge of choral and instrumental arrangement for church and band performance. Hrigory's new songs and vivid concertizing spread from Detroit along the national Ukrainian network, with a national organization emerging in 1958. Petro organized the youth bandurists' movement, which spread to Winnipeg and Cleveland. This initiative culminated in a large-scale concert at a major downtown hall in Detroit in 1969 with groups from several cities, under local guidance. The project lives on in summer workshop programs in Pennsylvania, and Cleveland still has a youth bandura ensemble. The Kytasty legacy has flowed into the innovative work of son Julian, with his projects based on neglected traditions and his remarkable collaborative work with Michael Alpert on the joint Ukrainian-Jewish musical heritage, *Songs from a Neighboring Village*.

One genre of songs was common to all European-origin groups: the immigrant's complaint about America. Usually set in the mode of irony or satire, such songs fill the catalogs of the record companies. They favor a working-class view and use English words to comic effect, and so are hard to translate, often using different registers of speech, from a European dialect to American slang. They tend to make fun of both

FIG. 4.5. Ukrainian Bandurist Chorus, Detroit, 1953. Photo courtesy Irene Kytasty Kuzma.

the simple "greenhorn," America, and, at times, the class structure of the group, since emigration shakes up the social order. A fine Italian example on a small Detroit label is Frank Amato's aptly titled 1952 number "L'Emigrante Disilluso," where the keyword is, of course, "money," given as "the most important English word." The song lurches between standard Italian and Sicilian dialect (marked with underlining). The internal regional and class distinctions within any immigrant community tend to be blurred, whether it's a generalized census check-off category or the American tendency to simplify ethnicity. Here's an excerpt of Amato's text:

> Un signore emigrante, e assai elegante <u>cu</u> la testa vacante discendente di
> <u>sangu</u> blu.
> Nell'America e <u>arrivatu</u>, ancora <u>nun</u> e un <u>misi</u> e già sa <u>imparatu</u> la <u>chiu</u> bella
> parola inglisi.
> "Muni, muni muni!..." [= money]
> Si e <u>imparatu</u> a di... Che sola voli <u>truvari</u>, e <u>prestu</u> <u>riturnari.</u>

> An immigrant gentleman, very elegant,
> A bit absent-minded and descended from blue bloods
> Arrived in America not even a month ago,
> And already he's learned the most important English word.
> Money, money money!
> This is what he learned to say.
> This is what he now wants to find, so he can quickly return.

Notice that the emigrant simply wants to make a bundle and then go back home, a common theme despite the standard "Statue of Liberty" rhetoric about finding the American dream.

To sum things up, Detroit was a very European city in my day, across a huge range of musics, from the dance hall to the symphony orchestra. By the 1940s, the groups were losing the older folk music styles they had brought with them. The close quarters of the city moved musicians and audiences toward more popular, Americanized sounds shared within and across neighborhoods that had similar taste. This internal energy circulated within a pressure-packed urban landscape that set off these European settlers from the influx—they might have said onslaught—of white and African American immigrants from the American South.

Appalachian Circulation

The idea of local traffic in the neighborhood expands to include crosstown connections in the case of the white Appalachian immigrants, the "hillbillies." They lived in five areas of settlement, often mixed in with European settlers. Their musical activity took them all over town, due to their very large numbers and mobility, since they did not face the housing barriers that African Americans endured. As recent arrivals, they did not necessarily get along with the older European Catholic communities. Since the whole of the United States could be their stamping grounds, white southern—"country"—musicians came and left Detroit freely, following job networks across America or falling back on a Detroit home base. There is a fine detailed account of this hotbed of talent in Craig Maki and Keith Cady's book *Detroit Country Music*. The authors' selection of local venues and national points of origin and touring is partial, but I've drawn a map from their listings that helps to locate these lively musicians' clustered origins in the border states, particularly Tennessee and Kentucky, and their circulation in the city. US Route 23, the north-south highway that passed through Toledo regularly dropped off immigrants in the Motor City. The Brooks Bus Line made a round-trip run in a single day from Detroit to Paducah, Mayfield, and Fulton in Kentucky and back again, nonstop. The highway was made famous by Dwight Yoakam's 1987 song "Readin' Rightin' Route 23." Its ambivalent lyrics knock both the horror of working in the mines and the tainted solution of moving north: "They didn't know that old highway would lead them to a world of misery." So it's no surprise that the map also shows the restlessness of country musicians' travel patterns, based on short-term opportunities and long-term connections of business and sentiment.

Within the city, the country music settings listed by Maki and Cady overlap and contrast with comparable information for Palazzolo's polka people. The Poles are clustered in their neighborhood, but can also be found in the downtown mainstream venues—clubs, radio studios. The country crowd played and record in the

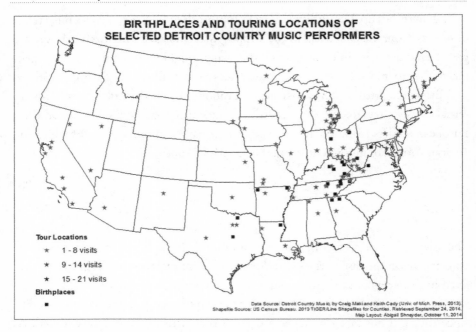

FIG. 4.6. Closely-packed birthplaces of Detroit country musicians vs. wide touring network. Data from Maki and Cady 2013, GIS map by Abigail Shneyder.

central locations, but they pop up all over the map as the Appalachian immigrants ranged across the endless white-dominated landscape of southeastern Michigan. It's just local traffic on a much grander scale.

The southern white musicians needed clubhouses for the local traffic trade, and they picked up real estate wherever they could find it. In the old neighborhood on Mound Road, Eddie Jackson's parents had a café and lived behind the building. They hired black musicians to play jazz and pop, so he got wide musical exposure even while living local. Lonnie Barron went way out to the actual country, buying the White Eagle Hall from Polish immigrants in Muttonville, a tiny spot that once housed a sheep slaughterhouse, out at Gratiot and 32 Mile Road. He used the space for barn dances, until he was shot dead by a jealous husband. People even started record labels out in those boondocks, as we see in the story of Clix Records, which tried to blend bluegrass with high school rock 'n' roll because "so many musical stories begin and end in marginal places," particularly for the white southerners of greater Detroit. In the 1950s, Dennis Coffey—later a Motown star guitarist—had a wide-ranging mental map of musical options, both for listening and playing: "In those days we were young, full of teenage enthusiasm, and thought nothing of driving all over Detroit or the suburbs to play our music. We were both totally fascinated by rockabilly . . . I would drive anywhere to hear a new guitar player. . . . I also practiced

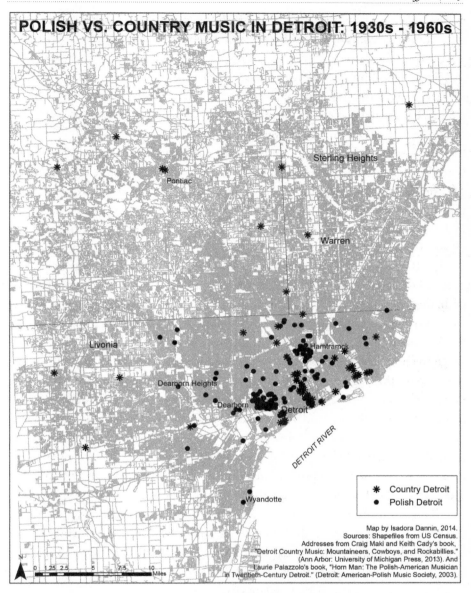

FIG. 4.7. Clustering of Polish musicians' territory vs. wide spread of country musicians' sphere of activity. Data from Maki and Cady 2013, Palazzolo 2003. GIS map by Isadora Dannin.

night and day and learned all of the guitar licks and solos that were being played on the radio." Notice that the radio is just another zone of discovery, a topic we will return to.

In surveying this Appalachian immigrant scene, I'll focus on a few key issues that cut across the chapters of this book: deep internal eclecticism that contradicts any notion of static subcultures, interaction with the many moving parts of the Motor City's music machinery, and wide personal variability in choices and career turns. Take for example, Mountain Red, "the Kentucky Troubadour," who worked for GM and Ford, entertaining at western-themed corporate events, a direct link to the city's industrial-managerial dominance. He also played for the Bob-Lo cruise ships on the river and at church and charity benefits, as well as coffee shops, bars, and cafes. No simple "honky-tonk" storyline covers this range of activity, matched and bettered by Mountain Red's competitors. One band "avoided bars and nightclubs for family-friendly fairs and events such as the State Sheep Shearing Contest in Manchester MI." In the 1940s, the Gus Sun booking agency landed the sponsorship of an agricultural machinery company that sent musicians all over the state in a variety show that included a contortionist and a juggler. It's an industrial translation of the medicine shows popular back in Appalachia. May Hawks, a 1950s woman star, was booked by the Michigan Milk Producers Association: "I played for the people who had the cows, who produced the milk, and for their banquets. I'd play a thirty-minute program then we'd have food. . . . Then we went to the haulers' meetings." Also wholesome was her frequent appearance in the public schools, starting in 1960: "I'd go for the early morning show, then on to another school for the noontime show, then I'd go to another show before they were closed in the evening. . . . I'd get [the children] up on the stage and have them sing." So much for the tears-in-the-beer stereotype of country music performance. Other venues for Hawks included Masonic lodges, Shriner functions, and the Detroit Yacht Club. The Michigan Raccoon Club also hosted bluegrass bands, starting in 1948. WJR Radio hosted southern white music (more on that below), but apparently "nobody got paid" for playing over the airwaves—it was strictly a promotional device. The first country music figure, Joe Steen, arrived back in 1932 for a job with Ford after leaving radio work in Louisville. He changed his name to Jack West and worked back into radio on WJR with his Circle Star Cowboys. Records did not offer much income support either. Artists would pay Fortune Records to make two to three hundred copies of a 45 rpm disc, and they would self-market them. As with the Poles and other Detroit groups, the lack of a major record label scattered musicians' efforts.

In a difficult economic climate, with the auto industry's ups and downs, country specialists kept their day jobs as long as needed, often on the assembly line, but also in a variety of other blue-collar jobs. Cranford "Ford" Nix moved ambivalently between the factory and the dance club: "I had my job back at Chrysler . . . and I never really intended on going into music full time. I wished I had." They also left town periodically or permanently if things opened up elsewhere. Steen/West headed for New York. Casey Clark, a prominent local star, moved to WNAX radio in Yankton, South Dakota. He and his band, the Lazy Ranch Boys, had been on the road, starting in Sioux City, with members peeling off for the South or turning back to Detroit. Another departure from Detroit came when May Hawks answered the call to Nashville, moving down in 1948. She had her husband commute down from Michigan, but she didn't want to stick it out in the country capital and retreated to Detroit's safer local traffic circuit.

In addition to taking advantage of every chance to play anywhere, the local country crowd reached out musically, to make their mix marketable. Jimmy Dickens had a half-Polish and half-country band. "We could play polka rooms or we could play the country rooms." Eddie Jackson, who was "too successful to leave Detroit" and played over five decades, stayed stable by being eclectic: country and western, pop tunes from the hit parade, polka, and Hawaiian music, taking requests from all comers. Women played active and versatile roles in this country music community as both sidemen and stars, like May Hawks, often through marriage and family networks. The Callaway Sisters mixed sentimental songs like "The Old Lamplighter" and "Red River Valley" with hymns, gospel, and the latest hits. All these Detroiters had to know every type of music and keep up with the times, since they had major competition from outside: Grand Ole Opry stars would fly up from Nashville, playing live at an 1,800-seat hall and grabbing attention on WJR radio.

Two fascinating figures display all the diversity that Detroit could offer: Chief Redbird and Vic Cardis. Born William A. Sanders in 1899, Chief Redbird grew up in Indian Territory (now Oklahoma) and was part Cherokee. He joined the Oklahoma Cowboys, already crossing musical and ethnic territory, after stints in rodeo and semi-professional baseball and working in the Honey Boy Minstrels. The Oklahoma Cowboys were a pioneering touring band in the depression era, recording fiddle tunes, blues, spoken word, old-time, and minstrel songs alongside newer pop songs and novelty numbers in 1926–31. They can be seen in a very early sound film of 1929, with Chief Redbird on backup violin, and, surprisingly cello, in the place of string bass. So it was as a versatile, established artist that Sanders moved to Detroit, where he expanded his range by putting together an all-woman band that included his wife. Every music community in Detroit worked up family networks. Around 1949, Chief Redbird emerged as a major star, performing six nights a week on Telegraph Road up in Pontiac as part of the expansive country notion of the local. He rotated themes for his floor shows, including sharp shooting and trick roping sometimes, lots of varied dance music, and leading a Cherokee stomp dance on Thursdays. Those were the days when there was still a "western" in "country western," allowing for white southerners to go redface at a Detroit club. But Redbird didn't just exploit Indian stereotypes; he also worked with the National American Indian Association, inviting their dancers, musicians, and singers. He took this identity seriously, hand-making a feathered headdress for every American president upon their inauguration, starting with Woodrow Wilson and ending with Jimmy Carter. His mash-up mode was quite deliberate. A 1955 song named "Yodel" began with Redbird pounding his tom-tom and telling a humorous story about a yodeling Indian chief who became a star on television. Chief Redbird was buried in his Native American outfit. He was not the only musician to work the Indian vein. There was the fiddler Chief Louis, an "almost full-blooded Indian."

All this lively intergroup commerce supports the image of Detroit as the city of open ears. While Chief Redbird's memory is hardly green, there is a touching 2011 tribute to him by a young local musician who got the old entertainer's violin from a bandmate of the chief's. "I never met the man, but I could feel his soul. . . . I only wish that I could play like him," croons Michael On Fire. "Maybe he was Chippewa, or Ottawa or Wyandotte, the Huron, the Iroquois, the Potawattomie." But Chief Redbird, like so many Detroit musicians, was a southerner, not from a Michigan tribe. Another old musician, Vic Cardis, carried the crossover story into Euro-American territory. He was of Hungarian origin but played with Chuck Hatfield as the Westernaires, playing pop standards like "How High the Moon" and "Stormy Weather" alongside "eastern European folk music," bringing his wife Dee into the band as they played at a club with a Greek owner, Jimmy Manteros. They infiltrated the Stockade, the hangout for Armenians, Greeks, and other Mediterranean musicians, and, in the local style, lived over the club. In 1955, as the Treble-Aires, the Cardises' final single was "When Senorita Comes to Hear the Senor Play," with a rumba beat, following the pattern of all Detroit musicians by edging into the Latin sound for non-Latin audiences. The Hatfields and Cardises moved west when the 1957–58 recession damaged Detroit's music business, ending up in Florida, where they again combined pop standards with Hungarian music. The career of the Cardises sums up the potential and the problems of Detroit for musicians: there was a large, working-class audience that would support both ethnic-specific and crossover jobs, but the club scene thrived in a city with a vulnerable single-industry economy.

Of all the Detroit country bands, the one with the broadest national standing was the York Brothers. Their career summarizes the scene in a number of ways. Coming up Route 23 from their birthplace in Louisa, Kentucky, wending their way through various states, they arrived in Detroit in 1939. They epitomized the two-voice, close-harmony male duo, such as the Delmore Brothers and the Monroe Brothers, that inspired the Everly Brothers. Their stay in Detroit was typically patchwork. In 1946 they were in Nashville, and then on the Louisiana Hayride down in Shreveport, but they returned in 1949. Two locally based songs became their signature hits and nicely condense the complexity of the city's musical interactivity. "Hamtramck Mama" appeared in 1940 on a typical local label, Marquette Music, which went back to 1900, supplying music first for player pianos and then for the booming jukebox business. It was Detroit logic to produce records to play on their machines. The opening couplet shows the brothers' quick understanding of cultural geography and caused a ruckus. It's about Hamtramck, that bastion of Polish pride, viewed through a "hillbilly" lens. As in Ted Gomulka's "A City Called Hamtramck," this song features the erotic appeal of the town's girls, but coming from an outsider, this move reads differently: "She's a Hamtramck mama, and she sure does know her stuff. She's the hottest thing in town, Lordy how she can love." Within months, the mayor of Hamtramck tried to get a court order to keep the song from the jukeboxes of his city, but that only drove up the sales. The York Brothers immediately followed up with "Highland Park Girl," placed in the other inner-Detroit enclave staked out by Henry Ford. While these two "girl" songs are in the country style of the day, the duo's 1950 "Motor City Boogie" crosses the line into rhythm and blues territory. They continued this direction in 1951, covering Wynonie Harris and the Dominoes, blending that bluesy sound with their own trademark brother-duo, southern style. "Motor City Boogie" is one of the great Detroit tribute songs, lending eroticism to the assembly line and the automobile in a way much more local than contemporary automobile songs like Chuck Berry's "Maybellene." The brothers ground the song by bringing back their earlier heroine:

> A Hamtramck Mama who's a friend of mine
> Learned the Motor City boogie on the assembly line.
> She does it mighty fine.
> The way she does the boogie, woogies me out of my mind.
> She's got a crankshaft boogie and a piston turn . . .
> The motor city boogie with an overdrive,
> The motor city keeps that gal alive.

On returning to Detroit, after hitting the southern capitals of country music, the York Brothers were willing to advertise the city's music-industrial power of attraction:

> If you're ever out Detroit way
> You better bring all your duds 'cause you're sure going to stay
> When you hear the motor boogie, they do it all around.
> They do the Motor City boogie, boogie all over town.

Unlike the celebrity status of the York Brothers and a few other country stars, most southern white musicians had a lower profile. Someone like Ed Bryant would play with his sons and son-in-law for church services, square dances, and parties, serving as a patriarch for an extended family. Family ties were strong. The Sunnysiders, a prominent bluegrass band, learned "old time music" from their fathers and grandfathers, just playing on evenings and weekends and "almost every pig-path in Michigan" that wanted to hear their kind of music. They could be specialized, but there was a tendency to be versatile. A major model was George Williamson, described in a 1981 survey of Midwestern southern white music as "an instrument maker (dulcimers, fiddles, banjos) who plays fiddle, mandolin, banjo, guitar, dulcimer, harmonica, bass, zither, and jew's harp and prefers Old Timey to bluegrass." Folklorist Mary Hufford says that "the best of the archaic musical strains are flourishing in Detroit, while the best of the post-war traditions are found in Appalachia and Ohio," which is somewhat surprising given the terrific dislocation of the immigrants and the pressures of industrialized modernization. That's because "music in general provides a significant rallying point for Southerners in an alien urban context." Among her prime examples of cultural preservation was Skeets Williamson, "a strong and unusual exponent of a very antique Kentucky style. His repertoire, firmly rooted in the nineteenth century [includes] 'Sandy River Belle,' an old tune alluding to a minstrel showboat that traveled on the Big Sandy." As with all local music making, players had to adjust to shifts in style to keep getting hired. Bill Gracey, a square dance caller, left Tennessee in 1942, found the usual factory job in Detroit, but still managed to find music work seven days a week. But his tired audiences began to move away from the demanding dance steps of the older style and didn't have the money for both a caller and a band, so by the 1970s, Bill was calling western-style square dancing, which blends the older steps with slower, more modern figures, using recorded music

As with so many Detroit communities, churches offered a strong support to people's sense of continuity and endurance. Hufford was impressed by the strength of the Old Regular Baptists, a small, enclosed group with only a couple of congregations, as an example of singing as part of faith. Ralph Caudill was even "reluctant to listen to a sacred hymn if it [was] rendered by a stranger," or to buy an album, he said, "because I don't know their life." Still, his singing circulated in the community, since he was "often given blank cassettes by friends, with instructions to fill them up." Beyond the church, local music traffic made a beeline for places that offered junctions for the far-flung white southern communities. Hufford summarizes the situation eloquently: "The shapes of Southern White communities are invisible—existing in the minds of Southerners, like so many subterranean streams. They surface at such visible junctures as Little Caesar's Pizza Palace in Southgate, the Rose of Sharon Old Regular Baptist Church in Flatrock, the Brooks Busline, Station WNRS in Ann Arbor, Old Homestead Recording Studio in Brighton, and Ilene's Restaurant in Ecorse."

Ilene's was a particularly important intersection on the roads that connected Detroiters to the South and to their scattered settlements in the city. Ilene (her last name was unknown) ran a family-style restaurant with no alcohol service. She literally grounded her customers, many of them musicians: "Ilene kept little jars of dirt in the restaurant, the dirt being from TN, KY, AL, NC and anywhere else that one cared to supply dirt from. The idea was that people could go there any time they were homesick and touch a piece of their home state. One day, with no warning at all, Ilene closed the place down and went back to Alabama," being as mobile as her customers, one of whom even wrote a song about her, "McKurgan's Bluegrass Opera":

> There was a touch of Alabam,
> Kentucky, Georgia, Tennessee,
> In bowls of dirt that meant the world to me—
> Ilene! Ilene! Ilene!
> How could you take our little piece of home?

African American Hubs

African Americans from the South came in huge numbers to Detroit, like all northern cities, but later than most. Their rich, influential musical life is sparsely and unevenly described. Jazz history is moderately well covered, particularly in the book *Before Motown*, with its steady survey of names, neighborhoods, and venues. There are few studies of individuals in the star-studded constellation of powerful names that emerged from Detroit's first major black neighborhood, which began in the poor Black Bottom and expanded to the ironically named Paradise Valley, with its entertainment hub on Hastings Street. Earlier in this book, I surveyed the situation for black students in the public-school music system, and later I'll talk a bit about media and Motown. Following the flow of this chapter, I will stay in neighborhoods, particularly important for a population that was the target of extreme exclusion and constriction. African Americans could not choose where to live without a legal fight and a struggle for financing, and their core zone might be destroyed at any moment by "urban renewal" projects.

Historically, the old center on Hastings Street takes pride of place, with its many clubs and dives. It was so central to the core of black music making that it got its own troubadour: a figure named Detroit Count (1920–70), whose two-sided single from 1948, "Hastings Street Opera," is one of the finest Detroit-based pieces ever recorded. He was born in Chattanooga and arrived in Detroit with so many others in

1938. He sang over his own piano riff in bars in the 1940s, switching to organ in 1953. Sunnie Wilson, a key figure in the entertainment and business life of Paradise Valley, describes Detroit Count vividly: "He drank quite heavily and never held down a job. The idea for 'Hastings Street Opera' came from two white men, two street hustlers. They put up the money and bought the Count a tuxedo, a hat, and some shoes. Though Joe Van Battle recorded the song in his studio on Hastings and leased it to King Records, these two fellas sold the discs on corners up and down the street. It became a local hit. He could stretch it out for a hour. A lot of the time, listeners would ask him to stop playing it, because they wanted to hear something else. When the Count was sober, though, he was no slouch on the keyboard. [He] worked just enough to get along. Everybody loved the Count." "Hastings Street Opera" is a title fully as ironic as Paradise Valley. Detroit Count, leaning on a steady, slow-blues piano backing, thumbnails as many clubs, bars, and joints he could fit on the few minutes of a 78 rpm disc. But, as Yusef Lateef said, "No one, not even Detroit Count, could recite with accuracy the number of clubs that existed in Paradise Valley in its heyday."

Detroit Count recounts his on-foot odyssey, naming each cross street to locate the bars he wryly spoofs, with remarks ranging from warnings to gentle comedy. It's so different from the auto-driven action hits about cruising and racing that rock 'n' roll would soon produce, or even from a local song that comes from driving out of your neighborhood into someone else's—like the York Brothers visiting Hamtramck.

Hastings Street Opera.
Boy, it's all down Hastings Street.
Henry on Hastings, corner bar, it's the onliest bar where you can walk in and get yourself a bottle of beer, turn your head and somebody else is trying to drink it up. Boy, that's a bad joint.
Down Hastings Street, Farmer, Ferry, Kirby, Frederick, Golden Bell across the street. That's the only place you have to shovel the sawdust off the floor before you can buy yourself a drink.
Sunnie Wilson's, the longest bar in town. That's the only place when you walk in to get a bottle of, you have to walk a mile through the joint to get it.
Joe's Bar. Old Folks Home. That's the onliest bar where ladies can buy a bottle of beer and he'll give them a dip of snuff.
The onliest place in town where you can get a steak sandwich and it tastes like fish. They cook everything in the same grease.
People's Bar, owned by Little Dave Open. Boy, that joint's a killer. That's the onliest place where the customers jump over the bar and run everybody off with two pistols.

> Cap's Cabin. Old Folks Home. That's the only bar where they sell free drinks to customers over 102 years old that are accompanied by their mother and father.

The joints on Hastings Street were not just about drinking but also very much about dancing, even to advanced bebop, nowadays considered abstract, semi-concert music. According to singer Leroy Mitchell, "Diz [Dizzy Gillespie] said the people in Detroit did more dancing to bebop than anywhere else they went in the United States. And Charlie Parker said the same thing. He liked to come to Detroit because we danced." Dancing would spill out into the streets at certain times of year: "There might be parades for the followers of Marcus Garvey and his 'Back to Africa' movement or on Halloween, grownups and kids alike would watch masqueraders make their surreal progress along St. Antoine. Clowns, red devils with curling tails, Zulus, men in evening gowns, women in tuxedos, each sex a parody of the other."

Fig. 4.8 shows the heart of the African American neighborhood in 1942, when immigration was at its peak for wartime industry. This haven of small-business growth and seedbed of immense musical talent lasted just twenty years longer, until the city gutted the neighborhood, building the Chrysler Freeway and paving Paradise Valley.

Paradise Valley was the site not just of music making but also music learning. Mentoring has always been crucial to the survival of African American forms, as

FIG. 4.8. Paradise Valley in its heyday, 1942, when music and entrepreneurial energy flourished in a dense, creative neighborhood. Photo: Getty Images.

FIGS. 4.9. The same area, now as the construction site for the Chrysler Freeway, which replaced Paradise Valley in 1964. Photo: Walter Reuther Archives.

Paul Berliner's seminal book *Thinking in Jazz* revealed. Berliner relied on Detroiter Barry Harris (he is cited on dozens of pages) for deep insights into how musicians transmitted the tools for both tradition and innovation in jazz. Many Detroit musicians also hail Harris as a mentor. Pianist Kenn Cox put it this way: "We had master artists in residence who were the greatest of mentors. They threw their homes open, and it was a daily thing, not the least of whom was Barry Harris." Bennie Maupin put it simply: "Barry Harris taught everybody. He did, he really did, because Barry had already figured out how things worked." I once asked Harris whether the public school training meshed with the on-the-job training in Paradise Valley. He said, "In school we just learned stock arrangements. As 'street musicians,' we really developed outside." Well into his eighties, Harris is still coaching weekly sessions for aspiring jazz musicians. Whole musician families—the McKinneys, the Joneses

(Elvin, Thad, and more)—along with Joe Brazil, Charles McPherson, Lonnie Hillyer, and others set up a network of mentoring that had profound effects on both Detroit and American music. Community members opened their houses to musicians for informal gatherings, as Bennie Maupin remembers:

> The wintertime in Detroit can be pretty brutal you know, so those basement areas and a lot of the houses are pretty fixed up so that people can go and relax, look at TV, have parties, and present music and stuff, and Jose Brazil was like that; he was an entrepreneur, he just extended his house to the guys and whoever wanted to come, you could blow. And this one night I was there and I hear a knock on the door, and it's like three o'clock in the morning—I open the door, it was Coltrane.

This idea of neighborhood music schooling included the churches as well. People sang gospel on porches and street corners back in the 1920s as early black immigrants made neighborhoods into homes. In a 2017 interview at age 103, gospel legend Thomas Kelly says people would "sing into the night," or until the police shut them down. In the late 1940s, just as Detroit Count was giving people the lowdown on street life, the Reverend C. L. Franklin was bridging sacred and secular sounds in a highly influential sanctuary nearby. Church music, which everyone agrees is central to the Detroit black experience, has hardly been dealt with, except as a seedbed for the singers, such as Franklin's own daughter Aretha. Franklin was powerful in both preaching and singing and was drawn to performers, both sacred and secular, running a salon at home and staging large public events. New forms of gospel allowed for influential stars like Wilson Pickett to start out with a solid church singing style that helped to shape the emerging popular music styles. Church connections spread across a national network, with people such as the young Sam Cooke arriving in Detroit in 1950 and shaking up the local sound. Out-of-towners mixed with locals at the momentous inauguration of Franklin's New Bethel Baptist Church the next year. Already back in 1945, Franklin had preached to the National Baptist Convention in Detroit, where delegates argued about whether the whooped or chanted sermon should give away to texted sermons, before C. L.'s sophisticated sense of a powerful, newer expression of sacred feeling took hold. By 1945, he "broke up the Convention" with "a perfect mixture of profound thought and emotional power." Even as Franklin was smoothing the way for newer forms of church singing, older ideas dominated, brought from the South. As vocalist Betty Carter put it, recalling the mid-1940s, "I got my desire to be a jazz musician from my school, not at church, because the church I was going to, if you want to be a jazz musician or stage singer, you were sinning, you were going straight to hell. So my parents didn't encourage me to be a jazz singer. It was the students at school that encouraged me."

A young African American musician's training might well be in the shape of a triangle: school, apprenticeship with older figures, and the church. Jackie Wilson combined a strong religious music upbringing with recordings of opera songs. The sacred music learning curve could be steep, particularly for pianists, who had to learn several skills: how to punctuate and dramatize the sermon and accompany standard choral hymn-singing that might also include "dramatic shifts in timbre and register, highly syncopated rhythm, and flexible improvisational structures tailored to the emotional peaks of the ritual in support of spiritual transformation." The new gospel styles only increased the need for versatility. For someone like Alice McLeod, who moved out into the jazz scene, married John Coltrane, and eventually shaped her own spiritual musical world, as Franya Berkman describes: "Her church training provided her with many of the requisite skills. . . . She was required to sight read, arrange spontaneously from a lead sheet, and listen and respond intently to a soloist or the pastor . . . to improvise musical statements and continually adapt her aesthetics, depending on the communal energy of the moment. . . . Alice was part of this time-honored yet undervalued tradition of female church pianists."

Berkman's spotlighting black women's contribution to Detroit's musical life is very relevant for a city that also produced Betty Carter and Dorothy Ashby in jazz and the many singers of Motown. Lydia Cleaver, director of the Harp and Vocal Ensemble at Cass Tech, remembers how important students' church training was for her group, through the end of the twentieth century: "There used to be more church connection, but more kids are unchurched—only ten percent now. It was much higher when I was in school. We came from churches where hymn singing was popular, so we were accustomed that kind of writing. Now even churches have shifted from hymns and anthems to praise singing."

The city's stellar talent pool was developed and launched on Hastings Street and the surrounding churches and homes, until the bulldozers cleared the area for the freeway, but musical energy spilled into newer neighborhoods whenever the city's restrictive real estate controls allowed African Americans a little more elbow room. Charles Burrell, whose classical training was described in the last chapter, moved with his family from the Black Bottom, which he termed "the super-ghetto of ghettos," to the middle-class neighborhood called the West Side. Betty Carter described the musical differences between the older East Side (i.e., Paradise Valley) and the newer neighborhood. Bebop was a West Side thing in 1945–46 "because the East Side was more or less the blues territory. . . . The West Side was more sophisticated, you might say, because there was a mixture of people there." In this newer neighborhood, "sophisticated" might also mean debutante balls at the Cotillion Club, founded in 1949, or membership in Walker's Singing String Ensemble, with an all-girl string section. Clubs and societies put on annual "clean and wholesome" events at the elite Detroit Institute of the Arts, and the Community Music School produced youngsters like Beulah Young, the only black female graduate of the Detroit Conservatory of Music, who became a piano teacher, church choir organizer, and NAACP activist.

Community Music School Building

FIGS. 4.10 and 4.11. The West Side Community Music School, undated photos. The formal dress is similar to the Cass Tech Harp and Vocal Ensemble. Source: *The Westsiders* (1997).

The neighborhood's most successful classical music product was James Frazier (1940–84), little known today despite his accomplishments. "The son of a sanitation worker, he was enrolled at the age of 5 in the Detroit Conservatory of Music because his parents considered it the best music school available and, he said, 'they saw it as a constructive way of keeping me of the streets and molding my character.'" Frazier rose to respect, conducting orchestras in American and Europe, from the Detroit Symphony Orchestra to the Leningrad Philharmonic. He wrote a Detroit-themed musical, *Twelfth Street: A Soul Opera*, celebrating the street that I lived next to for my first ten years, later the epicenter of the 1967 riot, and now called Rosa Parks Boulevard. Frazier died at forty-four of a heart attack before realizing his potential. He seems to be a symbol of the unrealized promise that African Americans could move boldly into classical music, beyond the opera stage. The middle-class aspirations of West Side music mirrored developments decades before in Chicago, with its much earlier wave of southern black migration. There, already in 1919, the National Association of Colored Musicians promoted black musicians who were classically trained. As in Detroit, musicians had to work day jobs to get by, and they came from many backgrounds: "Southern migrants to Chicago might be farmers like Muddy Waters or urbanites trained in classical and religious music," but "all were squeezed into a limited, segregated, policed market."

It's true that Detroit was always playing cultural catch-up to Chicago and New York, but eventually it overtook most cities with the range and renown of its African American musicians. In the 1950s, Miles Davis left New York time and again, partly to kick his drug habit, and crashed on people's couches in Detroit because the level of jazz was so high and there were so many places to play. What's important to remember is the "ethos of flexibility and eclecticism, in which music served the multifaceted purposes of religious expression, communal participation, and cultural and historical validation." In other words, people listened across boundaries, were open to picking up skills in every available musical context, and developed wide-ranging agendas that drove both aesthetic and marketing moves. As Kenn Cox recalled, "Every neighborhood had at least one bar, for starters, that had live music. It may have been a blues band, it may have been a rhythm and blues band, whatever. . . . As a youngster I could go into most of those bars. This was all over town. West side, north side, you weren't hurting for music anywhere. . . . There was a considerable amount of opportunity to play." John Lee Hooker attracted an older generation with his down-home blues and might have been disregarded by the studious bebop circle for his rawness and naiveté. Nevertheless, he also played in clubs with guitar, piano, and sax. Whether listeners came for down-home southern blues, progressive jazz, or rhythm and blues, musicians all agree that Detroiters were discerning—they would dissect your playing, which, as Cox says, "was a great help in developing as a young musician." Charles Burrell never lost his appreciation for the sharp judgment of Paradise Valley's audiences. He remembers the way people would reject even Yusef Lateef because he didn't play in tune, and how "the musicians were adamant about telling you, 'No, get off the bandstand' " if you couldn't cut it. What's important is that across generational, neighborhood, and taste lines, they listened to each other, particularly in musicians' circles: "The camaraderie that existed between all ages and musicians of all disciplines was quite incredible."

All the street and sacred styles of African American music merged in Hitsville USA, where the Motown magnet drew in the talent. Berry Gordy's studio on West Grand Boulevard, a short walk from where I first grew up. The house became a space that combined the pent-up musicianship of Paradise Valley, the new housing projects, melding a mixture of street smarts with church and public school music training. Those kids could leave the neighborhood and move toward centralized stardom.

To sum up the local traffic of Detroit's music, in every musical arena, the city acted as a magnet for incoming talent, from jazz figures like Frank Foster from Cincinnati; Sonny Stitt from Flint; Joe Henderson from Lima, Ohio; or the country crowd from the border states to the classical kids, like Kenneth Goldsmith from Greenville, Pennsylvania; David Cerone from Syracuse; and the Kavafian sisters from Istanbul. They all relished the city's resources but eventually hit the highway to fill the talent pools of bigger spaces on the emerging interstates. Touring kept the income stream going, crucial for the musicians of the 1950s who were trying to raise families on sixty-five dollars a week, according to veteran black bandsman Thomas "Beans" Bowles, at a time when the national average was ninety dollars. Though some left the city for good, others like the jazz musicians Kenn Cox, Roy Brooks, and Alma Smith came back after stints on the road and in New York, influencing later Detroit generations through their outreach work and example.

This chapter has focused on groups that had a strong connection to a homeland, all of them arriving in Detroit in a short time period. The European-origin clusters broke up and regrouped as people abandoned their entrenched neighborhoods for the endless flat highways of southeastern Michigan, building new settlements in the nearby, then ever more distant suburbs. The white southerners, already widely distributed, also just kept on moving. The sharp divide of race kept African American musicians more bounded, even as their music jumped across social roadblocks.

For yet another group, the Jews, things fell out differently, as noted earlier in my personal and family profile. They mostly came from eastern Europe, where a significant number of Jews had moved after a long series of diasporas, with no real "homeland," for two thousand years. Within Detroit, they occupied a middle ground between the "black" and "white" zones in a strongly anti-Semitic city. With its special heritage, musical concerns, and unique positioning, the Jewish community deserves a closer look, which follows.

City space grounded Jewish political and cultural life in twentieth-century America.
—LILA CORWIN BERMAN

Different voices seemed to cry out in disharmony for resolutions to a confusing
mixture of problems and questions.
—SIDNEY BOLKOSKY

5 Border Traffic
THE JEWISH LOCATION

*Americans are famously mobile, but cities have borderlands, zones between temporarily
entrenched populations that may dislike each other or find ways to collaborate. Since
the Dark Ages, European Jews have always been on the borderlands: between Franks
and Teutons in the Rhineland, between Germans and Slavs toward Poland, and across
the world as peddlers operating between white and indigenous peoples, including my
grandfather's first location in Rosebush, Michigan, in 1906. In Detroit, Jews lived at the
population center, between African Americans and the largely Catholic communities to
the north, always moving diagonally northwest, eventually out to areas that were once
farmland or lakeside cottages.*

*But a borderland is not just demographic: it is deeply cultural. Shelfloads of books
have mapped the marginal Jewish location, marked by the ambivalence of modernity,
which, surprisingly, made the group central to philosophy, sociology, psychology, and the
arts, from Marx to Kafka and Freud. From within an enclosed communal space, the
American Jews placed themselves socially and imaginatively toward downtown, even
while shifting to the suburbs. It's a special traffic pattern that deserves a close look.*

In 1867, Detroit Jewish pioneer Isaac Hart announced, "We have formed a Social
Club of about 45 members," who played cards and put on dramatic performances,
lectures, and concert balls. So from the first, the city's Jews set up not just a synagogue and a cemetery but also a social space based on expression as they moved

into Detroit from tiny outlying settlements, setting up trade networks, opening shops, and supplying local industry. Their population exploded with the auto revolution, jumping from 10,000 in 1910 to 50,000 in 1920 (including my great-uncles) and peaking around 90,000, putting the city in the top ten nationally. These Jews never really joined the working class. In my day, 54 percent were "managers/proprietors" and 10 percent blue collar, while for the rest of Detroit it was almost exactly reversed. Even among Jewish American cities, Detroit stood out in these class statistics. Importantly, the Jews affiliated heavily by family: compared to the 16 percent of American Protestants or 33 percent of Catholics who were regularly involved "with at least five related households," the figure was 71 percent of Jews. Being close to your family might make it easier to disagree with your fellow Jews, whose beliefs ranged across religious denominations and shades of socialism and communism, from Yiddish secularism to Hebrew-based Zionism. Dozens of subcommunities competed for members, forming collectives based on "sentiment rather than coercion."

All of the groups made their statement through music, which covered a huge range of repertoires and groups. But when it came to presenting the larger Jewish population to the mainstream, people agreed on certain resources and strategies. They had to. They were always aware of being marginal. I certainly didn't grow up feeling totally "American." Detroit had possibly the most anti-Semitic atmosphere of any American city. The presiding genius of the city, Henry Ford, notoriously paid for publication of the infamous, phony *Protocols of the Elders of Zion*, which accused the Jews of masterminding not just the economy but also music and the mass media, and he befriended Adolf Hitler. Throughout the 1930s, the inflammatory radio priest Father Coughlin, based in suburb of Royal Oak, spewed stories of the Jews' plots against America, broadcasting to millions nationwide. He was unchecked by the Catholic Church until the US government shut him down in 1942. At the same time, groups like the local Michigan Legion dreamed of taking matters into their own hands. In 1936, its commander "devised the grandiose plot to murder one million Jews by planting bombs in every synagogue across America on Yom Kippur." This encircling pressure was part of the reasons that the Jews huddled in the enclave I grew up in, responding to racialization with "spatialization." Anthropologist Sherry Ortner, writing about Newark, sums up an atmosphere much like that of the Detroit neighborhood I grew up in, calling it "a little homeland where it was OK to be Jewish and where Jews were not threatened. There was no mistaking the fact that this was a Jewish neighborhood. Between the physical marks of the landscape and the overwhelmingly Jewish population in most parts of the neighborhood, Jewishness was naturalized and normalized. . . . One did not have to defend it. One did not have to explain it. It was just the way things were. Younger children often literally did not know there were any other kinds of people in the world but Jews," which is exactly how my brother Dan felt as a child in Detroit.

In this chapter, I will follow the traffic flow of music through the Jewish neighborhood's circuits and out into the main cultural traffic lanes of Detroit. The community wanted to turn its border location to advantage. American cities "gave Judaism urban roots and city smarts." The digitized *Detroit Jewish News* makes it easy to take a core sample of years and look for patterns and trends. No one has ever mapped the musical life of an American Jewish community, and there's only one study of a single genre, on Philadelphia's klezmers and weddings. Detroit had so many different venues, styles, occasions, and orientations for its Jewish musical activity that I can only offer a modest survey. In what follows, three themes detail what drove the community's intense musical variety. We start with the internal microworlds of a growing and fractious community. In their synagogues and social halls, Jews developed musical expressions for a broad range of traditional and social agendas. Next comes the group's ambitious drive to make its mark in mainstream Detroit's musical life. Jews reached out in many ways to cross the city's highly charged social borders. Finally, there's the "classical core," part of the outreach, but also deeply diagnostic of the modern Jewish urban experience across Europe and the United States, going back to Mendelssohn and Mahler straight through Leonard Bernstein.

The Sphere of the Sacred

Detroit's synagogue affiliation rate was 49 percent (Sklare 1991, 112) That didn't mean that half the Jews were at services every week. Membership offered family and network sociability alongside spirituality, and it guaranteed a slot for your son or daughter's bar/bat mitzvah at age thirteen. My parents were synagogue minimalists, so it was hard for them to find a place for me to shine when my moment arrived in 1956. My father tutored me himself, as a master of sacred text that he only really practiced at home on Passover, around the family table. In shul (synagogue) the High Holidays period in the fall was the climax of the liturgical and attendance cycle. Congregations sold seasonal tickets to raise money for their yearly expenses, and in earlier decades they hired star sacred singers—cantors—as an added attraction.

In the mid-1980s, I directed the History of the American Cantorate project and interviewed some cantors who had worked in Detroit, surprisingly including the one who had officiated at my own wedding. Like many cantors of his generation, for David Bagley, Detroit was just one stopover on a long journey that included many posts, sometimes in far-flung places like Europe and South Africa, all while he was also working for the Israeli secret service. More typical of the cantors who left an imprint on Detroit was Louis Klein. I learned more about him from one of my graduate students, Garrett Field, a specialist in South Asian music, when he wrote a seminar paper about his childhood experience in a Detroit synagogue boys' choir. It happened to be at B'nai Moshe, the very congregation where I had my bar mitzvah.

Garrett and his brother were deeply affected by Cantor Klein. Born in Romania as the son of a cantor, Klein got to B'nai Moshe in 1958 via Belgium and London. He sang with Jewish chorales and orchestras in Detroit, on radio and television, and at a Catholic retreat, part of the Jewish outreach approach detailed below. A couple of quotes from Garrett and his brother (personal communication) show how the personal spatiality of in-group musical expression shapes experience and memory:

> As a young boy, raised in a conservative Jewish family, I could sense that the High Holidays and its distinct Ashkenazi-liturgical music were just around the corner, when the air became cooler and the leaves began to color. Soon I would

FIG. 5.1. The author being tutored for his 1956 bar mitzvah by his father. Author photo.

be on the *bimah*, the elevated platform of a synagogue, with my boys' choir cohorts, circled around the *shulchan*, the table on which the Torah scroll sits, accompanied by the *hazzan*, synagogue prayer leader, Louis Klein.

I remember the excitement and nervousness before heading on stage, when we sat with our families before the performance, like secretive spies with alternate identities: one second the humble and anonymous son of the Field family, and a minute later—zam!—a regular mini-cantor, belting out our sonorous renditions of traditional Jewish songs for the audience of fellow congregants. . . . I always felt a kind of closeness to them [the other choirboys], as though we had shared an important experience, that we had done something great and exciting and special and memorable. It was a kind of secret, proud friendship and comradeship.

Earlier, I surveyed my family's secular song system. Passover provided the space closest to the sacred. It was a holiday celebrated at home, and since family was almost a religion among Detroit's Jews, it created a moment of strong and intimate bonding. The homemade tapes I have of two Seder nights (1956, 1965) blend chanted prayer, sometimes boisterous ritual songs, and nonstop conversation around the edges of the table. After some ceremonial wine, my brother and I would drowse under the table, watching the grown-ups' legs and hearing their muffled holiday merriment. The oldest males would rattle off reams of text from the Haggadah, the Passover collection of prayers, tales, and songs, and the women would intervene, asking for changes in pacing or selection of tunes. In those days, melodies had not yet been standardized by institutional Judaism—summer camps, synagogues. We had family variants not heard in any other household, like a lovely minor-key melody for "Chad Gadya," the last song of the long evening, attributed to a certain cousin Hershel. It was all part of an intimate association with Jewish history and experience far removed from the sanctity and formality of the synagogue.

This sense of local musical knowledge was fading, but still present, in the synagogues as well. Some of the atmosphere of Alfred Kazin's description of the local synagogue of his childhood in Brownsville, New York, in the 1920s still hung around the Taylor Street Synagogue that my grandfather went to. Small congregations that remembered where they came from and wanted to pray with their *landslayt*, people from their European hometown, in the intimate, local style they cherished:

The little wooden synagogue was "our" place. All good *Dugschitzer* were expected to show up in it at least once a year, had their sons confirmed in it as a matter of course, and would no doubt be buried from it when their time came. . . . There were little twists and turns to the liturgy that were strictly 'ours,' a particularly nostalgic way of singing out the opening words of prayers that only *Dugschitzer* could possibly now. . . . There were scornful little references to the way *outsiders* did things.

This great internal religious variety differs from the large Catholic parish bulwarks that dotted the other Euro-American neighborhoods, with their centralized ritual and clergy control. Synagogues are powered by lay leadership, not a top-down chain of command, even within the major denominations of Reform, Conservative, and Orthodox.

Kazin describes the family closeness of his home, street, or even of the synagogue as not having much to do with God. In Detroit's Jewish enclave of the 1940s, living near Twelfth Street allowed us to be neither "ethnic" nor "religious," but just members of a kind of village with its customs, habits, and language. Anti-Semitism put the Jews in a circle-the-wagons frame of mind, so ninety thousand people could make a world. Yiddish was still heard in the shops, by the pickle barrels, or at home, from the old egg man at the door and from the family circle, since my immigrant grandparents lived upstairs and the great-aunts and uncles came to visit. They might gossip or play old world card games, calling out *far mir!* ("mine") when they took a trick. But they did not chant the grace after the Friday night Sabbath dinner or revel in *zmires*, the melancholy or joyous spiritual tunes around that table. This was before the rise of more Orthodox practices that began from the 1970s on, when formerly more secular Jews began to feel an urge to return to older ways of sacred musical expression and newer pathways to self-fulfillment.

Subcommunity Spirit

Beyond religious practice, Detroit's Jews deployed music to support the huge array of political and ideological groups. Each faction moved to its own beat, though the rhythms might coincide for a common communal purpose. Zionism had become a steadily rising preoccupation of Detroit's Jews in the 1930s and 1940s, sparking many focused concerts, such as the appearance in 1947 of Metropolitan Opera star and former cantor Richard Tucker, "with profits expected to exceed last year's $75,000, to complete a settlement in Palestine on Jewish National Fund land." That is roughly $800,000 in 2016 dollars, $10 per capita for the city's Jews, for just one event. Tucker's music must have been multipurpose—he was a trained cantor as well as an opera singer—alongside a gesture to the songs of Zionist dreams. The many, bitterly divided leftist subcommunities sponsored in-house evenings, but even they looked for collaborators, such as when they honored a valued visitor, Paul Robeson, the iconic African American performer-activist, in 1947. The sponsor, the Intercultural Youth Council, included Zionist, civic, and religious organizations.

Cultural programming in the Yiddish language—the vernacular of the great wave of immigrants—reveled in strong European roots, even as the language was steadily declining in daily use. American assimilation, combined with the liquidation of the Old World during the Holocaust, doomed long-term survival of this programming. Most of the events were leftist-oriented, but there was also the stalwart steadiness of enjoyable entertainment at Littman's Yiddish Peoples Theater, whose tireless founder-manager secured productions with the top actors from New York and even commissioned an elegant building back in the 1920s. The music at Littman's would have been as widely eclectic as in any period or location of a Yiddish theater, from Warsaw to Capetown to Buenos Aires—from the start, the genre was freewheeling musically.

Most Detroit Jewish balls, benefits, and concerts blended musical styles liberally, even when under the banner of a specific synagogue or social movement. Maybe it was about broadening the audience base, but this openness suited Detroit's Jews, as I suggested earlier with my father's song stock. Everyone's musical construction was as a compound of European and American elements. So, just to take 1947, an event at the Wayne University Hillel chapter might be called "From Boogie to Bagel." A Balfour Ball Zionist event featured Roberto Rodriguez and his Latin American band, while the competing subcommunity of Yiddishists, the Sholom Aleichem Institute, also hired Ponchito's Latin American orchestra. While the classical crowd was captivated by Mr. List, "who held the more than 500 people spellbound with the beauty of his interpretations of charming English and German folksongs," they also enjoyed his version of the "Negro spiritual Nobody Knows the Trouble I've Seen," while being "surprised and thrilled" at "the concluding number—'Eili, Eili.' This touching Jewish melody was sung by Mr. List with such brilliance and was so well interpreted in the spirit of Jewish traditions, that many in the audience regretted that he had not included other Jewish numbers in his program." These listeners wanted it all.

Internal eclecticism marked every group. Let's take the Jewish People's Chorus, of which I was a Junior Chorus member. I had only vague recollections of this until I got—from the Harvard Library, of all places—the program for its thirty-third annual concert, in 1958, held at a prime downtown venue, the Scottish Rite Cathedral (since 2013 renamed for Jack White, the Detroit rocker who bailed the place out). The "people's" designation is a giveaway for far-leftist leanings. According to Arnie Kessler, who sang alongside me, it was a communist front organization by the late 1950s, since the rampant anti-communism of the period cut off political activism. I had no idea at the time, but did know that my friend Fred Sweet, also there that evening, had almost been deported to Poland due to his father's leftist labor work. The program's notes position the group as simply being "a cultural organization that, since 1925, dedicates itself to the development and enrichment of Jewish music." Then it explains that the repertoire, sung in English, Yiddish, and Hebrew, consists of "folk songs, cantatas, oratorios, and songs of the worker." Cantatas and oratorios are highfalutin classical genres—think Handel and Bach—but had been domesticated to serve not biblical but political topics, especially Zionism and the workers' struggle. Folk songs included both eastern European items that might include love or comic songs, but also the emerging songs of Jewish settlers to Palestine. "Songs of the worker" could be American or international, as part of the Cultural Front approach that stressed solidarity with the oppressed everywhere. This Detroit leftist Jewish chorus differed in no way from similar groups across America, often with a New York hub that sent out directors, composers, and pieces to "provincial" cities.

The chorus always mixed sources freely. In 1957, they programmed the Soviet poet Yevtushenko's bombshell indictment of wartime Jewish massacre, "Babi Yar," even as the group invited Cantor Louis Danto from Pittsburgh, seemingly out of place for such a secular, or even anti-religious, chorus. They wrapped up with "The Lonesome Train," Millard Lampell and Earl Robinson's classic, folksy 1945 cantata on the death of Abraham Lincoln. How did we follow this up in 1958? The adult chorus opened with songs by New York–based choral luminaries Vladimir Heifetz and Jacob Schaefer. As early as 1943, Schaefer was honored by another leftist chorale, the Freiheit Gezang Farein. Next came a piece by the Detroit figure Julius Chajes (to whom we will return later), before a classic from the Yiddish theater tradition and an arrangement of a Passover Seder tune. After this round of internal repertoire, the program moved to Beethoven's "Ode to Joy," a nod to classical universality. The wrap-up returned to Jewish interests, with the Zionist song "Hey Daroma." So it's all "people's" music, justifying the group's title, but with the broadest possible coverage. Next, my Junior Chorus mined the American folk vein, starting with "This Land Is Your Land" and moving on to "Pretty Little Gal" before switching to a Yiddish and Polish folk song and a Palestine number (in Yiddish, not Hebrew), rounding out with "Hava Nagila," another Zionist item just starting to hit its stride as the ultimate Jewish (and universal) anthem of celebration.

Despite this dizzying aria of eclectic singing, the Jewish People's Chorus's grand downtown concert was hardly over. After intermission, the going got heavy with a Yiddish oratorio, "Von Viglid biz Ziglid ("From the Cradle Song to the Victory Song"), by the New York heavyweights Moshe Rauch and Wolf Younin, which "tells the story of two children born at the end of World War One and the struggle of their lives during the years until World War Two when at their wedding in 1939, the Nazi troops arrive to disrupt their lives and devastate the lives of their people. In twelve scenes, the story is told of life and death, their struggle and final liberation," through armed resistance, allowing for "the victory of life over death." This optimistic reading of the Holocaust turns up repeatedly in Jewish American telling of the tragic tale, lodging later in the way that *Fiddler on the Roof* and *Schindler's List* find some redemption at the end.

Notice that choreography plays a large role in this pageant-like production. The featured artist, Lillian Shapero, "evokes the romanticism of the eastern European village and represents the life of the working people" and their eventual struggle and triumph "in a choreography of a popular folk quality." Shapero, an American-born member of Martha Graham's troupe, had already been noted by 1934 as a "significant innovator" in addressing "Jewish themes through the lens of American modern dance." In 1947, she appeared together in New York with four other dance artists (Berk, Elakova, Hadassah, and Sokolow), and the notes commend her for "tempering the folk quality" of Jewish dance with "a new modern interpretation," since she had credentials in the more mainstream styles. Importing Shapero to Detroit for the 1958 Jewish People's Chorus concert was part of a live-from–New York approach that marked every kind of local Jewish cultural activism, from Yiddish theater to liturgical music and popular styles.

FIG. 5.2. Undated photo of Lillian Shapero dancing to Langston Hughes's poem "Good Morning Revolution." Photo courtesy Museum of the City of New York.

Dance was already embedded in the local Jewish world by 1943, when Nathan Visonsky gave a seminar on "the aesthetics and psychology of Jewish dance, as well as instruction in biblical, festival and folk dances and modern Palestinian dancing." Here again, the long trajectory of Jewish history intersects with local tastes, merging the folk, the sacred, and the Zionist in one seminar under the banner of "aesthetics and psychology."

In making sure that dance had a place at the table of culture, the Jews were right in step with the broader community. Detroit loved dance in all its forms, with many crossover programs between black and white, ethnic and Jewish organizations. Harriet Berg, a local dance pioneer who was in her nineties when I talked to her, described a citywide intertwining network of public and private instruction, dance companies, and outreach programs. "The Detroit I knew was a cultured Detroit," she said, and dance claimed its place in the mix in a variety of performance media and formats. All this busy cultural activity provided a positive atmosphere for the Jews to push out from their microworlds of music into the broader arena of Detroit's cultural activity, as a way of countering the intense animosity of much of the city's attitude toward the Jews and courting good will.

Insistent Outreach

Evidence for outreach goes back to World War II. The Jewish community was heavily engaged in building solidarity in the face of a crisis that was not only American but urgently dramatic for their own families in Europe. Miss Rose Biel, "Detroit songwriter and author of a number of poems, had some of her patriotic songs played in local hotels and over the radio," the *Jewish News* reported in 1942. In 1943, there were parties/dances for servicemen at Holy Name Church, the Downtown YWCA, the League of Catholic Women, and the Jewish Welfare Board. The Odessa Progressive Aid Society, representing one of the many *landsmanshaft* fraternal organizations of people from a particular European city, ran a concert for United China Relief, not an obvious Jewish cause, and there were many programs in support of Russia's war effort. Zinovi Bistritzky conducted a string ensemble alongside the Russian Balalaika Orchestra, while the paper chronicled a "troupe of Russian dancers in costume" with a mandolin orchestra. The Halevy Singing Society, an old concert choir, gave a special program at the Veterans' Hospital but made a bigger statement at a "mammoth Americans-All Rally," with "approximately fifty different nationality [ethnic] groups taking part to promote Americanism and good fellowship and to overcome hatred and misunderstandings among the various groups." This is a very clear attempt by the Jewish community to use the wartime moment to curb the anti-Semitic atmosphere. I doubt that African American musicians were included among the "nationalities."

Cantor Robert S. Tullman, who got out of the Nazis' clutches, was scheduled to sing after being reunited with his wife, who had escaped earlier. He was "found" by the prominent Rabbi Fram and invited for a Detroit appearance, not just at the Jewish Community Center (JCC) but also for the federally funded WPA Michigan Orchestra, which toured the state for cultural uplift and to keep musicians employed. That organization made a point of collaborating with all the city's ethnic groups—Poles, Czechs, Romanians, French—and of premiering Shostakovich's symphonies in solidarity with Russia. So even an in-group moment like the "discovery" of local hero Cantor Tullman became an opportunity for connection to the wider world at a moment of crisis. As the war raged, Detroit's Jews reached out to other ethnic groups, as in the appearance by the Detroit Welsh Male Quartet in 1943 at the JCC's series of open air concerts. More broadly, this era saw the advancement of the ideas that the Jews were equal players in American life as part of a trio of faiths. The local kickoff came at the "first Inter-faith Good Will Concert" of 1943 arranged by the Round Table of Catholics, Jews, and Protestants, the first in a chain of such musical events. The organization sponsored an appearance by the Vatican Singers as part of a ninety-nine-city tour, linking Detroit to comforting national trends, at a time when Father Coughlin was still raging on the radio.

Jewish musical groups could shine when national organizations came to the city. For the 1947 concert, here is the eclectic and ecumenical list of performers, starting with the Jewish Folk Chorus: the Detroit Fiddler's Band, Saint David's Catholic Church Choir, Saint Peter's and Paul's Russian Cathedral Choir, and the Detroit Lutheran A Capella Choir. The mixing of sacred and secular groups blurs the lines of affiliation of Detroit's musical and social communities.

No Detroit event was overlooked as a possible partner for Jewish music and musicians. In 1947, the Temple Beth El choir sang for the five thousand attendees of the National Federation of Music Clubs' convention. The *Jewish News* boasted that "it was the only one of 600 church choirs in the city to be selected for a concert recital." The music they sang, by nineteenth-century Berlin cantor Louis Lewandowski and contemporary Jewish American composer Max Helfman, was suitably mainstream. 1947 also saw a "Jewish Day" at the city's Flower Show, including concert music by Jason Tickton, Temple Beth El's "eminent organist" and Wayne University musicologist. He played alongside a film about agricultural development in Palestine, enjoyed by "tens of thousands of non-Jews" who stopped at the Palestine Garden to listen to organ music and see the film, a boost to Zionist attempts at mainstream acceptance. Even if Tickton played Jewish-themed music, the sound of the classical organ would have been suitably mainstream. The *Jewish News*'s long-term editor, Philip Slomovitz, sometimes adds revealing comments on all this interactive musical activity. Here's his take on a 1943 open-air JCC concert:

> The audience is worthy of mention. No swank first-night crowd, this, in tails and tiaras. Women in ginghams, men in slacks and open-throated shirts, smoking innumerable cigarettes, all listening to the music as music is best enjoyed, in comfort and informality. The very young and the very old were there, as well as all ages in between. Occasionally a delicate-faced Oriental, or a Negro, lent interest to the group. The [presumably African American] janitors who came in to adjust a lamp or open a piano stayed to listen.

It's strange to see perhaps patronizing self-satisfaction slip into these columns, particularly at such a dire historical moment. There's a sense of anxious straining for approval that arises from Jewish achievements in the charmed zone of classical music, which sometimes seemed like the very heart of the group's presence in American cities.

The Classical Core

Earlier, I noted my cradle-to-college classical immersion in family, concert, and school life. Here I want to ground my experience in the community's almost obsessive involvement in this musical arena. It's true that not every family was interested in concert music. For peers I've talked to, it's a foreign musical language. But publicly, Jewish Detroit invested in it heavily, much like its counterpart cities Boston and Cincinnati, which also have searchable newspapers, or San Francisco, as described by Leta Miller: "Jews were particularly strong supporters of the arts, both visual and musical. For the San Francisco Symphony, Jewish numbers appear in far greater numbers than their proportion in the population." As in those cities, every issue of the *Detroit Jewish News* makes sure to mention Jewish achievements, nationally and internationally, in prestige musical circles. In 1947, readers learned that there were "at present about 30 Jewish artists in the Metropolitan Opera alone." Reporters flagged stories about opera singers, soloists, and conductors regularly, with electrifying moments such as Leonard Bernstein's sudden triumphal debut. He came to Detroit very soon after, appearing already in 1945 at the Jewish Community Center to explain American music, part of the bridging exercises the community supported.

1945

- He wrote the music for "On the Town", the "Fancy Free" Ballet and the "Jeremiah Symphony."

- He is conductor of the New York City Symphony and is one of the most gifted and popular guest conductors in the country.

- He's not only one of america's finest musicians, but also one of its most fascinating personalities.

- At 27 years of age he is the talk of the country.

LEONARD BERNSTEIN

THE JEWISH COMMUNITY CENTER PRESENTS

LEONARD BERNSTEIN

Famous Young American Conductor, Composer, Pianist

Lecture With Piano Illustrations:

"WHAT IS AMERICAN MUSIC?"

☆ ☆ ☆

SATURDAY, APRIL 13, 8:30 P.M.

JEWISH COMMUNITY CENTER AUDITORIUM

WOODWARD at HOLBROOK

Admission: $1.50 Including Tax. • Tickets Available at Center Office

FIG. 5.3. Rising star Leonard Bernstein combines Jewish appeal and American music boosting in 1945. Photo courtesy Detroit Jewish Community Archives.

Detroit came late to arts patronage, not having the old money of Boston and New York, or even Pittsburgh and Chicago. It was a city without robber barons, which had to wait for the motor moguls to emerge, around 1915. They gradually realized that the city needed a symphony orchestra, which had tended to come and go, under the early German immigrant leadership that fueled all of America's concert activity. The symphony petered out in 1910. In 1919 the rising crowd of social climbers invited a leading member of the new wave of maestros, Ossip Gabrilowitsch, a Jewish immigrant who happened to be Mark Twain's son-in-law, to start up an orchestra. He asked to see the concert hall, and refused to come when it turned out that the patrons had not yet supplied him with one. Orchestra Hall was built in four months flat and remains an acoustic gem. Over the next stretch, funding for the Detroit Symphony Orchestra (DSO) waxed and waned, and when I was born, it had vanished. This wartime collapse was deeply resented by the *Jewish News*. In an article titled "The War As It Affects the DSO" by Herman Wise lays out the importance of the DSO to the Jewish people itself. It's an extraordinary statement in the midst of rationing, blackouts enforced by neighborhood street wardens (my grandfather was one), and rumors of the liquidation of European Jewry:

> Because we are in the war up to our necks is just one more good reason why the DSO must go on. . . . The Jewish people, particularly, should appreciate the universal importance of this musical organization, and even those not especially interested in instrumental music as such, must realize an obligation to support the highest artistic standards, the most universal values, and the deepest emotional interests which are tied up with the DSO.

Wise's words worked. In 1943, the local Jews stepped in: "Max Osnos, of Sam's Cut-Rate, has guaranteed 21 performances by the DSO, which keeps alive one of our great institutions, including twenty-one half-hour broadcasts over WWJ." WWJ had actually sponsored the very first radio broadcast of an American symphony, in 1922. Just a month later, the DSO paid for a public apology for those who couldn't get into the concerts: "Only 4,620 seats are available, which is hardly enough, due to the greater-than-ever interest in the DSO." One imagines a large percentage of the frustrated concertgoers were Jewish. But a few years later, when the mainstream moguls had started paying the bills again, the main patron pulled out. Henry Reichold of Reichold Chemicals balked when the musicians talked about unionizing. Again, the Jews came to the rescue. Having formed an informal ensemble called the Little Symphony with some DSO members, Barney Rosen stepped into the breach when the orchestra collapsed in 1949 in what became a two-year break. This included two of my childhood violin teachers, Meyer

Schapiro and Felix Resnick. Very quickly, the *Detroit Free Press* music critic, Dorsey Callaghan, said that "the Little Symphony of Detroit has emerged as the most significant development musically in over a decade." Meanwhile, to make ends meet, Rosen and Resnick spent the summer in a resort playing with the Carlos Cortez Latin Band, in Latin costumes.

"Carlos" was really Max Pecherer, a former violin prodigy. Taking classical musicians to unlikely places, disguised as Mexicans, was part of the border traffic for the Jewish community, which led to an odd moment when the Cortez band performed at Jackson Prison. The audience there included several members of the notorious Jewish Purple Gang, who probably recognized the true identity of the Latin Band members.

The Little Symphony continued its classical border-crossing work with concerts at the Jewish-owned, upscale London Chop House. Eventually, the group gained enough popular support to produce a huge Bach anniversary concert in 1950, bringing the ethnic hero Leonard Bernstein to conduct a sellout concert in the five-thousand-seat Masonic Temple. That was the musical magnet I had visited since the age of three to hear all the great classical figures. I'm not sure I was at the Bach

FIG. 5.4. Carlos Cortez Latin Band, including Detroit Symphony Orchestra's Jewish violinists. Photo courtesy Michigan Jewish Historical Society.

concert at age seven, since, as noted earlier, my parents were not big fans of that composer, but I have a vivid recollection of wandering at knee-level in the dense blue smoke of the Jewish concertgoers who met regularly in the lobby as sociable subscribers of the DSO when it returned in 1951. The classical music news played into the local newspaper's need to connect with its readers, such as the family of Florence Weintraub, presenting her graduation recital at the Detroit Conservatory of Music in 1947 and about to become a faculty member there. Deftly, the article blends the personal with the larger theme of ethnic triumph, not a minor issue in the period of widespread Jewish exclusion from American professional circles: "Miss Weintraub is being initiated into Sigma Alpha Iota, national music fraternity. She is the first Jewish musician to be accepted by the Detroit chapter of this professional group" (May 16, 47).

Acceptance was the aim of this cultural border-crossing, from local traffic to downtown dominance. The *Jewish News*'s preoccupation mirrors the mainstream media's eagerness to connect classical music to the emerging elite of the industrialists, seen as a triumph of the American way and of local display of good taste, as items the *Detroit Free Press* chronicles. The 1957 dates detail concerts I was probably at, in the newly constructed modernist Ford Auditorium on the riverfront. The new hall, shaped like a hi-fi loudspeaker, was torn down after only a few years' use, in Detroit's pattern of build fast and tear down soon. One breathless account of the fur-clad wives of the auto moguls stressed luxury but added an egalitarian description about the modest clothing of symphony patrons: "Everybody wore the best he had." This democratic urge might mark the mainstreaming of minorities, particularly the Jews, who made such an investment in the DSO. It also supports the all-Americanism of the concert description, which details the imported French conductor Paul Paray's diplomatic choice, in his final season, to program *An American in Paris* by George Gershwin, an immigrant Jewish composer:

> Only a great city could have produced Thursday night, when the Detroit Symphony opened its new year. . . . The orchestra is uniquely Detroit. Even to the most worldly Detroiter there is still a thrill to living in the home of one of the world's great orchestras. And as the limousines and the jalopies rolled up to the canopy in front of Ford Auditorium in the soft, hazy night there was a sense of expectation, and a little awe. It was not a particularly dressy throng. Everybody wore the best he had because it felt good that way, whether it was mink or blue serge. It was not a gabby crowd, either. More on the dreamy side, and you could hear clearly the slow sounds of boats signaling each other on the river behind the auditorium. The crowd began arriving more than half an hour

before concert time, to sit quietly and savor the delicious sights and sounds of a symphony orchestra cranking themselves up.

As always, the opener brought out a full complement of limousines, furs, jewels and dazzling gowns. Symphony board chairman John B. Ford, Jr. and his wife gave a dinner party beforehand. Mrs. Edsel Ford in a long black chiffon gown and a matching stole, edged in ermine. Amid the thicket of minks and sables was Mrs. Henry P. Williams in her elegant trademark, a short chinchilla wrap, worn over a short black lace gown.

He [Paray] swung into the rhythmic changes of the [Gershwin] music with the abandon of an old-time Dixieland jazz band. . . . The entire orchestra went "way gone." . . . Paray may be a Frenchman to the core, but inside that core on Thursday night he was as American as cottage cheese and apple sauce.

Some Jewish-mainstream overlap peeks through these concert descriptions. It's true that we ate a lot of cottage cheese and applesauce at home. People's houses were often the site of the classical consensus, as in these parallel 1962 notices from the *Detroit Free Press* of events at Jewish and non-Jewish music salons:

From the Society Column: The Daniel Goodenoughs will be putting up Paul Doktor and Yaltah Menuhin before their Grosse Pointe Morning Musicale program at the [all-white, ritzy] Country Club; they've been hosting since the programs started during World War Two.

Mrs. Tom Borman will open her home to stimulate interest in a concert at Masonic Temple. Mrs. Adler, wife of Rabbi Morris Adler, will address the concert workers. Sponsored by the Detroit Chapter of the American Women for Bar-Ilan University, with Mischakoff, Olefsky, and Russell Skitch, bass-baritone, for scholarships.

Grosse Pointe was and remains the iconic ritzy suburb of Detroit, with the country club contrasting with the mere "home" of the Bormans. But the classical music boosterism that informs both announcement links the Jews with the upper crust. The musicians Doktor and Menuhin were well known to the Jewish music community, as were all Jewish musicians of any prominence, local or national. Mischakoff and Olefsky were stalwarts of the scene, as concertmaster and principal cellist of the DSO, as well as being activists within the Jewish community's music network. This type of classical convergence of subculture and mainstream was traditional by 1962, when a column paired socialites of suburban WASP Birmingham with two other pianistic personalities of the Jewish community, profiled below, Mischa Kottler (of course represented by his Mrs.) and Karl Haas, cited below as a key arbiter of classical taste:

"Concert Party to Include Soloist's Wife." Mr. and Mrs. G. S. Godell of Birmingham have made up a party for the Detroit Women's Symphony concert. Listing of guests, such as the Herbert Pontings, who have just returned from Honolulu and will be leaving soon to spend the winter in Ft. Lauderdale. The Boyds will entertain the group at dinner at the Detroit Athletic Club. Mrs. Mischa Kottler is listed, and the soloist, Ernst Victor Wolff of East Lansing, is accompanied by Karl Haas.

Classical music as a domain of lady patrons writing checks from their businessman husband's bank accounts is very well known in American music studies, going back to the Gilded Age and its domestication and feminization of the arts. These women were permanently attached to the cause. When longtime patron of the DSO Marjorie Fisher died in 2016, she left five thousand dollars to each member of the orchestra. Opera was another meeting ground for Detroit's women of culture, as in the mixed Jewish and non-Jewish committee that planned a season in 1943 for Philadelphia's La Scala Opera. But to create a local, competitive talent pool, an in-house artists' nursery was a productive choice. We can return to the Music Study Club, founded in 1927 by a group of Jewish women on the model of the 1887 upper-crust ladies' group called the Tuesday Musicale. The MSC held regular meetings in members' homes, many of which I attended and played at, and it offered scholarships and visibility to the best of the youngsters. Every year, the winner played a special concert at the Detroit Institute of the Arts, backed by the orchestra of the Jewish Community Center, of which more below. The concert's proceeds "represent the principal source of income for the club's scholarship fund, by which many nationally and internationally prominent musicians were aided," says a 1957 article, citing the current winner, Ruth Meckler, who went on to a major pianistic career (later as Ruth Laredo). Her father, Ben, taught with my father at the all-black Miller High, and she's in our home movies. The MSC tracked its members, even to the point of asking them for payback as their careers advanced. Isidor Saslav, approached to return his scholarship money, instead offered a free recital with his wife, Ann, a pianist. I was deeply enmeshed in this network. At a concert in 1960, no fewer than three of my friends—Rita Sloan, Richard Luby, and David Levine—soloed, and the next scheduled event starred my violin teacher, Gordon Staples (who will reappear below for his after-hours connection to Motown).

Staples often worked with cellist Paul Olefsky, who had his own chamber orchestra of DSO members, labeled "non-sectarian," an odd phrase that needs an explanation. Olefsky was aiming for the quality of the cosmopolitan chamber orchestra of New York's prestigious 92nd Street Y: "While the body is backed by Jews, its orchestra's concerts are attended by discriminating patrons of all creeds and faiths, Olefsky notes." "Non-sectarian" codes the intense drive of the Jewish community, through its patrons and musicians, to both support and blur their origins. It could be a scene that played out in Vienna, Berlin, or St. Petersburg decades earlier. Everywhere, as urban Jews gained access to modern public culture, classical music became a driver for their attempts at upward cultural mobility. Detroit's talented Jewish youth were patronized as ethnic standard-bearers, but they were not socially isolated. They rubbed shoulders with children from all over the city, of every background, at the homes of the top teachers, at the famous and famously competitive summer camp at Interlochen, or in the school and all-city orchestras, from first grade through the acme, at Cass Tech. Kenneth Goldsmith, a distinguished violinist, came from Greenville, Pennsylvania, to Detroit and really appreciated both the musical opportunity and the ethnic diversity. He got to know the future virtuosi Armenian American Kavafian sisters, Ida and Ani, when they were all still in elementary school.

As this Armenian case shows, the Jews were not the only Detroit subculture trafficking on the social borders with classical music. Already back in 1943, an alliance of central European groups sponsored a performance of Smetana's popular opera *The Bartered Bride*, including "Czecho-Slovak organizations, the Austro-American Society, the Polish Friends of Arts, and the Michigan Slav Congress in conjunction with the Detroit Friends of Opera," a mainstream organization. The Women's Symphony, founded in 1947, might be another example of subcultural crossing. Predictably late, Detroit had joined a movement that saw a dozen female-only orchestras established in the 1930s. But there were speed bumps in this express lane from the local neighborhoods to the downtown. The parents of the Kavafian sisters, themselves accomplished classical musicians, had to present themselves as "ethnics" at a 1957 event sponsored by the Ladies Auxiliary of the Armenian Veterans Association. It was held at the downtown International Institute, a showcase for multiculturalism that my family went to regularly for colorful celebrations. "Mr. and Mrs. Yenovk Kavafian, concert duo from Istanbul, to play at the musicale-tea at the International Institute. Her husband runs the Oak Park Dondero High School orchestra. Armenian pastries will be served by costumed committee members." So the Kavafians and their fellow Armenian Americans were forced to dress up as exotics, despite Yenovk's standing as music director at an important suburban high school.

In the years before the 1960s, it was even harder for African Americans to merge onto the service drive onto the musical freeway. I've already suggested that the problem dates back to Miller High in the 1930s. The testimony of bassist Charlie Burrell is poignant. He made it into the classical world, but only by literally taking the bus out of town, to his relatives in Denver. Burrell's musical dedication was so intense that it even won over the dreaded Detroit police force: "I used to go to Belle Isle every morning with my car at 5 o'clock and practice from 5 until eight . . . and then go to school. . . . And the policemen used to bring their horses over to listen. . . . They'd get the horses accustomed to this noise. And every now and then they'd bring me a sandwich, or a piece of watermelon. I'd thank 'em. That was for 3–4 years." Burrell had access to the classical music greats: "Every Saturday in the summer we could go to the Institute of Art and see the biggest name musicians in the world. I remember seeing Andre Segovia there, Heifetz, Piatigorsky, and dozens of others, for 10 cents. That was all part of the education, too." Burrell and other African American young musicians in the 1930s could also take part in a number of "separate but equal" organization for young black players. Cellist Ardine Loving, "recognized as an outstanding 'elite artist' talent in her native Detroit," played in the Detroit Negro Symphony and the black Lyric String Ensemble and was a "respected cello soloist and radio personality." Then there was Burrell's membership in the National Youth Orchestra, "an offshoot of the [federally funded] WPA. It was designed to help the young people of that era get work. The little orchestra was all Black—it was designed to help the Blacks, because Blacks still didn't integrate with the Whites. . . . There were no working integrated units in that era." If Burrell wanted to earn money with his talent, he had to find a venue within his community that would appreciate concert music: "My first real job playing classical music was at Ebenezer Church in Detroit. The first thing I did was the Messiah. Handel's Messiah. That was the first legitimate job I had had playing by myself. I mean on bass." Burrell's use of "legitimate" is telling, since he had been able to perform in jazz clubs at an early age. He wanted something else, but he realized it would take a massive effort of discipline, not just talent. He learned from the unfortunate fate of his friend Flournoy Hocker, who was unable to get over the speed bumps, even though he came from a privileged black household: "His parents were affluent, because his dad had a good job, I think in the post office. . . . He went down to take an audition with the Symphony in Detroit, and he played rings around everyone. But the conductor told him, the time isn't right. Okay? Go back and wait for a while. And Flournoy couldn't take that pressure . . . and went home and blew his brains out. That helped me to become more strengthened in terms of: they were not going to make me commit suicide if I got to that point." Burrell and Hocker's plight was widespread. In Chicago, jazz great Milt Hinton gave up on classical placement and switched to jazz, while other black musicians "settled for post office jobs with music work on weekends." As mentioned earlier, even Ron Carter, with his classical Cass Tech training, gave up on orchestra hiring quickly, switching to jazz. Hocker's postal service dad was safe in his slot, and some of his colleagues in Chicago were even able to play music as amateurs while on the job: the post office had two black choral groups and orchestras.

By contrast, the Jewish youth of my circles, especially pianists and violinists, knew they could get ahead. Every year, twenty of the top violin students flowed into the home of Mischa Mischakoff, one of America's greatest concertmasters. He had been hand-picked by Arturo Toscanini as the leader of the NBC Orchestra and came to Detroit as a courted celebrity. He treated the students severely as he shepherded them to professional success. The violin was, in a deeply felt way, the "Jewish" instrument, from klezmer street musicians and classical virtuosi in tsarist Russia to Carnegie Hall. Alfred Kazin's moving memory of listening to records in his poor Brooklyn kitchen overlaps with my family's profile and my inner core of musicality as a child violinist. Despite his doubts about the religious faith of his neighborhood, Kazin makes a soulful segue from the almost sacred sound of the stringed instrument to Kol Nidre, the chant that drew many Jews, even alienated ones, to the shul once a year:

> The effect of the violin on almost everyone I knew was uncanny. I could watch them softening, easing, already on the brink of tears. . . . Any slow movement, if only it were played lingeringly and sagely enough, seemed to come to them as a reminiscence of a reminiscence. It seemed to have something to do with our being Jews. The depths of Jewish memory the violin could throw open apparently had no limit—for every slow movement was based on something "Russian," every plaintive melody even in Beethoven or Mozart was "Jewish." I could skip from composer to composer, from theme to theme, without any fear, ever, of being detected, for all slow movements fell into a single chant of *der heym* and of the great *Kol Nidre*. . . . When Mischa Elman played some well-known melody we sighed familiarly at each other—his tone was so *warm*; he bubbled slowly in my ears like the sound of chicken fat crackling in the pan.

No doubt it was hearing Elman at an early age and also delighting in *grivenes*, those schmaltzy cracklings, that made me ask for a violin teacher. I did not get to Mischakoff, studying instead with Shapiro and Resnick, two of the DSO members who had kept the orchestra alive. Maybe it was the weekends moonlighting as Panchito's Orchestra that made them nod off occasionally as I played my scales.

Mischakoff was part of a cluster of major music figures, along with a "troika" of pianists, Mischa Kottler, Karl Haas, and Julius Chajes.

Their life stories reveal the European origins of classical music across the United States and highlight the modern upward mobility of Jewish and other immigrant musicians. In the Motor City, these refugees or émigrés found a home at the end of tortuous pathways. Mischakoff felt the need to escape from Soviet cultural crackdowns, while Kottler had an even trickier trajectory. Born in 1899 as Mikhail Salyagin in Kiev, he had already toured Europe as a prodigy by age ten. He came to America with his family already in 1913. Rachmaninoff himself heard Kottler in New York and advised him to head back for studies in Europe, where he worked with Emil von Sauer, a pianist whose teaching lineage stretched back to Beethoven. Marrying another Kiev-born pianist, Kottler finally returned to the United States in 1929, in time for the Depression, which forced him to play in theater orchestras, jazz bands, and cafes. Kottler finally got to Detroit via Jean Goldkette, a prominent bandleader and music promoter. Goldkette had a similar history, arriving in Detroit after a childhood in Greece and Russia, studying at the Moscow Conservatory as a

FIG. 5.5. Two stalwarts of the classical establishment: Mischa Mischakoff, two ladies' club admirers of his Stradivarius, and Julius Chajes. Photo courtesy Detroit Jewish Historical Archives.

child prodigy. For immigrants in America, music, classical and popular alike, offered a kind of escalator—step on it, and you could rise, without capital. Kottler stayed on the classical side, working for the DSO and producing nationally broadcast concerts with the WWJ radio orchestra—every major American station with cultural ambitions had one in those days. From time to time, he inserted Jewish music programs.

Karl Haas (1913–2004) also rode the transatlantic road to success and starred on radio. Starting out like Kottler in Europe and studying with piano great Arthur Schnabel, he was blacklisted as a German Jew and somehow got to Detroit in 1936. Known as a pianist and as director of Interlochen's prestigious music program, he turned his mellifluous voice into career gold. His radio show, *Adventures in Good Music*, started on WJR in 1959, went national in 1970, and played until 2007, two years after its host's death, winning Haas the first-ever slot for classical music in the Radio Hall of Fame. As a youngster, I really disliked his oily tone and sometimes simplistic introductions to classical music, but it was a brilliant formula. He interacted with the third member of the troika, as did everyone else in Detroit, the omnipresent Julius Chajes (1910–85, rhymes with Y-S, with ch as in Bach), who deserves a longer look. He came from those Viennese Jews who, like Mahler and Freud, were immigrants to the cultural capital from the Czech and Polish regions. A prodigy, he gave his piano debut and composed his first piece at the age of nine. Like Kottler, he studied with a Liszt pupil, Moritz Rosenthal. Sensing the danger of the Nazis, he pushed off for Palestine already in 1934. The celebrated Rosé Quartet played Chajes's string quartet at his farewell event. Palestine did not take, and by 1938 he had arrived in New York, where his sacred text settings won award and performances.

It was in 1940 that Chajes's life took a decisive turn. He was offered the chance to start a major music program at Detroit's JCC. This summons came from the redoubtable Fred Butzel (1877–1948), the "Dean of Detroit Jewry." Butzel is worth a close-up of his own. When he died, flags flew at half-staff across the city. His forebears were German Jews, among the earliest successful settlers in Detroit, rising to prominence as lawyers and judges. They wrote the corporate law for the fledgling auto industry. Unlike his hard-driving brothers, Fred was more interested in civil rights issues and classical music, though he kept up a half-hearted law practice. The number of organizations he founded and sponsored is vast, from Henry Ford's Boys Republic for "wayward" youth to Zionist development projects, with a special interest in African American causes. Butzel was also an accomplished pianist and hosted evenings of chamber music in his two-grand-piano living room. With this intensive Germanic investment in music and his passion for institution building, it is hardly surprising that Butzel would conceive the ambitious idea of a music unit within the JCC that would rival or surpass any other program in America. Chajes was the right man for the job. He was ambitious and knew how to talk up patrons. He found a ready partner in his new wife: Marguerite Kozenn, a trained soprano and music activist. Also trained in Europe, she adapted readily to the Detroit scene, becoming the artistic head of the mainstream Detroit Conservatory of Music (1957). Together, they not only reigned in Detroit but toured widely. She was an honorary counsellor for the Salzburg City Tourist Center, showing how tenaciously tied she was to the couple's European roots, as this 1947 account from the *Jewish News* shows:

> Marguerite Kozenn, dramatic soprano, and Julius Chajes, composer-pianist, are leaving today on the French liner S. S. Colombie for a two-month concert tour. They are scheduled to appear in Paris, Zurich, Vienna, Prague and Bucharest. In their radio concerts, Miss Kozenn and Chajes will present, upon special request, American music such as Negro spirituals and American Indian songs, as well as contemporary American music by George Gershwin and Virgil Thomson.

It is striking that two émigré Europeans would represent American music across the Continent after the Holocaust, an impressive feat of adaptability and marketing savvy. The combination of standard black and Indian musics and contemporary composition seems part of the postwar export blitz of American culture, often supported by the State Department. One wonders if the Chajeses presented Jewish music on the tour, as Julius was an expert at promoting that cause and his own compositions.

Back in Detroit, Chajes was everywhere. As early as 1943, he was bringing the Center Symphony Orchestra to play both for the Dental Society and at the Pinsker Club's concert and dance, where they opened for "Music by The Imperials." Already by then, local music critic Callaghan could hail Butzel's hiring move: "The Jewish Community Center has more than justified the establishment of its music department under Julius Chajes. It is surely becoming a force in Detroit's cultural life." This is high praise from the mainstream, exactly what the Jewish community wanted. The Center Symphony Orchestra was a well thought-out organization. Built on students and amateurs, it was fortified by professionals often from the DSO who raised the performance level, and the pros could earn extra income giving lessons at the JCC. The list of world-class performers invited by Chajes runs on and on, and the reviews stress the high caliber of the concerts. He coordinated closely with figures like Mischakoff, Kottler, and Haas to build a citywide following in concerts around town and on the air. The music program was just part of the JCC arts structure, with counterpart programs in chorus, dance, and the visual arts. Creating an internal music structure put the Jews in the position of being an ethnic minority that could pose as a cultural city within the city, parallel to the many townships and suburbs that ran flagship music organizations. For example, in 1952, six communities on the western edge of Detroit held mass concerts, including Belleville, home of the Belleville Three, the future founders of Detroit techno. The events included a 110-piece symphony band, 250-voice choir, and 60-piece orchestra.

The spread of the classical music gospel into every Jewish communal nook and cranny was not just a Detroit specialty. The pages of the Boston and Cincinnati communities' newspapers brim with similar announcements and the doings of

FIG. 5.6 Rita Sloan, a future music star supported by the JCC and Music Study Club, part of my classical circle. Photo courtesy Detroit Jewish Historical Archives.

local celebrities. In the latter city, there was already a Jewish Center Symphony in 1932, but it was just for amateurs, people "interested in playing symphonic music for pleasure, recreation, and furtherance of their musical knowledge," and welcoming of "all denominations, occupations and ages." Chajes may have had more of a patronage base could rely on the triple threat of pianism, conducting, and composing. He also was restless to open up new repertoires. Whereas the Cincinnati programs stayed solidly with classical chestnuts, Chajes stressed new works and a strong agenda of Zionist-themed composition, often his own pieces. Twenty years on, the *Jewish News* trumpeted the orchestra's success: "It was a source of amazement to many professional musicians that the task . . . of transforming a volunteer organization into a powerfully-functioning symphony—should have become the model non-professional musical organization in the land." Whether the ensemble really was such a national model is hard to say.

Chajes arrived on the scene at a critical juncture in Jewish concert music. The original urge to create a "national" style that sprang up early in the century in St. Petersburg and Berlin had been stymied by revolution, Nazism, and the lure of Palestine. Some came to the United States and worked in Hollywood. Others created art music within synagogue life, a trend that peaked around this time. Composers—even as prominent as Ernest Bloch and Arnold Schoenberg—affirmed or ignored their Jewish identity in ways too complicated to detail here. Chajes had been trained by the modernist composer Hugo Kauder in Vienna, who had his own original ideas about musical modes. When he went to Palestine, Chajes absorbed the emerging compositional language of Near Eastern–tinged writing. So by the time he came to America, he had many resources and the ambition to forge a personal style that would also be "Jewish." In the United States, marketing directs or derails careers, as many émigré composers found out. Chajes was modestly successful in building a national reputation but hugely influential in Detroit, a place that, if not provincial, was a tributary with respect to the mainstream centers of Jewish music—New York and Los Angeles. The composer turned out no-nonsense reflections on his orientation. Here's a straightforward summary:

> There is a renaissance in Jewish music now with a complete school of musical artists. This school consists of two branches. The first is the modern style coming out of Palestine with all its gaiety and the hope of the pioneers. The second is the liturgical chanting as a basis following the school of Ernest Bloch who is recognized today as the greatest Jewish composer alive and one of the world's greatest. I use both styles . . . depending on what I happen to be writing. (Quoted in Goldblatt 2012, 105)

In another article, he adds a third type: music based on eastern European Jewish folk songs. But like many musicians of his time, Chajes saw that Old Country music as dated and flawed, and too tied to the Jewish fondness for musical elements shared with non-Jews, such as the melodic interval heard at the opening of "Hava Nagila" (try singing the first five notes), a resource in the music of many peoples that somehow became "Jewish." Chajes saw the music of the Sephardim—the Mediterranean Jews of Spanish origin--as more "authentic," on the odd basis that "they were not wanderers," hardly a viewpoint that would stand up in Jewish music studies today. But since the "Hava Nagila" stereotyped sound has been used by everyone from Hollywood and Broadway to Jewish composition, it crept into the pieces Chajes wrote in eastern European style anyway. His analysis was insistently inconsistent, since he thinks the Jews of his Polish-Russian background did preserve ancient synagogue tunes, despite borrowings. He only sees modernity and Europeanization as the problem, even if he himself was a fine product of that musical education. His dislike for eastern Europeanisms was probably grounded more in memory than in musicology. In a review of *Fiddler on the Roof*, which had its tryouts first in Detroit in 1962, the composer writes about the childhood shock of surviving a brutal 1920 attack on Lwów/Lemberg, his Polish hometown, by Ukrainians, before the family fled to Vienna: "I'll never forget the screams and shrieks of the unfortunate people which were burned alive." Here, Chajes overlaps with my story, my mother's family having survived pogroms just to the east, in Ukraine.

Chajes tried his hand at all three varieties of "Jewish" composition he listed: the liturgically based, the Yiddish folk-song-inspired, and the new Mediterranean-grounded Palestinian sound, as well as a fourth: the more abstract concert music of his Viennese training, which was performed less frequently in Detroit. For that style, he describes himself as being "a late romantic" who wrote music based on "the ancient Greek modes," a nod to the theories of his mentor Kauder. The composer's flexibility served him very well in building a career in the United States, and even allowed him to get an endorsement from Bloch himself as being "musical and honest, a very rare thing nowadays." In 1978, the eminent violinist Henryk Szeryng placed Chajes as a national, rather than American or European, composer, making the bold claim that "his music is to Israel what Chopin's was to Poland, De Falla's to Spain, and Bartok's to Hungary." Chajes's goal throughout all his work in Detroit was "bringing up the standard of Jewish music to a level which can proudly measure up to the level of the music of other nations," a somewhat defensive position one finds in various sectors of Jewish music's evolution in the twentieth century. But the phrase sweetly summarizes the border-crossing ambitions of his community.

Chajes's concerts in Detroit summarize all of the trends sketched out above. Soon after arriving, he produced a patriotic song in 1941, even before America entered World War II. "Song for Americans" begins with this awkward verse by one Herman Wise:

> America, America
> Let me praise you day and night
> Grateful through and through
> I will strive for you
> Cherishing my freedom true.

Here, Chajes is being personal as well as collective, I imagine, since he had found a safe haven from the Nazi storm. This patriotism carried through in moments such as the concert for the 1948 installation of JCC board members, as it began with a call to colors by Boy Scouts, Girl Scouts, and Camp Fire Girls, singing the American national anthem. Then the officers appeared, followed by a children's and modern dance presentation, a piano concerto movement by a boy wonder with a cadenza provided by Chajes, and the JCC business meeting, punctuated by part of a Mendelssohn Symphony. The communal was totally embedded in the classical.

The Zionist stream flowed steadily as well. The program for the 1966 world premiere of the composer's oratorio *Out of the Desert* looks like a still from a Hollywood film, with lone riders on camels amid the dunes. The ending of a scene in his undated script for *A Visit to Palestine* narrates the successful arrival of Jewish refugees to Palestine. It suggests that Zionism will bring unification, peace, and romance to the incoming Jews, embodied in dancing the hora, an eastern European genre (like "Hava Nagila") adapted for Israeli life. "They shout 'Palestine, Erets Yisrael,' they look toward the shore. The five young people form a circle and start to dance and sing 'Horah.' More and more join, so that almost all dance and sing, the German near the Pious Jew, Michael near Miriam." Later, the composer supports his own music: "I did not know we have such beautiful music." "And we can be very proud of it." "How long will they sing?" "A couple of hours." These oratorios were not light listening. Chajes also took his music to Israel itself, playing his Piano Concerto—rather than a Jewish-themed piece—in Jerusalem with the Kol Israel radio orchestra in 1953. It was an early year for Israeli composition, when German-origin immigrants dominated the musical scene. Perhaps he wanted to burnish his credentials as a Viennese composer there, not that he didn't also play that piece with the Detroit Symphony orchestra around the same time. In Chajes, the internationalism of classical music overlapped with the dispersed fate of the Jews and their culture.

The year 1966 saw the annual Jewish Music Festival, broadcast on radio, with no fewer than six events sponsored by the local chapter of a national promotional organization, the Society for the Advancement of Jewish Music. Four local cantors were enlisted for the event, which interspersed art music with sacred song, a couple of Yiddish pop tunes, and some Zionist numbers. Music papered over the cracks between the rival factions of Detroit Jewry. Chajes worked even in the religious sector, by serving as music director for the German-heritage Temple Beth El while collaborating with Conservative synagogues. As fragmented and divisive as the community might be, its musical multilingualism made it possible for people to find common ground. The family of Rita Sloan, an important Chajes pupil pictured in Fig. 5.6, found it comfortable to bring their daughter to him as a teacher, since they were from Warsaw and could speak Polish with him as they adapted slowly to America in 1949, coming straight from a displaced persons camp in Germany. This was also true for my wife, Greta, a very late immigrant to Detroit from the USSR and Poland in 1960, who studied with Chajes.

Chajes's outreach projects multiplied. But already back in 1942, as part of the wartime strategy detailed above, Chajes figures in a complicated Michigan Orchestra program that gestured in all directions: opera arias, two classical warhorses—the *Blue Danube* waltz and *Marche Slav*—and a piece by one Eastham, based on American folk tunes, alongside Chajes's own biblical piece. In the middle, Capt. Donal Leonard of the Michigan State Police held forth, doubtless in a patriotic wartime vein. A similar format appears in a 1954 joint concert with the Central Woodward Christian Church Choir, that combined Brotherhood Week with the Jewish Music Festival, so that Chajes could have his most successful piece, "The 142nd Psalm," appear as an ecumenical gesture. The president of the JCC, Judge John V. Brennan, punctuated the performance with remarks that must have urged brotherhood for a city that sorely needed it. All this constant border traffic paid off for Chajes in a resolution of 1961 by the Detroit Common Council to honor this "composer-conductor-pianist" on his fiftieth birthday and the twentieth anniversary of the Center Symphony Orchestra, with "grateful thanks for his many contributions to the cultural development of our community." Eventually, this energetic conductor/pianist/composer/promoter became more than just a Jewish figure in Detroit. By 1950, he had secured another base, joining the faculty at Wayne State University.

What was his music actually like? Two pieces currently available online can stand in for Chajes's compositional work. "The 142nd Psalm" was composed back in Vienna in 1932. It got its premiere and a prize in Berlin in 1937 from the Jewish Culture Association (Jüdischer Kulturbund). It represents the last gasp of European Jewish creativity and communal life, and its ecumenical craft could book the composer a 1939 performance at the New York World's Fair with the renowned Schola Cantorum, a non-Jewish chorus. This broad appeal extended to the Festival of the American Guild of Organists and at other Jewish and non-Jewish sites. The YouTube performance of "The 142nd Psalm" is by a Presbyterian church choir. Program notes that the composer possibly wrote himself position Chajes as "a skilled craftsman in the art of counterpoint [who] like other leading American contemporaries, achieves a "modern" sound by using the ancient modes, avoiding chromaticism," a general term that would include both the "Jewish" sound he avoided and the Viennese style of the generation before him. The strategic setup between the Jewish and the current American sound even marks Chajes's Zionist pieces, such as *Israeli Melodies*. Its set of vignettes of settlement blend a muted "Eastern" modal sound with the national style developed by Aaron Copland and others in the period when Chajes was finding his compositional and communal voice in Detroit. These were styles and topics on the American musical mind in the 1940s, as shown by the subject of Leonard Bernstein's talk for the JCC in 1945 (figure 5.3). Clearly, Julius Chajes had figured out how to consolidate the classical and the outreach approaches of Detroit's Jews in his tireless, versatile activities.

Julius Chajes resembles many a Detroit musical figure: locally prominent, good at finding traffic lanes for his travels into the city's mainstream, and always keeping an eye out for national and international opportunities. Within the Jewish community, he integrated the three sides of musical energy this chapter presents: internal institutional strength and diversity, outreach across cultural borders, and a strong commitment to the classical core of modern Jewish musical investment.

Emma Schaver

Although I know Chajes's students, my path did not directly cross his, but I did have a personal connection with the final highlighted community figure, Emma Lazarof Schaver, who was a family friend. Schaver was a bit of a diva who crossed over from the opera world, where she had some initial success, into the world of Jewish causes and music. Born in 1904, she came to America as a baby and got to Detroit by 1914, where she married Morris Schaver in 1924. Like so many Detroit Jewish businessman, he was a successful supplier to the auto industry, in this case offering overalls, and became a nationally prominent Zionist, visiting the White House. Emma was incredibly active in the 1930s, singing with the local choral societies and on a joint recital with famed tenor Tito Schipa in Detroit. She toured Latin America with the Cincinnati Opera in leading roles. She did a recital of "English, Yiddish, and Palestinian Songs" in Pittsburgh in 1931, and the same year found her in Toronto doing Hebrew religious-themed songs on a program that had a lecture called "The Chinese and Japs Talk to Hoover." I remember going to Schaver's concerts, which were in a genre well known at the time but obsolete today. She can be compared with a male counterpart, Sidor Belarsky, with whom she performed. They offered what seems now like an unlikely blend of classical concert music, Yiddish folk and popular songs, religious numbers, and Zionist items, all with serious piano accompaniment and no sing-along atmosphere. Pianist Rita Sloan, of my classical crowd, says, "We all looked down on Emma Schaver and thought she was pretentious and we didn't go to hear her sing," and even though the members of my family were good friends of hers, I shared Rita's evaluation. Her vocal and emotional appeal and her repertoire were generationally bound.

But Emma found another valuable sphere of activity when she visited displaced persons camps in Germany just as World War II ended. She was a member of the first cultural mission sponsored by the World Jewish Congress and the UN's refugee administration. There, she overlapped with a friend of hers, my aunt Ann, profiled earlier, as another Detroit Jewish woman encountering the horror and the survival struggle of the Nazis' victims. Schaver toured the camps, singing her wide repertoire of Jewish songs for the survivors, saying, "When I saw the condition of the people, I volunteered to stay longer," ultimately staying six months because, she said, "I felt I had something to do there. She was impressed by the resilience of the refugees: "There was action, energy, and a beehive of activity. It was an amazing experience." As a result, Emma produced the first recording of what we now call Holocaust songs, giving her a special historical position, and produced a small songbook as well, one of the very first to present that repertoire. On the album, she boldly presents her distinctive style. There's a certain declamatory, operatic quality that sounds overblown to our ears, even to mine as a child, but it's very effective dramatically and was a sound of her time and community. It's influenced by those Red Army Chorus recordings that circulated among Detroit's Jews—including my family. It works well for singing the "Partizaner Lid," the wartime anthem of the Jewish resistance to the Nazis, a hymn that became essential to postwar Holocaust memorial events. Schaver starts rhetorically rather than melodically, with a militaristic backup, then moves into the tune itself. Only after the first verse does the rhythmic, intense chorus enter. It is a militant and rousing reading of the song that suits the early days of stressing survival. It also heralds the optimism that would be transferred to the Zionist cause she held so dear. In the groundbreaking anthology she published, Schaver leaves interpretations of these charged and cherished songs open, but insists that singers learn the words : "The interpretation of these songs is left entirely to the performing artist, but close familiarity with the text is indispensable, for the spirit of the text will dictate dynamics and tempo."

FIG. 5.7. Emma Schaver's 1948 anthology of Holocaust songs. Author collection.

Julius Chajes and Emma Schaver understood how to use musical training to broker a relationship with Detroit and the world in a way that met the need they and their audience felt to remain true to the full range of Jewish sensibilities. They were born early in the twentieth century, so insecurity and uncertainty blended uneasily with their cosmopolitan training and outlook in their quest for Jewish cultural meaning and influence. Many other musicians of their era took that background on the road. The story of the great American songwriters—Gershwin, Berlin, & Co.—who crossed the border permanently is very well known. A local version would be the career of Seymour Simons (1896–1949). Musically gifted, Seymour ignored his father's insistence that he become an engineer at Ford. Instead, he moved into music, writing songs and becoming a booking agent who collaborated with national stars like Nora Bayes. He and the left-leaning Jay Gorney, who was about to write "Brother, Can You Spare a Dime/" met at the University of Michigan, and Simons co-wrote that American songbook favorite "All of Me," with Gerald Marks, another Michigan Jewish boy. Simons remained connected to good works in the Detroit Jewish community and the national USO,combining hometown and ethnic affiliation with outreach aspirations.

In sum, the Jews of Detroit balanced the pressing spiritual, ideological, and aesthetic values of their dense, divisive internal life by making a sturdy and studied effort to cross their neighborhood border, flowing steadily into the mainstream musical traffic of the city. The modern Jews followed this urge everywhere they settled, in the great age of emigration from Europe. For Buenos Aires, Pablo Palomino describes the Jews' parallel moves into Argentine classical music and into the more popular spheres of concert life: "Jewish musicians performed Jewish music at events held by non-Jewish reformist political parties with which they shared a universalist outlook. . . . Some *hazzanim* [cantors], bridged the sacred and profane by singing also with tango and classical orchestras." Palomino says his examples of crossover "make clear the bonds that connected Jewish musical life across ethnic identities, national boundaries, and political allegiances." Modern city life gave the Jews everywhere a chance to move out into the broader world of music with all the resources, selective strategies, and multiple agendas that characterized this mobile minority.

In the United States, Detroit Jewry made more of an impact on the American scene than historians have admitted, says historian Lila Corwin Berman: "The fact of the matter is that for a medium-sized Jewish community, Detroit Jews played outsized roles on the national Jewish stage, serving as leaders of national Jewish organizations and emerging as trend-setting philanthropists," such as Morris Schaver and concert patron Max Fisher. Locally, "Jews came to believe that they could play a broader role in the fate of the city, and, at the same time, they felt more empowered to assert that their own agenda should be central to the city's future." It is this border-crossing mentality that allowed the Jews, a threatened but economically dynamic group, to make their voice heard in Detroit through the music they produced and patronized.

6   Merging Traffic

Beyond personal construction sites, public school circulation, and neighborhood music, compelling forces led to converging traffic on the civic highway. This chapter selectively surveys the urge to merge. Many groups shared the same idea: to unite Detroiters through music. This need for corporate, civic, and labor intervention into people's musical lives goes back to a nineteenth-century American drive for unity through music, the flow of urban migrants—rural or foreign—and a general push for discipline and order in the streets and squares of public life. Meanwhile, media kept bringing people together at a dizzying pace as new technologies and formats multiplied.

The appeal to solidarity through music can be top-down or bottom-up, springing from working-class or countercultural activism. Strong individuals can shape this drive for unity, or the work can be widespread and anonymous. The activity ranges from national radio shows to local cafes and college hangouts, from church basements to the factory dining hall. Strong and canny commercialism also encourages the pooling of talent in a city as rich in trained musicians as Detroit. The most successful local enterprise was Motown, brilliant at integrating the experience and skills of dozens of creative spirits.

Meanwhile, on the front doorsteps and in the millions of cars streaming through the city there was the newspaper and the radio, joined by the TV set, as channelers of the flow, acting as sometimes neutral, sometimes partisan, musical traffic cops.

Corporate Convergence

Good music as well as good cars comes from the factory of the Ford Motor Company.
—FORD TIMES, 1913

As the auto boom expanded, Detroit's industrial leaders joined a national drive to boost worker morale and company visibility by setting up bands, orchestras, and choruses. It was an on-ramp to merge the population into the industrial lane. Auto companies embraced this approach to recreational convergence, from small outfits like Nash and Studebaker to the giants, Ford, General Motors, and Chrysler. Some of this variety of Motor City music has been stored in archives, but not much, so we have only a sketchy sense. Chrysler simply deleted its records after merging with Fiat, but GM and Ford are helpful in looking for the lost music of the Big Three. These two major players agreed on one area of uplift and outreach: the idea of a chorus of workers. It was a national trend, since GM featured alongside Texas Company, Hotpoint, Electric Companies of America, Burlington Mills, and Stanley Home Products in a 1953 national radio Christmas broadcast, each with its own home-grown singing employees. Local corporate collaboration also brought companies together, as at the "Industry Sings" events that combined the Ford and Great Lakes Steel choirs with GM, as late as 1959. To date, there is almost no literature on the way that American factories and modern corporations saw music as a way to boost the morale of their overworked and sometimes rebellious employees, who came from many nations. It goes back into the nineteenth century. In Connecticut, the fife and drum tradition got a new lease on life in the mills, after Civil War marching bands melted into the civilian workforce. The need to make this in-house tradition into a kind of sonic logo spread from factories to the retail economy. In 1957 Detroit, the singers of the iconic J. L. Hudson department store, the Hudson Carolers, a forty-five-voice group, was considered crucial for Detroiters as a morale booster that was "particularly significant this year with the world at unrest." The store also sent its in-house band in the spring and fall to Detroit school auditoriums.

For corporate music, Ford set the pace for musical organization, just as it did for auto construction, but let's start with General Motors compact idea of industrial sponsorship before turning to Ford's more detailed and diverse musical production line. The GM Chorus started back in 1933, an invention of the boss, William S. Knudson, a Danish immigrant who had probably heard a lot of choral singing. He hired Edward Ossko, a busy music organizer who ran the old-time German group, the Harmonie, and energized programs in local churches. So it was not hard for him to align the corporation with civic and Christian concerns in a convergence of American values. He conducted a 1938 production of "The Life of Christ in Prose and Song" for the Detroit Bach Chorus, even as he ran the GM singers. This was the last gasp of the nineteenth-century German-Christian-dominated music scene. The auto ensemble also celebrated the holiday under Ossko that year, combining their 250 voices with the sixty players of the GM Symphony Orchestra and the company's actors, the GM Players. The show was written by "well-known Detroit newspaperman Rex White," converging the press with the corporation and civic religion. For the next Christmas, 1939, the city of Flint, so endangered today, could celebrate by combining its 400-strong GM chorus with "several thousand" other factory workers to sing carols. These dates coincided with massive sit-down strikes, whose songs are detailed below, so workers could merge in song in two different social keys. Christmas was clearly a red-letter day on the corporate calendar: just a single division of GM, Inland Manufacturing of Dayton Ohio, fielded a nationally broadcast concert by a group of 170 workers' children, folding families into the business model. Also on Christian themes, Ossko was taking the GM group to Flint to perform "The Cross Victorious" with that city's Civic Symphony. Christmas became a bit more multicultural by 1964, which saw a "West Indian carol in a calypso rhythm," and by 1973, with the durable GM chorus down to seventy-five members, the press release announced that carols "from around the world will be presented in their native tongue."

Who were the members of these robust choirs? A press release says this: "Composed of office and factory workers in Detroit GM plants, the chorus is one of the largest industrial musical organizations of its kind in the world. Men and women from 18 to 75 are numbered among its membership, and the organization has received many favorable comments from such internationally known opera stars as Kirsten Flagstad, Lily Pons and Lotte Lehmann, who have appeared in concerts with the chorus in Detroit and Flint." Bringing in divas was a regular feature of GM's musical agenda, aligned with the national trend of "making America musical" that promoted classical music alongside sentimental, seasonal, and popular song. The scope of the corporation's effort to raise the musical taste of its employees is impressive, especially a moment from 1935, in the middle of the Depression. GM staged a concert for 4,600 employees at the Masonic Temple, Detroit's prime venue, and broadcast it on NBC over sixty-five stations nationwide. The diva was whisked to Detroit from the cultural capital, New York City: "Lotte Lehman will step off the Met stage in her Elsa Lohengrin costume directly onto the Detroit train to make the event." In those years, the GM chorus also regularly appeared with the Detroit Symphony Orchestra, cementing another civic network.

The national radio broadcasts ranged widely, but stayed close to the corporate agenda. At midpoint, the shows featured GM executives pitching progress, like this postwar prosperity prose from Charles Kettering: "1946 will see us enjoying new comforts, new conveniences and new jobs undreamed of today, for the world is far from being finished." To properly celebrate its product, GM even commissioned an orchestral work, to be played alongside Haydn and Ravel at a 1946 on-air concert, *Moto Perpetuo* by Don Gillis, a staff member of the GM Symphony of the Air. Its premiere aligned with the nationwide celebration of the fiftieth anniversary of the American automobile. It was a fitting contribution by a company that was keeping Detroit and the nation in perpetual motion, on the assembly line and the vastly expanding highway system. Like the Jewish community but for different reasons, GM quickly picked up on the rising star of classical music, Leonard Bernstein, and featured him with a work by Marc Blitzstein, a surprising choice, given the latter's leftist and gay profile. But GM chose a patriotic wartime work, *The Airborne*, commissioned by and dedicated to Blitzstein's wartime unit, the Eighth Air Force, to extend the patriotic theme that the corporation had been pushing during the war. As "a patriotic service," GM produced *Cheers from the Camps* in 1942–43, with an all-soldier cast. "In this 'moral program' for the folks back home, the boys in khaki will show the best of their entertainment talents." Each week was broadcast from another camp, spotlighting specialists such as aviation engineers. "The soldiers have not forgotten, in their grim training for war, the talents they had in civilian life. There will be comedy from boys who can laugh as well as fight, martial music by camp bands, quiz contests, dramatizations, entertainment of all varieties." Pointing out its own contribution to the war effort, with "90 plants in 38 cities fabricating about 10 per cent of all metal products for war," GM had the total cooperation of the USO and the Department of War for this entertainment initiative. Not often do corporations get a chance to wrap themselves so completely in the national flag, and even beyond, with shows beamed to Canadians, who like Americans, reveled in a mix of music and musicians to integrate their fragmented nations in wartime: "Of special interest to Scotsmen will be the skirl of the bagpipes from the bands of the Saskatchewan Horse Regiment," who played the French-Canadian folk song "St. Anne Reel" and a Scottish ballad, sung by a Chinese bandsman. Variety percolated down to the local levels of the far-flung GM music network. Any division of the company might have its own performing group, like the seventy-five-voice Pontiac Male Chorus, which appeared in 1936 with the DSO in the city's premier park, Belle Isle. The program was deeply American eclectic, opening with Ossko's "Theme Song—Pontiac Chieftains," blending the local sad history of a defeated Indian chief with industrial cheerleading. Along with the classical *Finlandia* of Sibelius, the chorus offered the usual standby plantation songs—"Dixie" and "Kentucky Babe." I sang some of those now-banned songs in grade school. We kids would solemnly intone Stephen Foster's nostalgic words, joining our little souls with the fate of a dying black servant: "I'm coming, I'm coming, and my head is bending low, I hear those gentle voices singing 'Old Black Joe." You could hear that and many other mainstream classics in the movie house, where the whole audience sang along, following the bouncing red ball up on the silver screen. School, cinema, and factory—it all added up, in the equation of nation-state + industry = American culture.

General Motors' bland combo of Americana and classical music pales in comparison with the colorful mix sponsored by the Ford Motor Company, originally designed, like the cars themselves, by old man Henry. He was very much a hands-on driver, not just in management but also in social engineering, with his staff of investigators barging into people's houses to see if their moral tone was up to his standards, alongside his well-funded fulminations against Jewish bankers. Ford—the man and the corporation—cared deeply about music, and the story goes back to the early, heady days of the auto explosion that shifted the traffic in Detroit's streets and society. Some of Ford's tinkering with the musical machinery only had local effects, but parts of his design had national implications. I, and millions of other children, might not have been square dancing in the schools if Ford hadn't started the old-time music craze in 1925. He liked to project his personal preferences and obsessions onto society at large. It's a story that's been well described but deserves some review in terms of this book's blending of the personal and the social, the subcultural and the mainstream model.

Paul Gifford says that Ford was longing to bring back the music that played in the roadhouse where he met his wife. The area was somewhat suburban but still, to his mind, a place in the country, the reservoir of American values. The bands there played all kinds of music, American and imported, roots, pop, and classical, but what stuck in Ford's memory were the duets of fiddle and hammered dulcimer, playing what he called "old-time" music, dance tunes from the British Isles. He filtered out the cosmopolitanism of what he had heard, to favor a kind of racial purity that tinged his thinking. In a book he sponsored, he denounced "the importation of dances which are foreign to the expressional needs of our people. With characteristic American judgment, however, the balance is now shifting toward that style of dancing which best fits with the American temperament. There is a revival of that type of dancing which has survived longest amongst the northern peoples. The tide has swung in favor of such dances." The problem is that square dancing, Ford's favorite form, was not really an Anglo-Saxon white style. It was "a child of immigration and cultural exchange, with elements [of] French and English ballroom dance; English, Scottish and Irish village dances; African American ring dances, early nineteenth-century stage dancing, and more." But old Henry was right about a revival of interest in "old-time" music, since he helped to create a craze was that fueled by the auto mogul's insistence on what he saw as an "authentically American" style. Ford "lit the match that fired a frenetic, national phenomenon during the winter of 1925–1926."

Ford hired and promoted a bunch of musicians from different parts of the country, starting in his own backyard in 1923. His imagination was set ablaze by a visit to a rural fiddler, Jasper "Jep" Bisbee, whom he sent off to be recorded by his great friend Thomas Edison. But somehow, Ford couldn't find the hammered dulcimer sound he needed for his romantic recall. His inner circle suggested a substitution: the Hungarian cimbalom. The advisor was E. J. Farkas, a Hungarian-born engineer who rose to the top with practical solutions to automotive problems: "My contribution to the mount was another rubber washer to the bottom which would check it from going down but very little coming up. I figured you had to snub it like you would on a shock absorber". Ford trusted people like this to get him what he needed. Somehow, they scrounged up a cimbalom in Flint, and Farkas scouted for a musician in the Hungarian Roma ("Gypsy") community of Del Ray, near Ford's headquarters. Billy Hallup filled the bill. He was from Cleveland, part of a nexus of Roma musicians in the industrial cities that were magnets for central and eastern European immigrants. So Henry Ford created a rather odd band, since he combined the cimbalom with a Michigan hammered dulcimer he eventually found, putting it in a piano case, adding string bass, piano, and a fiddle. "Ford was so excited about getting dancing that he walled off part of a building to make a ballroom big enough for seventy couples, and spent an hour or two there every day before going to the business office. Meanwhile, Hallup was busily learning Appalachian fiddle tunes even while he threw light classical—Strauss waltzes and the like—and what we'd call today lounge music into the mix. It was a very stringy, hammered sound, a fine example of eclecticism and modernity masquerading as Old-Time." There are a handful of recordings of Ford's band of the period, which muddy the old-time waters further by adding a sousaphone for sonic strength. One track combines three old standbys of the fiddle-tune tradition still played for dances today: "Pigtown Fling," "Flowers of Edinburgh," and "Farewell to Whiskey."

This band really reflected the two sides of Henry Ford's nature. The sentimental and dogmatic support of his idealized America combined with hard-headed business practices. Since his old-time-music push coincided with a drop in Ford auto sales, dealers were told to capitalize on his band's newfangled radio broadcasts. They fitted the showrooms with loudspeakers, holding public dances to draw people to the gleaming new cars. It's a different model for "dancing in the street" than the one Motown would provide later. Dancers could drive right out of the dealership in new Fords, merging music and traffic onto the ever-expanding highway system. It wasn't just the old-time musicians who spread the gospel of music as national refreshment. The 45–55-piece Ford Band, with its vocal quartet, had already started at the dawn of the Auto Age, in 1910. They went on state and national tours for towns, cities, and dealerships, again mixing the civic and the commercial. Bands changed their uniforms to keep their image fresh, as opposed to the frozen-in-time approach of Ford's original pastoral imaginary. These shows formed part of a century-old fascination with music in the town square, at parades, in the schools, and in the colleges, with their highly popular glee clubs. America was a singing and marching society that slowly shifted its taste to incorporate newer styles of dance and pop song. The radio served to detach the music from the moment, relocating it in the living room instead of the park or dealership, but the idea of an all-purpose musical product that went on physical or sound-wave highways lingered for a very long time in American society.

Live performance helped to gather workers and their families outside the dreadful conditions of the foundry and assembly line, humanizing the harsh realities of work. The Ford Novelty Band, begun in 1935, offered side-splitting slapstick and comedy routines. The group emerged from the Trade School German Band, so it must have carried over the stage stereotypes and comic business of vaudeville, which had drawn crowds for decades. This outrageous outfit could even be too effective for its own good: "In Flat Rock, a man died laughing watching them," according to a deadpan *Ford Times* report of 1948. Could this have been when "a blank pistol set the trumpeter's pants on fire?" This scattershot gang of entertainers had by then played at "over ninety clubs, sewing circles and sports events, church programs and stag parties, Republican rallies and Democratic rallies, insane asylums, and universities," as well at Briggs (later Tiger) Stadium and for fifty thousand spectators at the State Fair. You can't get much more corporate bang for your buck than investing in a few zanies. But life was hard for the touring entertainment workers. The workers had to clock in time at no extra pay as they pushed trucks out of rural mud. A 1916 odyssey in primitive motor vehicles involved 225 people across Michigan up to Ontario. It was a sixteen-day slog, with seventeen trucks poking along just for "kitchen work, baggage carrying, office work, electric lighting, refrigeration, and so forth" (February 22, 1925). It all sounds somewhat like the mobile troupes that constantly crisscrossed the young Soviet Union at just the same time, with similar agendas of ideology-laced entertainment. The socialist circuits lacked Ford's commercial pizzazz but offered a similar sales pitch about progress and technology, blended with strong nationalist sentiment.

Like GM, Ford also funded on-air classical music showcases, but the company liked to spin off units across a wider sound spectrum. Most of the bands were workers-only, even including the Ford Hawaiians, who offered an authentic island touch not available even among Detroit's diverse demographics. The Ford trainees from Hawaii were enlisted for a 1925 radio show with "a Chinese string quintet with two guitars, one steel guitar and two ukuleles." The write-up makes a point of saying that four of the five Chinese-origin musicians were Hawaiian-born, thus being American citizens. The balance between mainstream and "exotic" music runs through the whole enterprise. Whereas the Ford Dixie Eight kept the minstrel show–plantation sound alive with songs and tap-dancing, the Hungarian Gypsy Orchestra of five immigrant Hungarian workers dovetailed with the cimbalom in the old-time "American" band for a more colorful listening experience. The balance between mainstream Americana and specialized sounds is remarkable, offering a panoramic snapshot of corporate music making. Some are only names, with no real documentation: the Ford Motor Company Clarinet Quartet, Mercury Rangers, Ford Ramblers, Glass House Quintet, Morgan & Flowers Act, and the Ford Rube Quartet, which poked fun at hayseeds, in a time-honored stage style. Back during the first world war, the aptly named Michigan Electrotype and Stereotype Company sang "coon songs," the new pop version of the old minstrel show material, alongside uplifting "Negro" spirituals. The race of the singers remains unmentioned, but either way, some of the performers were probably in blackface.

The Ford News lovingly details groups dear to old Henry's heart. The St. Andrews Highlander Ford Kiltie Band revels in its community connection, but cold calculation lurked behind the cheerful façade of the company concerts. Formed from a Detroit band that started way back in 1849, the Kilties played under the corporate logo in 1932 and these rules: "Each member was credited with 8 hours working time for each 24 hours on the road, and then was given a like amount of time off with pay." Authenticity was important: the members had all been born in Scotland, had served in British pipe bands during World War I, and wore uniforms ordered from Scotland. In 1939, this ensemble swept the group and individual prizes at both the American and Canadian national piping championships, including the best-dressed category. The resonance of the eleven pipers and nine drummers must have been thunderous. This triumph of a "northern" white sound would have been music to Henry's ears. Scottish songs had been spotlighted in American school and home songbooks throughout the nineteenth century, set off from the grotesquerie of African American appearances on stage and sheet music covers. This long history, unlike the music of the newer immigrants, dominated the Ford sensibility. An all-Scottish Ford program featured ballads "that echoed from the strongholds of the clans centuries ago." Included was a talk in "Scottish dialect" by Victor Mitchell of Henry's mouthpiece, *The Dearborn Independent*, called "Slandering the Scots." Apparently, that paper's slandering of the Jews, which had begun to subside, could now be swept under the rug. Ford was building on a long-standing Detroit attachment to Scottish music, a fascination that started early and lasted long. In 1947, the St. Andrew's Society celebrated its 103rd anniversary, marking the moment with singers, a violinist, and Highland Dancers and their Pipe Band, all converging on the Burns Statue in Cass Park to lay a wreath.

Like every other Detroit story, what the auto archives reveal about the industry's musical intervention into the lives of its workers, the city, the state, and the nation points to the paradoxes of American cultural activity. It was a period of large-scale movements to invest in music education. The private sector was trying hard to mold the workforce into a standardized social class in the interest of efficiency and expansion and saw music as a tool for integration, against the tide of rising unionism. The rapid expansion of the media—radio, recordings—and the interstate road network drove this corporate control effort. Yet older forms of live music making persisted: the community choir, the vaudeville show, the picnic and excursion, the traveling circuit from clubs and hospitals to trade shows and country fairs. Radio, the more homogenizing force, could push the idea of uplift, as with GM and Ford's classical hours, matched by other companies' efforts: the Firestone Hour, the elite NBC Orchestra under the glamorous Toscanini, and the weekly Metropolitan Opera broadcasts. Locally, though, in diverse Detroit, Ford supported a variety of formats and genres, some based on audience interest, some just on Henry's whims. An organization as massive as Ford—a hundred thousand workers in the vast River Rouge complex alone—could still have a personal stamp for its branding. Curiously, Ford's drive for musical diversity did not match his business model, which relied on standard models for all buyers—"they can have any color, as long as it's black"— whereas GM's pioneering push for variety and novelty seemed not to extend to its corporate musical patronage, which stayed with the tried and true classical and concert formats.

Driving on the Shoulder: Workers' Music

Please, Mister Foreman, slow down your assembly line,
Please, Mister Foreman, slow down your assembly line.
See, I don't mind working, but I do mind dying.
—JOE L, worker / labor activist / soul music singer, ca. 1970

In Detroit either you go to college or you go work in a factory. Give a bottle of whiskey to the foreman and you got a job on the line.
—MARK NORTON, rock singer and journalist

Ford, GM, and their many competitors were in denial about the rising labor discontent that fueled the huge unionization push of the 1930s. Even as workers took part in company choruses, they created their own parallel musical system. Converging in their union halls, at picnics and demonstrations, and in their major sit-ins and strikes, the industrial workforce wrote and performed songs in clusters of creativity of different sizes and orientations. There were small units inside UAW locals and more radical repertoires outside the union, within the many splinter groups, from early Communist Party and Trotsykite cells of the 1930s to 1950s through the black workers' movement of the 1970s. Surprisingly, there's not much trace in the archives about all this full-throated singing and picking, so I can offer only a sketch, not a portrait of those who sang truth to power. Nor is there anything like a general history of workers' music in the United States to draw on for comparison. Of course, there is the cherished image of those inspirational traveling troubadours, Pete Seeger and the Almanac Singers, Woody Guthrie, and the rest. But how much that syncs with local experience is unclear. I was struck by a reply I received from the historian Hayden White, who grew up in a Detroit labor household. I asked whether his circle of country music-loving Appalachian immigrants made use of "folk music:" "Oh, we thought that was above our station. It came from another world. We thought Woody Guthrie was phony." In his circles, they danced to Ernest Tubb and Bob Wills. Probably the situation was more balanced. Workers, like seemingly most Detroiters, had open ears and, as we'll see below, freely mixed types of music as both entertainment and resistance. It's a very American way of dealing with rich resources of song.

Millions of workers converged musically on the job or in private, so you have to look at both collective and individual expression and then chart the ways they flowed together. For mainstream factory workers, the only self-generated document I've seen is a 1948 songbook of UAW local 937. It's from the Royal Typewriter Company in Hartford, rather than Detroit, but is probably like union song in the Motor City. The Hartford factory had shifted musically, from the company-sponsored all-American fife and drum corps to a new worker consciousness based on popular music. The texts offer the easiest possible access road: parodies of well-known American songs. It's a tried and true technique, known most famously from 1909's *Little Red Songbook* of the International Workers of the World. The Royal local's source songs were well-known from childhood: "Take Me Out to the Ball Game," "She'll Be Comin' 'Round the Mountain." Or they could come from the old Scottish song stock: "Annie Laurie," "Roaming in the Gloamin.'" These songs overlap with Henry Ford's idea of acceptable tunes, here turned against corporate control as weapons of resistance. It's a far cry from "Maxwelton braes are bonnie / Where early falls the dew / And it was there that Annie Laurie / Gave me her promise true" to the UAW version: "There are union men and women / Who walk the street today / Whose only sin is asking / For a decent rate of pay." Even more subversive was converting a military anthem, "The Caissons Go Rolling Along," to the union's purpose, as "The Decency Song," while keeping the militancy of the original. The text speaks directly to singing as social action. It transforms "Over hill, over dale / As we hit the dusty trail / And those caissons go rolling along" to "U. A. Dub, U. A. Dub / U. A. Dub-Dub-Double-U / We're a union that sings as it fights." It's a kind of low-intensity parallel to Pete Seeger's famous banjo inscription: "This machine surrounds hate and forces it to surrender." Older popular song also inspired worker poetics, from "Easter Parade" (now "Picket Parade"), "Sioux City Sue," and "Little Brown Jug." The refrain of "Pretty Baby" was refitted as "Join the union." Sometimes parts of the original shine through its parody, as with Royal's version of "For Me and My Gal," which starts "The sun is shining / For me and my gal," moving into "There's just one union / For me and my gal / The Royal Union / for me and my gal."

To stand in for the wide range of worker and leftist expression, two forgotten figures suggest the full spectrum of engaged musicking: Maurice Sugar and Sid Brown, contrasting types who, coincidentally or not, both emerged from the Jewish community. Maurice Sugar was born in isolated Brimley, a hamlet in Michigan's sparsely settled Upper Peninsula. He was the son of a Jewish peddler who turned shopkeeper. That happened all over the world, including in Michigan. My own father's father started out that way in the similarly small village of Rosebush. Sugar's biographer Christopher Johnson thinks that "Sugar learned from the lumberjacks his first lesson in the power of labor united," and he heard those exploited woodsmen belt out songs like this:

> Oley Olsen is a jobber
> Who will go to hell some day
> For working men long hours
> And cutting down their pay.

Or, more poetically:

> Bear and wolf,
> The louse and the bedbug,
> The devilish strawboss,
> They thirst for our blood.

Meanwhile, in the time-tested Jewish way, Sugar's mother tried to distance her boy from the surroundings by insisting on piano lessons, which he ignored. He was far more interested in the music at the little dance hall, where he heard different classics: "Turkey in the Straw," "The Irish Washerwoman," and "The Girl I Left Behind Me," which "wafted across the railroad tracks to his open bedroom; on occasion he managed to dance, clap, and sing with the music on the spot." This is exactly the repertoire that shaped Henry Ford's aesthetic and which he pushed relentlessly through his house band and his car dealers' sidewalk phonographs. Deep in the Upper Peninsula, Sugar also heard pop tunes blaring from mechanical devices, in the saloons. He and his bitter enemy Henry Ford agreed on one thing from their Michigan childhood: the importance of popular music to the masses of working people.

The studious and observant Maurice left the lumberjacks and got a law degree. Moving into Detroit's labor scene at the dawn of the automotive revolution, he became a Socialist lecturer, inspiring radicals with fiery speeches in 1916, just when the big factories were shooting their smokestacks into Detroit's darkening skies. Sugar paid many dues, sitting out World War 1 in jail for defying the draft, joining protesters in the constant battles against the corporation, and rising to be the UAW's general counsel from 1936 to 1947, until he lost out in Walter Reuther's purges of the far-left ranks of the union. Sugar is crucial to the story of leftist music, because he wrote some highly popular songs of the struggle. It seems he was more influential than canonical figures such as Pete Seeger, and Seeger himself acknowledged Sugar's skills in a *Sing Out!* column and a 1970 letter: "Another great song. I've read it and I'm going to sing it. . . . I've already mailed copies to SING OUT! And BROADSIDE. Wonderful to know you are alive and kicking as ever. Keep up the good work" (Reuther Archive). Even before Seeger arrived on the labor scene, the Communist paper the *Daily Worker* praised Sugar in 1938 both for being "a central figure in Michigan's progressive circles" and for the power and impact of his songs, of which two stand out: "The Soup Song" and "Sit Down." He wrote the first in 1931 after coming home from a meeting of miserable homeless workers, "white and black, native born and foreign born of many national origins," in darkest Depression Detroit. Like the UAW workers' homemade efforts, "The Soup Song" is a parody of a song every child could sing: "My Bonnie Lies Over the Ocean," another Scottish-origin item. Here's the beginning:

> I'm spending my night at the flop-house,
> I'm spending my days on the street.
> I'm looking for work and I find none.
> I wish I had something to eat.
> *Chorus:*
> Sooo-oup, sooo-oup, they give me a bowl of soo-oup
> Sooo-oup, sooo-oup, they give me a bowl of soo-oup.

Sugar's biographer says, "Very few songs of the Depression enjoyed such wide currency." The lawyer himself said he heard it everywhere he went on a national speaking tour. Remembering the song late in life, Sugar was particularly proud of a moment in 1937 at the pivotal Flint Fisher Body strike. He was given a tour of the plant, and after seeing the posh executives' offices, he "was taken to plant kitchen where long lines of workers stood with soup bowls in their hands, waiting to have them filled from the gigantic soup cistern . . . and all the time they were singing the 'Soup Song' with gusto."

By 1937, the Flint action was just one of many major events that the rising union movement choreographed in the Detroit area, and songs played a major role in raising morale. "Small picket groups headed by a banjo-strumming union leader move back and forth between the Hudson plants and the Chrysler factory," a newspaper reported, and they were singing Sugar's emphatic song "Sit Down," which helped to drive the new strategy of workers simply sitting down on the factory floor and refusing to work until management recognized their demands:

> When they tie the can
> To a union man
> Sit down! Sit down!
> When they give him the sack,
> They'll take him back.
> Sit down! Sit down"
> *Chorus:*
> Sit down, just take a seat.
> Sit down, and rest your feet.
> Sit down, you've got 'em beat.
> Sit down! Sit down!

A 1937 recording made just after the strike, with small mixed chorus and piano, presents the song in more of a jaunty hymn style than a Woody Guthrie–Pete Seeger style.

Sugar's songwriting dovetailed with the UAW and more radical organizations in Detroit, who sponsored cultural programming in clubs and theater projects. Both the earlier John Reed Club, which spawned the Detroit New Union Theatre, and the later UAW-CIO-sponsored Union Theatre of Detroit put on worker-friendly dramas such as Clifford Odets's *Waiting for Lefty* or a play on the struggle to free the unjustly imprisoned Scottsboro boys. They might well have used Sugar's 1938 song on the subject, printed in the *Daily Worker*:

> Black workers, white workers, lis'n to me
> They aint goin' to kill those Scottsboro boys,

I'm tellin' you they're goin' free, they're goin' free.
Chorus:
Hear my cry a-ringing
Ringing thru the land
Hold those bloody fingers
Drop that bloody hand

Sugar wrote the music himself, with somewhat of a fanfare flourish and a punchy rhythm that matched the hard-hitting lyric. These labor theaters moved around the city, performing at schools, hospitals, union halls, and picnic grounds. But the workers did not just sit still for agitprop plays. The only event I could find a record of in the Reuther Archives is a 1937 gathering at Eastwood Park, where the entertainment was Milt-Bernie and Their Orchestra and Chrysler's "Sit-Downers" Swing Band. Maybe that band played a pop arrangement of Sugar's "Sit Down" song, but it was more likely that the picnickers were dancing to a Benny Goodman number. Since all of the white southern musicians in Detroit had day jobs, most of them in factories, it is not surprising that they might bring their music into the workplace to lift morale. The fine traditional musician George Williamson worked at the Fleetwood Plant, and on a couple of occasions he and another well-known player, Mabel Dorman, drove around the factory on a cart, playing old-timey tunes for a special occasion honoring outstanding workers. The nationally renowned banjoist Wade Mainer, who lived to the legendary age of 104, moved from Asheville to Flint in 1953. He remained incognito while polishing brake shoes for 1954 Chevrolets until his record came out. "The people in the shop . . . they'd *heard* of me, but they didn't know who I was, but I was workin' around them all the time—everyday". Then all his workmates bought a copy. Doing factory work to support playing music was not new—that's what he had done back in North Carolina—only there it was a cotton mill instead of a car factory.

Maurice Sugar's summary is the best I've found of music on the job: "They frequently improvised musical bands, featuring accordions, mandolins, guitars, mouth organs, and now and then a saxophone. These bands went sled-length for folk songs . . . lots of hill-billy stuff . . . and lots of parodies." A photo from the 1937 Flint strike backs up his description, though the three guitars and banjo present a slightly different lineup. It is a pity that we don't seem to have the workers' own accounts of what music meant to them in that era of Detroit's labor wars, though perhaps there are oral histories somewhere that I have not yet encountered.

By the late 1960s, the early militancy of the UAW had given way to a status quo that masked both the decline of Detroit's economy and the militance of black workers, who formed DRUM (Dodge Revolutionary Union Movement). At their

FIG. 6.1. Workers' band during the 1937 Flint sit-down strike. Still from uncredited footage at https://www.youtube.com/watch?v=kVrxruRTtDA.

demonstration for greater black recognition in 1968, it was African garb and bongo drums that set the tone, not song parodies or fiddle and accordion bands. New cultural currents were moving through the city.

The Counterculture Corridor

All we ever thought about was flying in the face of authority.
—LILY TOMLIN

In contrast to factory activism, the circle of my youth that gathered to sing leftist songs in the 1950s was pretty middle-class, but sympathetic to labor and struggle. We knew Spanish Civil War songs, Seeger, Guthrie, and Leadbelly standbys, and even Russian repertoire from the Red Army Chorus records, leftovers from the US-Soviet wartime alliance. I picked up a round-bellied mandolin in a pawn shop and strummed along. We picketed the Detroit Institute of the Arts when they canceled Pete Seeger's concert during his blacklist days. Earlier, I noted the Jewish People's Chorus, of which I was a member, as another haven for progressive singing. My two musical circles, the classical and the lefty, rarely overlapped. I only remember one party where I tried to bring them together. One of the people who might have been there was Sid Brown. In 2005, Sid wrote a "mini-memoir" called *Still Wobbly After All These Years*, inspired by the centennial of the IWW (the "Wobblies"), who produced that influential *Little Red Songbook* in 1909. He starts by praising the union's strategy of writing parodies: "Such a provocative and pragmatic idea! . . .[Their songs] definitely had more transformative wisdom, wily wit, exciting incitements and parodic popularity" than Mao's Little Red Book.

Sid chose the guitar, which gave him access to songs from many sources, but where could he find them? "Back then, before the 'folk revival' of the Sixties, the only place to get folk music books was at the Communist Party bookstore," a place I did not frequent. Ending up at Cass Tech, Sid found "the Stalinoid resource center," just a block away, where he dropped by regularly to peruse *Sing Out!* magazine, Marxist classics, and Commie literature. He scored a copy of the IWW songbook, which he says he clutched in "my blistered, yet-to-be-callused guitar-picking fingers and began to figure out all those three-chord wonders. I didn't do it on my own, for music making works/plays best as a collaborative effort." Like the massed members of the UAW, Sid banded together with his buddies in song, becoming a "precocious little putz" who was a "fairly adept guitar picker and picketer." We must have been on the line together at some point, since he mentions the action against the downtown Woolworth's store as a signal victory for collective action. I too walked down a few blocks from Cass Tech to join in. That area, around Wayne University, became known as the Cass Corridor, after the main thoroughfare that led to nearby downtown Detroit.

Sid Brown personalizes the ways that ideology merged with the musical traffic lane that became called the counterculture. Knowing a bunch of songs and trying to play them on mandolin and banjo was not enough: "Playing the same tune for fifteen minutes eventually got old, so we started improvising." This led Sid and his friend Arnie Kessler to be bold enough to walk into white southern clubs to see how you could "really" play those instruments. They even went to a few big country music shows. Sid was adventurous and influential: "He had a certain charisma and brought others in. He was kind of a wild man as a kid, ran with a bad element, and turned people on to playing music, says his friend and mine Arnie Kessler. Sid would go anywhere for music: "We heard Greek music before *Never on Sunday*," the movie that helped to launch Greektown as a tourist destination. "Sid learned bouzouki. Got to know one of the players and followed him back to Greece and made a movie about him."

Sid and his buddy made the familiar Detroit move of trying out New York, back in 1958 or 1959. By then, major jazz musicians like Lateef were already being drawn to the magnet of the East, and many never came back. "I remember hitchhiking with Sid. There was some girl in NY I wanted to see. Slept on the ground, looking for a ride. Big station wagon pulls up, almost full. We were worried about throwing the instruments in to the car, but he said 'don't worry about that'—he was the guy who built Seeger's long-necked banjo. He gave us the name of Eric Darling," a major folk figure, so they hung out with him. But it was too early for these amateur

Jewish boys to find a niche in New York; they went back to the Cass Corridor. It was a fluid moment for a generation that wanted to try out new sounds within an industrial city.

> Wanna-be-Beatnik coffeehouses opened up and we did regular jams, including one mind-blowing and ear-revelating session with Yusef Lateef. A bongo-banging poet referred to us as the "Trotsky Trio," though we billed ourselves as "The Motor City String Banned." In dark dingy and depraved dens such as the Unstabled, we alternated sets with an improv ensemble which included Lily Tomlin. We few folkies *schlepping* a fretful array of perhaps 20 guitars, banjos, mandolins, washboards and washtub bass plucked 20-minute blues, bluegrass and Greco-Middle-Eastern improvisational mélanges. Honoring the past's rich folk traditions and creating "newness and now-ness" through improvisation was energizing and empowering.

Or, as Kessler puts it: "The Weavers came to town. We already had complete contempt for the Weavers. We had been doing folk music for six or seven months. We were such assholes."

Today's battles over cultural appropriation did not seem to be an issue for activists like Kessler and Brown. Whether the stance was innocent or disingenuous, Sid defended a certain working-class and neighborly rationale for the musical exploration of Detroit's streets: "What 'right' or credibility did city kids have singing songs of sharecropping or moonshining. But Detroit's auto factories were filled with émigrés from the farms and hills of the South. These workers . . . were the parents of the kids I went to school with. They were sometimes our friends, but always our neighbors, and why shouldn't we honor diversity and add our riffs and licks to the stew brewing in our multicultural melting pot?" Kessler narrows it down: "Detroit was a hotbed of unionism. All those circles moved in similar directions." I'm still not convinced that the side street of the counterculture moved on to the service drive of workers' music. But I support the idea that everything irregular—not part of corporate or ethnic initiatives—had a tendency to bump into each other and interact. The folk scene was small, as was much of Detroit's counterculture, overlapping the huge sectors of African American musical energy and immigrant recreation. Enjoying an atmosphere of integrated activism along the Cass Corridor and elsewhere, people got along: "We felt we were in a backwater—things happened at the University of Chicago, New York, California. In Detroit, if you wanted some folk music, and George Tysh liked jazz, you got together. There was more cross-pollination than elsewhere. If you were in politics, and there were people in the arts, you hung out with them anyway."

FIG. 6.2. A homegrown hootenanny at our house, 1959. Al Young on banjo. Author photo.

My brother's generation flowed into the Cass Corridor easily. His junior high buddy Al Young, now a distinguished African American writer, hung out with everybody, very deliberately, moving in the 1950s from the Central High band and orchestra to jazz circles and then into the folk world before moving on to the college-town coffeehouses of Ann Arbor. Another classmate, Mary Tomlin—later Lily—was drawn downtown and honed her acting skills in plays by Ionesco and Beckett, as well as trying out sketches and improv comedy. "I would do anything to be around that place," she says. But those shows didn't get much audience response, according to Dan Georgakas: "We could only do plays on the weekends, so during the week it was a coffeehouse, and you could have lectures, folk music, and so forth. When the play was over, before midnight, jazz would come on, jazz after midnight. The jazz was the successful part of the enterprise, making money, always crowded." There were also folk music shows after hours.

Experimental jazz began to flourish. By the time John Coltrane brought his new style in the mid-1960s, he alienated some of the African American audience that was loyal to his late-bop virtuosity. Ralph M. Jones gave me a vivid account of a 1966 concert at the Bowl-A-Drome on the fashionable West Side: "There was a huge line going down the street to the Drome, people in their Sunday best, with their girlfriends, showing off how hip they were. He played for two hours straight, ballads, 'My Favorite Things,' but when he started with Rasheed Ali and Pharaoh Sanders,

THE UN-STABLED

16 TEMPLE

"A RAMSHACKLE COFFEE HOUSE IN A RUNDOWN
NEIGHBORHOOD —FINE THEATRE" –VARIETY

OPENING MARCH 12th
David Compton's

OUT
OF   **FLYING PAN**
THE

with

BARRY LEVINE and MARY TOMLIN

AND

Simpson's

A RESOUNDING TINKLE

with

BARRY LEVINE, MARY TOMLIN and SYLVIA KING

DIRECTED BY... **Edith Carroll Canter**

AFTER THEATRE –MARTY BURKE–Irish Folk Songs	
JAZZ–WEDNESDAY	AFTER HOURS JAZZ
11:00p.m.–2:00a.m.	FRI.–SAT. 2:30a.m.–?
Robert Allen	**Sam Sanders**
866-8069	**832-8740**

FEBRUARY 29, 1964   9

FIG. 6.3. Unstabled Theatre Program of 1964, with Mary (later Lily) Tomlin and listings for the after-hours folk and jazz programs that floated the place. Program courtesy Dan Georgakas.

people got up and left." Only Jones and other musicians stayed. The audience "went through the same thing with Yusef Lateef. Big crowd, but when they heard what they were playing, got up and left. A lot of people in Detroit didn't want to hear new things. It drove musicians out of the city because of the attitude there. The venues weren't there to support this new music. Musicians would fight each other for the scraps." It bothered Jones, who was starting out, but he learned from Lateef to "keep moving forward." And jazz did survive, as we've seen.

The Cass Corridor tried to support an alternative experimental scene that was racially integrated, but the problems could be more than just financial, says Georgakas: "The city government didn't say: the black arts could be a draw, like Opryland. No, they suppressed black arts. This club [the Unstabled Theater] was integrated, and they didn't like it. They did drug busts, heavy police surveillance for the jazz programming. Concept East was more black nationalists, and the police were less concerned, because there wasn't racial mixing." Georgakas and his friends started an integrated magazine, *Serendipity*, to go along with their theatrical initiative. But local black arts movements also wanted their own creative outlets to rival the mainstream world that overlooked them: "There were all these black poets who couldn't get into the 'best poems of 1958' or the 'beat' anthologies; they had their own circle, Broadside Press," started by pioneering black poet, editor, and cultural activist Dudley Randall. As Randall's collaborator and biographer Melba Boyd put it, "Detroit is a production-oriented city. The attitude of the cultural community, whether nationalist or Marxist, was more focused on what one does rather than what one says, which provided an ideological flexibility." African American musicians, writers, and artists overlapped and sometimes integrated with the general counterculture movements of the late 1960s, with leaders such as Kenneth Cox and Charles Moore expanding opportunities and searching for collaborators. Jazz musicians did not just go to jam sessions and look for gigs, as Charles McPherson points out: "In Detroit, to be hip, you didn't have to know just about Bird, you had to know about painting, philosophy, and if you could talk, and you had something to say, you were hip." There are scattered writings and oral histories of this period, but not a bird's eye view that would help to map the crisscrossing side streets, intersections, and merging traffic of the counterculture.

As things moved along, energetic outsiders were drawn into the small vortex the city offered, such as the notorious John Sinclair, who traces his pathway with characteristic frankness in *Guitar Army*:

Graduated high school in Davison, Michigan in 1959 . . . got turned on to the beatnik scene . . . wandered the streets of the north side black ghetto in Flint, trying to be black moved to Detroit in 64 from Flint, attended grad school in American lit at Wayne, got busted for weed . . . helped organize the Artists' Workshop as a neo-beatnik self-determination center for musicians, poets, photographers, painters, filmmakers, dope fiends and lovers of all kinds, published a poetry magazine (*Work*) and an avant-jazz magazine (*Change*) out of the Artists' Workshop Press, served as the Detroit correspondent for *Downbeat* magazine.

Sinclair was riding a wave of countercultural activism. Already back in 1963, a coalition of black and white writers and artists started the Red Door Gallery, followed a year later by the Detroit Artists' Workshop Society.

Musician and activist Cary Loren says that "it was a truly interracial organization," and that "in fact, the Workshop came about directly after all of the founders were witness to Dr. Martin Luther King, Jr.'s 'I have a Dream Speech,' which he debuted in Detroit before presenting it more famously at the march on Washington. Everybody in that audience remembers it as a pivotal moment in their lives." In a parallel move in the late 1960s, musicians Kenn Cox and Charles Moore founded an influential initiative called Strata, which put out cutting-edge record albums and produced other forms of cultural activism for about ten years. Local luminaries like Lateef mixed with white kids, as Sid Brown said, with everyone talking about art, poetry, and literature, just as they did in their own gatherings of jazz musicians. Everyone wanted to be up on the latest, from Camus to Coltrane. Writer George Tysh, a charter member of a

FIG. 6.4. The founders of the Detroit Artists Workshop, ca. 1965, in front of the Detroit Institute of Art. *Left to right*: Doug Larkins, George Tysh, John Sinclair, Robin Eichele. Photo: public domain.

number of groups, says: "Charles Moore and all those others played 'the new music.' After Cannonball Adderley finished their sextet, Charles Lloyd came with us, played all afternoon. The Art Ensemble of Chicago played a workshop, did residencies. This was 1965–66." Suburban kids connected with the counterculture quickly, orienting their music toward the cosmopolitanism of the Cass Corridor: "We sculpted a new sound, attempting to capture and combine components of rock, jazz, folk, and electronic music," recalls Herman Daldin, who cites his group's ties both to the local music scene and the Artists' Workshop.

Producer Don Was points out the mutual respect between the seemingly separate sectors of the city's musical energy: "Rock 'n roll was developing a deeper consciousness. . . . Shows at the Grande [the hottest venue] were modeled on Fillmore, Cream playing with John Lee Hooker; the bills were mixed up and exotic. Jazz groups started putting rock groups underneath, and the rock guys were talking about sheets of sound from Coltrane." Was went on to front the indie band Was (Not Was), produce five Rolling Stones albums, and write prize-winning film scores. As the current head of historic Blue Note Records, he's in a good position to look back at the Detroit scene of his youth. He remembers the dynamism of the 1960s as being the strength of the city's profile: "The guy who epitomized Detroit music the most was John Lee Hooker: raw, without pretention or affectation. Same with MC5 and the Stooges. The music was not dressed up for anything, just essential energy."

Things shifted just after this high point, particularly with the 1967 "riot," or the "uprising" or "great rebellion," as it's being called today. There were Afrocentric moments, like the group called Tribe that reacted to Motown's 1972 departure and the exciting concepts of Sun Ra, including lyrics such as "Ancestors call out with beats / To those with ears and soul," with a goal of "fusing the Diaspora of sounds / Into unity for those who know." The Artists' Workshop itself shifted away from jazz to the Sinclair-promoted MC5 and proto-punk. Musicians from Sid Brown to Charles Moore moved away, and Ann Arbor's campus scene benefitted, with the beginning of its influential and eclectic Blues and Jazz Festival and the emergence of figures such as Iggy Pop. Sinclair felt the full wrath of the city's police, ending up in jail more than once for drug offenses.

By the mid-1960s, Detroit's modest attempt to build a counterculture corridor turned into an on-ramp for exiting the city. Like so many jazz musicians, Sid Brown and his buddies tried either Chicago or New York as outlets for their evolving music from 1965 to 1968. Promoting their self-produced album by using Chess Records' famous studio in Chicago, the group drew the attention of record promoters in New York as the Spike Drivers, "a folk rock/psychedelic band that went on to semi-fame and misfortune." Their album was reissued in 2002 by a German label looking for obscure Motor City music, and Brown's very amusing notes detail the misfit between the innocence and hubris of his provincial bandmates and the machinations of the record industry, a collision that sank the band. Despite playing with Tiny Tim and opening for the Animals at a vast New York music festival, "they came as close to making it as possible and still failed. Not rock stars, just minor asteroids." Brown claims they taught Mike Bloomfield Greek, Arabic, Persian, and East Indian scales. The Spike Drivers' own music itself is strikingly unidentifiable, in a Cass Corridor way, with hints of the Mediterranean flavoring a psychedelic folk-rock sensibility. In songs with titles like "Strange Mysterious Sounds," bouzouki lines skitter off electric twelve-string bluesy guitar riffs with "sha-la-la" backups flitting in and out. Or a high girl's voice in Baez style floats over a Motown bass line with rock guitars nearby. The whole project reads like a parody movie, a cross between Christopher Guest's *A Mighty Wind*, the Coen brothers' *Inside Llewyn Davis*, and Rob Reiner's *This Is Spinal Tap*.

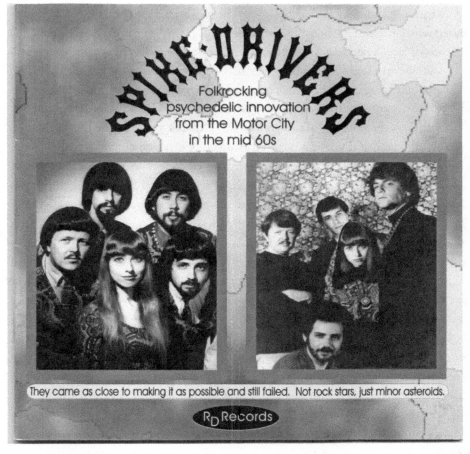

FIG. 6.5. Reissue album of Spike Drivers songs. Counterculture collides with rock culture on the folk-rock highway, late 1960s.

The Spike Drivers' failure to find a commercial niche was just one episode in a shift away from a countercultural meeting ground located between the leftist/labor activism and racial difference that marked Detroit's way of life.

The Motown Model

I don't need to sketch out the history or the impact of Detroit's major contribution to American music, still easily recognized worldwide by its name and its sound. No other city made space for a black-owned, homegrown music machine that fused musical sources and workforces on principles that consciously paralleled the auto industry. Although Detroit was home to dozens of small labels and some very fine recording studios, it never produced a studio like Chess Records in Chicago, which even the Spike Drivers tried to work with, or Stax in Memphis. Detroit's little labels were more scattered, and were run by open-eared white promoters, notably Jack and Devora Brown of Fortune Records. The output of small, scattered, sometimes single-interest labels depended on the remarkable local recording studios, such as United Sound Systems, rather than on a single Detroit-based label. Unlike the sketchy equipment of Fortune Records, USS, like the auto industry, specialized in improved technology and productivity. Ed Wolfrum, the inventor of the Wolfbox, a device that shaped the Detroit sound, was an engineer, and he praises the city's ingenuity, which merged advanced tech with a high level of musicianship: "What you have to recognize is that Detroit had a technical culture to begin with, because of the automobile industry, but it also had a musical culture, pre-Motown, that was exquisite as well, at the same level." Wolfrum didn't realize just how good the local product was until he worked on the west coast, where he was stunned at how backward things were from the hardware standpoint. The stuff they built in Detroit—"homebrew"—was far superior. "The guys here were sharper." Don Was agrees: "In Detroit, you had to figure it out for yourself. So you put microphones in different places—you don't apprentice with guys in lab coats, like in NY or LA."

Dennis Coffey, who worked all over the city in studios and for small labels, was one of the musicians who reaped the rewards of the crosstown convergence of local enterprise that would eventually merge into the Motown express lane: "In Detroit in the early sixties, it seemed that small independent record labels were popping up all over the place, like dandelions after a soft summer rain. . . . I'm not sure why I started getting all those calls for sessions, but I think it was because I was one of the few guitar players in town who could sight read music, play tasty guitar fill-ins, and punch out hot solos."

For Detroit's wide-open spirit, Coffey claims, race was not an issue. Music came first, even in 1967: "We always had both black and white musicians in our sessions, so at the time we didn't feel the riot as racial. In fact, we weren't really sure what the hell was going on, so we just completed our songs, grabbed the tapes, and got the hell out of there." But beyond the studios, the record companies themselves did not fully reflect the well-developed small-business sense of Detroit's African American community. There were some small-scale black record company owners, such as Robert West, first to sign the future superstar Wilson Pickett, as a gospel singer, and the proto-Supremes group the Primettes. But Berry Gordy's rise from the assembly line to corporate triumph stands alone. Even while on the factory floor, instead of submitting or singing, he sped up his work so he could have a few seconds to think up new pop songs, unlike the UAW's drive to slow down the line. In getting out of the factory doors and into the industrial zone that still functioned in the 1950s, Gordy consciously merged the city's musical traffic. He drew in players from all streams of the city's talent flow, a plan that allowed him to build his own lane. The Motown founder was hardly alone in his ambitions. It's often noted that steady work at the auto plants allowed for even black workers to have some disposable

FIG. 6.6. Fortune Records, a mom-and-pop, lo-fi label that fostered local music, in 1973. Photo courtesy Marian Krzyzowski.

income for housing, entertainment, and investment. Even if they got the dirtiest and most dangerous assignments and their interests were disregarded by the union, this African American proletariat could develop into a middle class that combined a love of music—church and club—with a strong business sense. After all, Detroit's black populaton was more highly industrialized than in any other northern city. Already by 1920, nearly 80 percent of the city's male, African American populaton found manufacturing and mechanical jobs, and by 1930, 14 percent of auto workers were black.

Among those who turned to music as a business, Joe Von Battle stood out, with his successful recording company, even convincing the Reverend C. L. Franklin to make his popular sermons available on disc. Sunnie Wilson created a small entertainment empire and became the unofficial mayor of black Detroit.

Similarly enterprising, the Gordy family held regular meetings to make loans from a shared kitty for development projects like Berry's dream of a record company. How he converted this creative drive into corporate cash has been well documented. What's important here about Motown is its canny sense of how to merge the many musical sectors of Detroit's sprawling scenes into a nationally viable product. That Gordy got this done in an industrial way has been noticed, at least since the cover photo of Suzanne Smith's *Dancing in the Streets*, showing Martha and the Vandellas riding a pink Cadillac on the assembly line. Coffey details the industrial connection as an insider: "Even today it's kind of difficult to find anyone in Detroit who hasn't worked on an automotive assembly line at one time or another. Some people said we punched out records day after day with the same corporate sound. But I've worked on a factory assembly line at General Motors, and I can guarantee you that Motown was different. Making records at Motown was a very creative process."

As an outsider looking to join Motown, funk superstar George Clinton had a helpful perspective on Gordy's business model. Before rising to iconic status in the 1970s, Clinton drove to Detroit from New Jersey with his bandmates. He was discounted at first, if only because of the different heights of the group: "That unevenness fucked up the sense of visual perfection, and that kind of thing mattered then to Motown, because all kinds of perfection did. The Temptations were all six feet tall and thin and moved together like they were parts of a watch. Motown was a machine." Clinton worked for Golden World, one of the more freewheeling studios. Coffey was there at the time and marveled at the expansion of the record business in Detroit, even as he notes the cutthroat competition: 'It seemed like anyone and everyone in Detroit was in the record business. I think the early success of Berry Gordy and Motown helped to drive it. . . . It was like a gold rush on the streets of Detroit. . . . Some people struck it rich, but a lot of people spent a lot of money for nothing." Clinton found that smaller labels could be a great warm-up for starting your own game: "If I had gone to work at Motown, that would have been one kind of education, where I was sitting at the knee of these industry giants. Golden World was another kind of education, where I was sitting at my own knee, and skinning it often."

But eventually, as happens so often in American business, there was a shakeout. Just as the Big Three of the auto industry eliminated the smaller car companies, "Motown was starting to feel pressure from the other Detroit artists and was eager to eliminate the competition. The result was they bought most of Golden World." And Gordy used his management power every bit as ruthlessly as the automakers did, as Coffey says: "In the end the Motown musicians had nothing but disappointment and disillusionment to show for being loyal company men—no pension, no security, no nothing."

A large part of Gordy's success was about being inclusive. Clinton acknowledges that Motown's working practice of musical and social convergence influenced him, citing Smokey Robinson's success: "Express everything that's in you, and then find multiple singers and musicians who can help you articulate those emotions in different contexts." Coffey thumbnails the blend that Motown brewed, which relied on a very local mixture of backgrounds and talents: "It was a regional sound that reflected the lives and experiences of the musicians who played it. The music had a funky feel, but because of the complex chord changes in the songs the music went beyond being just another regional blues sound. Most of the vocalists at Motown had a slick, urban sound to their voices, which was different from the blues singers and southern funk singers who came out of Stax in Memphis and farther south. This vocal sound provided Motown with enormous pop crossover appeal." Gordy especially knew how to integrate the city's vast talent pool of jazz musicians: "Jazz guys could always come up with a nifty riff or slick lick that propelled the music over the top." Don Was sees Motown's success partly in terms of its local setting: "Motown to a certain extent was jazz guys trying to sound like NY but doing it different. You're more likely to do that in a provincial setting." But people weren't just "jazz musicians." Future Motown musicians were meant to be eclectic, as Thomas "Beans" Bowles says: "In the studio we had all elements from the city. It wasn't like it is now, when it's all segregated—we all played in the same places. We did our own thing and got together on the stage. Somebody might get up and sing the blues, do a little bebop, sing a ballad, you could hear a gospel song. Everything was done at the same night club—you didn't have to go all over town."

The public school training, the church choirs, and the informal jazz mentoring all played their part, but there was also the city's deep interest in having open ears. Adam Rudolph, who knew Yusef Lateef very well, told me that Lateef's interest in non-Western instruments was not connected to his moving into Islamic thinking but was because he was "an evolutionist" who was always picking up new instruments and equipment his whole life. He told Rudolph he wanted to have a long career creating music, and to do so he would have to study as much as possible about all kinds of music to be able to vary his musical palette. "Detroit guys were always very studious," drawn to "research and development." But you didn't need to be a jazz experimentalist to be big-eared. The musicians like Coffey who moved into popular music also searched restlessly for sources, long before hip-hop artists began "digging into the crates." He and his partner Mike Theodore looked up obscure instruments in a music dictionary, found someone who played one, and used it on a session for a new sound. "We used everything from bagpipes to bass saxophones, bass clarinets, and bassoons, and we had fun doing it." So when George Clinton chose Bernie Worrell to come to Detroit to help invent funkadelic music, he made sure to choose someone with an openness that would suit the city, as Worrell himself analyzed "I mix musics; I don't stick to one thing. I can hear the same scale or mode in a classical piece; you can find the same mode in a gospel hymn. Same mode in an Indian raga, same mode in an Irish ditty, same mode in a Scottish ditty, or whatever you want to call it. Same mode in Latin music, African. It's all related. It's how you hear it."

One example of the Motown model of convergence strikes close to home even for me, the classical kid: the little-known album *Strung Out* (1971). This one-off effort combined classical strings with a funk beat. The story of this album knits together threads spooled out in earlier chapters. I have a personal interest in this commercially unsuccessful Motown venture, since it featured no fewer than three of my 1950s violin teachers from the Detroit Symphony

Orchestra: Meyer Shapiro, Felix Resnick, and Gordon Staples. Oddly, Staples got the credit for the album, *Gordon Staples and the String Thing,* which was arranged by Paul Riser, a fellow Cass Tech musician, who brought in yet another Cass person, the harpist Patricia Terry-Ross. *Strung Out* offers a snapshot of the musical merge that was Motown, blending public school training, symphonic skills, and the streetwise synchronization of the Funk Brothers. The cast of characters appears on the playfully integrated cover photo.

Paul Riser, the arranger, was two years behind me at Cass Tech, but he appears in my yearbook, playing in the Symphony Band. By the time he got to Harry Begian's famous group, Riser had already been under the baton of a great leader, Harold Arnoldi (1926–2002), back in elementary school, starting at age seven. He was even too small to handle all the positions on the trombone. Arnoldi later created the Weekend School of Music for Detroit's kids and became the director of bands at Wayne State University for thirty-three years. In Detroit's mode of merging the corporate and the civic, Arnoldi was also director of entertainment for the Detroit Lions for fifty-one years. Paul Riser, who came from a highly religious family, "hated

FIGS. 6.7. Cover of *Strung Out*, Motown, 1971. My violin teachers are there: Gordon Staples, Felix Resnick, and Meyer Schapiro, alongside Pat Terry-Gordon, harpist from Cass Tech.

rhythm and blues with a passion," even though it was taking over the Detroit sound, because of the strict atmosphere of his home and the formal musicianship at school. His move to Cass Tech only intensified this trend, as he learned music theory, arranging, and orchestration. It came as a surprise for Paul to be slipped into the Motown machine, on the recommendation of a classmate, Dale Warren. It was a tough initiation into the commercial world, but he was only following the road traveled by so many high school classmates. "I came with a lot of discipline from Cass Tech. I had no street smarts. The Funk Brothers were drunk, and high when they made the music, but they were a brotherhood. They didn't take to me very well initially. I was considered a longhair, better than they were, because I was out of the classical genre. I learned quick, because it takes so much discipline. Not that I respected the music, but I respected how much work it took to get to the end product." Cornelius Grant of the Temptations, among many witnesses to Motown's work process, confirms that musicians "punched a clock" at the hit factory. It was so important to hang around Hitsville that when you came back to Detroit from touring, you checked in at the studio before going home. Song-building started with the Funk Brothers, who would lay down rhythms all day in a chain of three-hour sessions, never leaving the "snakepit" studio.

Considering their importance, their workload, and that they got no share of Gordy's profits, it's not surprising that these incredible musicians might be surly or not enjoy directions from a middle-class, Cass Tech–trained eighteen-year-old. To build a new work station on the Motown assembly line, Riser turned to string writing, his main contribution to the sound. He was drawing on a rock 'n' roll tradition that went back at least to Leiber and Stoller's "Stand By Me," a hit for Ben E. King in 1960. Riser says he enjoyed working with string players, because they could read music notation and were disciplined by their classical training. The horns were less manageable, and the rhythm section did not take instruction. He even found them a bit menacing. Dennis Coffey backs up the tense background to Detroit studio work for the rhythm section: "Most of us at Motown carried guns at one time or another because we worked at all hours of the night. We worked in recording studios and clubs and lived in dangerous times. . . . We were all very visible and felt vulnerable because most of us drove brand new Fleetwood Broughams."

Riser's gambit of bringing in the singing strings really worked for Motown. He managed to convince even the singers who grew up far from classical music. Apparently, the Temptations hated "My Girl" until they heard it with strings in the mix. He most enjoyed the work when he could push that sound, his favorite being a symphonic arrangement of "Ain't No Mountain High Enough": "Not only did it elevate Motown, but it elevated me. I was finally able to open up musically." Eventually, Berry Gordy himself would call Riser "one of the great unsung heroes of Motown."

To build a strong string section, Riser turned to the Detroit Symphony Orchestra, whose struggles and survival are described above. By the late 1950s, the DSO had stabilized under the imported French conductor, Paul Paray, and its ranks included three of my own violin teachers. Meyer Shapiro and Felix Resnick had helped to save the DSO in one of its low points by organizing the Little Symphony as a temporary replacement. In eleventh grade, I came to Gordon Staples, a more recent arrival, who worked his way up to concertmaster by 1968. Staples had followed a winding trail to Detroit, from Los Angeles, Vancouver, Philadelphia, the Navy Band, and the New Orleans Symphony Orchestra. Riser found a ready partner in Staples: "Industrious and assertive, Gordon made a lucrative cottage industry out of not only supplementing his classical work with studio work on pop sessions, he became the go-to contractor for the best players who were most adaptable to playing those styles of music." The idea of a "cottage industry" as a supplier to the main factory is classic industrial practice. What's distinctively Detroit about this setup is seeing a young black arranger working for an African American hit factory succeed by hiring white musicians from the elite world of classical music. As a unit supervisor, Staples "was a strict disciplinarian . . . very outspoken and serious." Dennis Coffey worked with Staples even before their Motown collaboration. He describes his "buddy" Gordon, whom he brought in to sessions for a short-lived label funded by an Italian who would simply put the cash on the table for expenses. At Motown, Coffey even felt that Staples had his back: "Not only was Gordon a superb player, but he was an effective leader. If other members of the string section gave 'The Rock & Roll Kid' a hassle during the session, they'd have to face Gordon the next day at the rehearsal for the symphony." The merger with Motown did loosen up the classical string players: "They'd let their hair down a bit, have a drink, crack jokes and relax," apparently glad to be away from the formality of symphony life and the tyranny of the conductor.

Pat Terry-Ross, harpist on *Strung Out*, came on recommendation from Riser, who knew her at Cass. He remembered her as the timpanist in the band, showing the versatility of the training. She agrees that the combination of work and pleasure made the Motown experience enjoyable: "It was always fun and relaxed. We would read through the charts several times, then start recording. It was especially enlightening to see how much we 'classical' musicians enjoyed playing R & B with the same dedication to accuracy/perfection/musicianship that we brought to the concert hall. . . . We would all listen to playbacks. . . . We never sat back waiting to see if a producer would let things slide. Nobody ever felt like, 'Oh, this is just Motown so we don't have to play in tune."- Pat was teaching elementary school at the time, so she ended up doing recording sessions from midnight to four on Motown's graveyard shift and then getting up and going to class. The Motown link developed into an invitation to join the DSO as a substitute, so she got to play concerts and go on tour, closing the classical circle that Riser had formed with Staples & Co. Pat gets a solo turn on one track, a Burt Bacharach song called "The Look of Love" that is far from the bebop harp she heard from her mentor, Dorothy Ashby. The cover photo for *Strung Out* makes a deliberate graphic statement about merger. Shot at the home of the owner of the Roostertail, a core venue for Motown stars, it shows some players are in formal dress, some in casual 1970 outfits, and the visual horseplay echoes the loosely constructed sound the album sought to project: classical + funk = pleasure.

The music itself is a mixed bag. The title tune opens with the strings' tune-up sounds, the only classical reference, quickly balanced by a deft bass beat by the great James Jamerson. Things settle down, so the song needs the B section, with the blended vocal styling of a house backup group called the Andantes formed for the occasion. Then the A section comes back for the wrap-up. It was not a winning formula. The album went nowhere, being lost in the Motown shuffle, and was only lovingly resurrected in a 2009 reissue. The whole album is deeply mainstream, designed partly to cash in on a trend towards instrumentals in pop music: "Disc jockeys like to use them as intros and outros during their shows." It was the age of soundtrack retreads and cozy mellow-string albums, such as Detroit's own San Remo Golden Strings, featuring some of the same symphony musicians. There was an easy listening list, and items like Mason Williams's *Classical Gas* had sold well in 1968. But however "soulful," this mainstream project was "a bit esoteric for R & B radio," says Miller London, a Motown salesman at the time. As Riser says, "No one had a clue what it would do in the marketplace. They just put it out and whatever noise it made was strictly on its own."

This Detroit music factory, like the auto industry of the day, might do consumer research, but could also just crank out products and see what happened, and the auto companies began to mistime the market. George Clinton sees this approach as a kind of provincialism: "Detroit was a strange mix, country but also real slick, with Motown and the car companies. The result was a style that was about a half step back. . . . Detroit was off the rack. Even Motown artists bought their clothes that way. . . . The Four Tops were sharper dressers, because they had left Detroit for a while and came back more hip." But ultimately, Clinton thinks the Motown model faded because the company was too fixated on playing it safe, as youth and music drifted into a more political, rock-based phase: "As the world changed, Motown didn't know exactly what to do with itself. . . . Motown had built its empire on love songs, with a little bit of self-empowerment thrown in there for good measure. Motown wasn't equipped for change . . . couldn't really understand either social change or the growth of rock and roll. . . . They would have stayed at the top longer if they had understood the importance of getting a little dirt on their hands."

Eventually, like the automakers, Berry Gordy disinvested from the city, moving his plant to Los Angeles in 1972, a moment that people talk about as a defining date for the closing of the golden age of Detroit music that this book centers on. But for the savvy musicians who learned the lessons of the streets and the studio, the 1950s and 1960s laid the foundation for durable careers. George Clinton took the basics of rhythm and blues onto the funk highway. Dennis Coffey moved from the industrial model to a personalized sound that served him very well: "They didn't call Motown the hit factory for nothing. I used to collect all the records I played on, but after a while there were just so many that I couldn't keep track of them. I played on at least one hundred million sellers for Motown and the other companies that used me." Gordy and the others had figured out how to merge all the musical resources of a great industrial city—the southern-based blues, the metropolitan jazz, the European classical sound, the public school training, the solid church foundations, the technological edge—all in the service of an egalitarian commercial convergence. This mixture became mythic over time. Almost three generations later, in 2016, a new American Girl doll was announced: a 1960s African American Detroiter named Melody, "a singer in her local church, with her backstory set against the civil rights movement and the rising popularity of Motown." Bruce Springsteen has succinctly summarized the appeal of Motown's merge to America's youth in his memoir of playing on the Jersey shore in the 1970s. The town of Freehold had three warring music crowds: the "rah-rahs," homecoming kings and queens, who danced to pop and beach music, the "greasers" who danced to doo-wop, and the "black kids" who preferred R & B and soul music: Motown was the only force that could bring détente to the dance floor. When Motown was played, everyone danced together."

White newcomers to the music scene—the MC5, the young Iggy Pop, Bob Seger, Glenn Frey, Mitch Ryder—grew up with the concept of the Motown merge but understood the facts of the city differently from older African American jazz and R & B audiences, the counterculture of Sid Brown and the Cass Corridor, or a middle-class Jewish leftist/classical kid like me. As Dave Marsh put it, "the dream, for the MC5, was that of toughassed downriver kids who came from factoryville to the big city, became neo-beatniks [and] prehippies." Like Dennis Coffey, these white kids, often from the nearby suburbs, roamed all over the Detroit area looking for music. Often working part- or full-time in factories themselves, they were part of a scene that hummed in synch with the auto industry, as the MC5's Wayne Kramer explains: "In those days there were a lot of clubs to play in. The auto factories went 24/7, so there were clubs open seven days a week, five sets a night, forty-five minutes on fifteen off." You could even find the hottest music in high school in the late 1960s, with a priest as music producer: "Father Bryson . . . got the Supremes and the Temptations, Shadows of Knight, Bob Seger. People would come from all over the Metro area, from the west side, from all the suburbs, because of the acts that were playing there," though if the MC5 came onto a parochial school stage, a melee might break out. But turbulent as the rising rock scene might be, it was overtaken by the real violence of the 1967 riot. The event marked a turning point in the musical traffic, with local action shut down by urban planning and white flight and so many musicians heading to the off-ramps, out to better neighborhoods in the suburbs and beyond, restless Americans all.

The MC5 broke up in 1972, just as Motown moved out. Glenn Frey had already moved to Los Angeles. The Motor City started spinning its wheels musically until the next breakthrough, techno, also invented by isolated suburban kids—in this case African Americans—who came into a declining city and saw possibilities in technology. That was not a new idea for Detroit's musical mergers.

FIG. 6.8. Screen shot from the MC5's video "The Motor City Is Burning," 1967.

The Media Merge

Detroit's music lanes also merged on the radio and the pages of the daily newspaper. Both versions of mass media were dominant in city life, with local television programming making inroads in the 1950s. Film also brought everyone together at the long double-feature Saturday sessions of my childhood. But once the age of live movie-house entertainment ended somewhere in the 1930s, there was only national, not local, culture, at the city's 134 theaters. Suitably, there were twenty-four Motor City drive-ins.

Radio came early to Detroit, open to all the streams of the music flow. Alongside pop songs and music for southern and ethnic subcultures, the city boasted the world's first live broadcast of a symphony orchestra, back in 1922. This new medium operated in two ways: to allow small groups to support their local micromusics on air and to bring communities into earshot of each other and the mainstream. The tension between commercial needs and individual or group agency was palpable. Inevitably, race cast its shadow over the soundscape. The airing of African American music split listeners and station owners. Already by 1945, WJBK "received letters from some in the listening audience complaining that a popular DJ "played too much music recorded by 'Negroes.'" The station fired back, saying that "music is music, and it doesn't matter who makes a good thing." Whether this defense came from idealism or a cool assessment of the economic clout of a vast black listener base remains open.

By the mid-1940s, WJLB tried to cover both positions by starting an *Interracial Goodwill Hour*, having hired an African American station manager who thought white DJ Bob Maxwell's southern-tinged speech would be good for promoting rhythm and blues. By 1949, the station gave up this blackface by replacing the *Goodwill Hour* with LeRoy G. White, the city's first black DJ, who was popular with all demographics. Dorothy Ashby, the influential bebop harpist mentioned earlier, was a featured folk singer on WJR and hosted its jazz discussion show *The Lab*. Ashby also had a regular program called *The Folk Scene* on WCHD. That station aimed to serve "the Negro community" with complete coverage of relevant local and worldwide news alongside "balanced entertainment, including the BEST in pop music, rhythm and blues, gospel, folk songs, spirituals, classical, and jazz." Once again, a balanced and thorough listening diet was prescribed by the media, in this case, an African American station looking out to the wide world of music and news.

Deejays of all types shared an interest in opening listeners' ears. That inspired musical merge and change in the Motor City. In the mid-1950s, aspiring musician and writer Al Young "sat up nights . . . listening to the all-night jazz show, barely audible on my radio, from CKLW, Windsor. . . . I paced the floor in my socks and jotted down ideas on musical score paper." That sounds specialized, but he also listened to WJBK's Bob Murphy, who started in 1949 and became Al's "favorite disk jockey. . . . Murphy's idea of putting a show together was to line up a stack of records that suited his fancy, no matter what the genre, and take it from there." This big-ears approach carried straight through the 1970s and beyond. Everyone talks about the influence of the famous DJ Electrifying Mojo, who helped to spark the Detroit techno revolution by introducing African American listeners to a huge range of unfamiliar music. He "knew he was playing to black people, but he insisted on playing this music anyway, because this is not what black radio was playing in the day. He went completely against the grain, and he had #1 ratings across the board." Don Was talks about how that stance worked, citywide: "Mojo is a great demonstration of how you can actually bring disparate people together. He had this thing of people flashing their lights and honking their horns [responding to his patter]. It shows how music transcends listening habits and creates cultural unity," and in Detroit style, listeners could even come together in their separate cars.

Back in the 1940s and 1950s, in Detroit's familiar way, progress and fallback merged. In 1949, DJ Bill Randle was canned for playing Nat "King" Cole at a time of day when black artists were not allowed. The station owner heard this affront for himself while listening to the radio as he was getting a haircut in a black barbershop. In 1962, DJ Fred Weiss was fired after being heard on an open mic saying "those g-d-n' are gettin' plenty smart," after the black paper *Michigan Chronicle* demanded his removal. But in 1963, Martha Jean Steinberg, an African American woman, made

FIG. 6.9. WCHD radio ad, 1964. From *On the Town* magazine, courtesy Dan Georgakas.

news by becoming a major DJ. She said that entertainment was a path to visibility for the black population, along with labor. Television was quick to follow broadcasting trends. Already in 1953, WXYZ TV aired Detroit's Only All Colored TV Show, with live music by jazz guitarist Kenny Burrell and his quartet. But controversy never died down. As late as 1964, when Larry Dixon became the first black DJ in Michigan to host a dance party show on television, white viewers watched their black and white TV sets closely. Some complained that a mixed-race couple was seen dancing, and the show was forced off the air. The situation of veteran bassist Dan Pliskow (1935–2015) is telling. He played thousands of jazz gigs, chronicled in a vast website of tapes and photos now at the Library of Congress. But he told me right off that he couldn't say much about the great days of Detroit bebop, since he never got called: mostly, whites called whites for jobs, and blacks called blacks. Yet he managed a musical merge anyway, on television: major jazz stars came to town to play at the top venues, and the bassist would be invited to accompany them in the studio. He'd have to be at the station for a 6:15 AM rehearsal, do a show at 7:15 PM, then put in a full night gigging and get up at 5:30 AM to be back at the station.

Many of Pliskow's gigs were ethnic celebrations, and those sounds spilled onto the airwaves. People wanted to hear familiar songs when they turned on the radio. Every American big city had "a station that speaks your language," literally offering ethnic groups a voice. Back in 1940, a Detroit DJ might throw in a polka or an Irish jig to go with the wacky advertising jingles. But subcultural sounds were threatened by the rise of pop. In 1948, WJBK cut out foreign-language shows, as well as its light classical studio orchestra, to switch to an all-pop format. This was hardly surprising, since broadcasters had to respond to the teen madness spawned by postwar pop music. In 1947, sixty-five thousand kids blocked Woodward Avenue to get to Grinnell's downtown music store, where a DJ was doing a remote broadcast with Detroiter Frankie Laine. A police riot squad had to be called out. This sound of postwar pop moved from the radio to the high schools, influencing many budding musicians. Jazz great Betty Carter remembered, "In my school, I was active more in singing commercial music, the music that was heard on the radio every day." After all, "Detroit was a 'breakout market,' a town where others measured the performance of new product." This was partly due to the sheer wattage of station CKLW, across the river in Windsor, Ontario, which could be heard beyond Al Young's bedroom, across the whole upper Midwest. In funk star George Clinton's early years in Detroit, "once a song got onto CKLW, it pretty much guaranteed that it was going to move up the ladder, market followed by bigger market." As Detroiters, we kids saw the new-model cars before anyone else in the country and heard the hits first. Ethnic broadcasting seemed like a dead-end street at a time of assimilation and the rise of the youth market. When your young audience and advertisers conspire to take specialized music off the air, it becomes invisible to members of a group, as classical pianist Rita Sloan recalls about the late 1950s: "I didn't hear much ethnic Jewish music; I hadn't gone to any weddings with Jewish music, we didn't have television, it wasn't on the radio." The intersection of ethnic celebration—weddings—with media can be important. The catering-hall-to-radio-studio circuit is mutually supportive, and if one side declines, it can affect the other.

But things turned around with a political shift. The new ethnicity of the 1960s, a backlash to black activism, brought back specialized styles, as in one station's 1967 slogan: "WIID Is As Ethnic and Proud As You Are. Why Not Hear for Yourself?" The majority of the time slots were Polish, but the list of one-hour segments includes Yugoslav, Ukrainian, German, Italian, Belgian, Jewish, Greek, Armenian, Arabic,

Latin American, and West Indian. Ethnic programming was a two-edged sword for musicians. It gave them a platform but took away jobs, and no one doing live radio work was getting paid much anyway, as both polka and old-time southern white musicians tell it. At WIID, there was only one slot for "Nashville" anyway, but other stations provided much more sustenance for Detroit's white southern immigrants. WJR regularly broadcast a wandering country musician named Happy Hank who eventually settled in Detroit and whose shows were distributed to other regional radio stations.

These talented DJs could tug on a community's heartstrings through music. A 1974 study details the deep impact of targeted broadcasting. DJ John Morris received many letters from grateful listeners, revealing the resonance of music: "The people who write to Morris validate their own existence; his comments on their letters reaffirm their aesthetic taste, values, and cultural norms; and his on-the-air response to their requests often marks for a brief moment the very landmarks of their lives: their birthdays, their weddings, their special anniversaries, their deaths. But most importantly, Morris's music takes them back home." The listeners "moved their belongings, but not their hearts. And they go back as often and in many ways as possible," on the daily bus route to Kentucky or on the radio. Morris's show allowed these alienated migrants to escape "the dreary grey city, the brown slushy streets, the monotony of the assembly line, the invasion of privacy, and all the unspoken silent hurts that an anonymous city hands out to its transients." One listener's letter summarizes the sensibility and urgency of the broadcast: "Dear John: My home is in Virginia. I'm now living in Blissfield Michigan. . . . I try every weekend to listen to all four hours of the show, even if it means bringing a portable radio out into my vegetable garden." Music on the air became a home away from home.

Within the southern white community, as with so many others, older listeners were offended by newer styles, while youngsters were drawn to the media magnet that usually sat smack in the middle of the living room. Harriette Arnow's epic novel of Appalachian immigrant life in wartime Detroit hammers home the generational shift. From the mother's point of view, country music is just noise: "She worked on, though the Miller radio played mountain music with a loud, nosey twanging that she hated." Gertie sees her daughter slipping into a daze of songs and soap operas: "Clytie had gone more deeply into the world of the radio people. More and more she would sit on the floor, her arms about her drawn-up knees, her eyes drugged, unseeing, her lips soft, while she listened to tearful declarations of love, long amorous sighs, mysterious rustlings, wicked, forever wicked mothers-in-law, brassy-voiced villainesses, sobbing misunderstood wives, and noble cheated upon husbands." Gertie has to concede to the radio's power after a family crisis, when her husband strikes her son: " 'Clytie, turn on th radio good an loud, it won't bother me none. It'll give Reuben in his room somethen to listen to.' Gertie turned to follow, and opened her mouth to protest when the radio screamed, demanding that she go at once and buy one package of General Kapitan's cigarettes." But the radio could also offer all the comforts of home, both to white southern immigrants and to their children, as writer Lori Tucker-Sullivan recalls:

> I remember my mother preparing Sunday breakfast in our small kitchen, hurrying to get us fed and ready for church, while the radio played country hymns from a radio show in Renfro Valley, Kentucky, a reminder of my parents' southern upbringing, which they left behind when they moved to Detroit in the 1940s.

The impact of mass media is so varied across a city's social landscape that the letter from the Blissfield radio listener or Arnow's fictional Gertie helps to flesh out the meager surveys. Detroit's radio and television stations were experimental laboratories in the shaping of American media and individual identity. Pheeroan akLaff reports this: "Travis Biggs, my brother's fellow-genius of the neighborhood, became arranger-producer of the Motown variety at 18. He got me a date with a blues singer, and I'm 15. This was not uncommon at the time. I heard it on the radio, a 45 with 2 different songs, in 1970." Here, radio is a way to get moving into the business lane as a producer or performer. What the media offered could be a strong stimulus for neighborhood musicians. Three brothers, sons of a Baptist preacher, founded an unlikely black rock band called Death after they saw the Beatles and the Who, even though they considered what they saw to be "white boys' music." In an entirely different neighborhood, "John Cage had his first connections with the innovations of radio broadcasting in Detroit. That was when he was still a real kid, and his father was working with the early automobile industry in Detroit and Ann Arbor." It's not common to associate John Cage with the Motor City, but there he was, in time to pick up on the superior technologies of the local sound studios.

Even after the great days of rock 'n' roll and the early innovative DJs, radio remained a junction of styles and tastes. It was part of the open-ears aesthetic that everyone mentions as being distinctive to Detroit. Judy Davis, who ran a show for years on WDET, a public radio station, kept the tradition of open ears alive: "The idea was to be universal—edutaining format. Even in basic rock you could find quality but also introduce classical. I didn't want to do just a white take on jazz and other music in Detroit—I wanted authenticity. The white people in Detroit love black culture. I lined up community jazz and blues people for djs, bringing people back to radio." I already noted the way that Pheeroan akLaff could get some airplay on commercial radio, through his brother's work, but he was also listening hard to the kind of mix that Judy Davis talks about, and it shaped his evolution as an exper-imentalist: "I listened to Kenny Constant's avant-garde jazz show on WDET, also heard electronic music. Everything that happened in the late sixties and seventies was a kaleidoscope of music that gave a window into the programmer's head." Judy Davis adds that even a mainstream radio DJ like Frantic Ernie would make room for the White Panther and MC5 promoter John Sinclair.

Many Detroiters credit DJs for opening, not narrowing, the passage of music from the ear to the brain and the heart. Even going back to the 1940s and early 1950s, "music was dumped on you in an undifferentiated mass. Jack the Bellboy would play Sinatra, Spike Jones, Benny Goodman, The Third Man Theme. And we just soaked all of that up. Bob Murphy's idea of putting a show together was to line up a stack of records that suited his fancy, no matter what the genre, and take it from there." This varied flow of music hit new ears as each new listening generation tuned in. Writing about hearing DJ Dave Dixon in 1967, Chris Morton says, "For the first time we could listen to an eclectic mix of blues, rock, folk, and jazz, all within the same pro-gram." (Morton 2016, 40). In Detroit, the producers, purveyors, and consumers of music all had big, open ears. Even the most local of the commercial music media— the corner jukebox—allowed for a broad flow of musical traffic. As John Hartigan saw in a southern white neighborhood: "The jukebox ratified the heterogeneous ra-cial setting. . . . [It] epitomized the synthetic crossings of racially marked musical genres that Detroit has long been known for."

The Journalism Junction

Beyond records, radio, and the jukebox, Detroit's three daily newspapers offer a pan-oramic view of the city's musical life. Drawing on a sample of just one, the *Detroit Free Press*, you can see how that mainstay of modernity, the "paper" thrown onto the front porch by kids like me, moderated the cultural traffic on the weekend en-tertainment page. Side by side in print, many of the venues and genres merge in un-likely ways. Back in 1943, there's a sense of both the tension and the pleasure around the appearance of African American music. Lucky Millinder's band opened for a feature film, *Seven Days' Leave*, "the first army musical: It takes a lot of self-control to keep from squirming in your seat when the sepia band hit their stride on the Michigan stage." On the same wartime weekend, the page offered the reader the chance to learn that electrifying music: "SWING!!! Piano, singing, dancing Harlem style. Colored teachers." Which would it be—squirm or learn? The neutral news-paper offers all options. Still in January of 1943, specialized concerts and services sit next to general civic moments of merging. You could go to a show featuring "I

Will Do My Best," a song that is "expressive of Detroit's war effort, by the local composer J. O'Reilly Clint," or you might be patriotic at ecumenical parties and dances for servicemen, at Holy Name Church, Downtown YWCA, League of Catholic Women, and Jewish Welfare Board. The midwinter event of the Detroit Society for the Hard of Hearing was also eclectic, with both "old-time and modern dances," mixing Henry Ford's mania with the young people's jitterbug. Nearly ten years later, a new dance club in the elite white suburb of Birmingham would still be featuring "the ever popular square-dancing" (September 7, 1952). At the museum, the high and the low rubbed shoulders, with composer Bernard Heiden conducting the Detroit Chamber Orchestra even as Jean Granese offered "something new in strip-tease" at the Avenue. In my day, pornography, or even a sex scene in a novel, was very scarce. Even *Playboy*'s centerfold was radical, so live burlesque offered a legitimate libidinous outlet.

Looking at the entertainment page reminds me a little of the view of Detroit's parades we got, courtesy of a family friend with a downtown office, right on Woodward Avenue, the city's showcase and dividing line. You could see Grinnell's music store, the famous Vernor's Ginger Ale factory, Sanders's luscious hot fudge sundae parlor, and many other points of interest as groups and bands trooped by to celebrate local and national milestone moments. From the *Free Press* window, the sweeping view of the city's cultural intersection mixes mainstream and minority, elite and populist equitably. The equivalent to the parade might be events like the1947 convention of the National Federation of Music Clubs, at which the orchestra premiered John Powell's symphony on American folk tunes, with groups including the Tuesday Musicale, the Negro Chorus, Detroit Madrigal Club, and the Catholic Dun Scotus Choir. Race and religion blended under the baton of mainstream culture, and Detroit kept an eye out for national recognition. Some of the same music club ladies were open-minded at their more private, well-meaning events, like a Musical Good Neighbor program at the Southeastern Woman's Club, at which Mrs. John Linson gave a talk on Hawaii, while Mrs. Robert Busby sang songs of India and Mrs. Eldred Fraser presented Latin American music. This manicured and controlling view of the world of music seems both inclusive and patronizing. At least Ford's Hawaiian Band starred native islanders, as did the Covered Wagon Inn, which, despite its country and western–sounding name, featured Hawaiian singers and dancers every Friday and Saturday as late as 1962. Not a bad run for the island craze that began in the 1920s.

The *Free Press*, true to its name, was happy to list ethnically diverse entertainment. The listings reveal the pattern of musical traffic, both into neighborhoods, as Detroiters drove in for a night's fun, and out, as subcultural musicians found their way into local hotspots or prime spaces. The Cedars, the premiere Middle Eastern club, advertised Arabic music on oud, violin, and darbuka, along with "accordionist Rieta Ray in the interludes." The Tamburitzans, mainly Croatian, played regularly just one block into Canada from the tunnel under the river, with "a Galore of Food." That fits the classic American definition of ethnicity: music and food. Also in 1962, white southerners could stay local every Saturday night at the All Star Hillbilly Show and Square Dance at the Big Barn Frolic, in the Dairy Workers Hall. Grez's Hungarian Village offered its annual gypsy concert in the dead of winter, with Ziggy Bella and his twenty violins taking off the chill with singer Mari Roumell. Serving up subcultural styles just from July to October of 1957, the *Free Press* listed French Canadian chanteuse Lucienne, at Young's Lounge, "who may soon have her own show on television." Here, a specialized singer was using a local nightspot as a springboard for broader media coverage. It's one of the rare musical mentions I have found of the large but unnoticed Franco-American community. Meanwhile, Cantinflitas riffed on the great Mexican entertainer Cantinflas, appearing at "Detroit's only Latin-American nightclub, El Tenampa," a draw for insiders and non-Mexicans. September 6 alone saw a stunning set of ethnic, black, and white music on display, either separately or blended, as at the Brass Rail, where the Nighthawks spotlighted Al Horvay, son of Hungarian village orchestra leader, who "specializes in gypsy and folk music and jazz."

Elsewhere in the area, New Orleans–themed Jack Teagarden was up against Jewish American comedian Jerry Lewis and black singer Eartha Kitt at the Elmwood, a major nightclub just across the river in Canada. All the while, the four downtown burlesque theaters were going strong every week, employing live musicians. A single major night club, the Flame Show Bar, could combine Tony Fernandez, a Cuban singer, with Miss Sharecropper (later the R & B star LaVern Baker) and white jazz singer Anita O'Day, "whose song style is sultry as the weather." The Flame, one of the most important clubs in Detroit's music history, billed itself as the "Midwest's beautiful Black and Tan," a term that meant black talent and mostly white patrons in a location at the intersection of musical traffic. The Flame's Idlewild Revue starred Della Reese, T-Bone Walker, and "the singing 4 Tops," an early sighting of Motown in the listings. Other black and tan clubs were located in Paradise Valley. The *Free Press* doesn't give space to the incredible list of Hastings Street joints celebrated by Detroit Count.

The variety that the 1957 weekend *Free Press* offered is dizzying, in retrospect. On June 7, there's a true traffic jam of talent: BB King, the Modern Jazz Quartet, Dick Contino (accordionist with a fourteen-piece orchestra), Mel Torme, Big Maybelle, Storme De Laviere ("the only girl in the 'Jewel Box Revue' of 25 female

FIG. 6.10. One day in the life of Detroit entertainment. *Detroit Free Press,* September 6, 1957.

impersonators"), contortionist Jimmy La Blond with pop Vocalist Mona Morgan, and "dynamic singer Larry Marvin, 'the modern minstrel man.'" It's antique and modern, as if a vaudeville palace and a night club combined to present all of American entertainment at one intersection. You could contemplate buying tickets for highbrow events—violinist Yehudi Menuhin or the Ballet Russe de Monte Carlo—but also might consider the "Motor City Parade of Harmony," a barber-shop quartet extravaganza, or Mickey Katz's Borscht Capades, designed for a Jewish audience that wanted to skip the symphony and see Yiddish parodies of pop songs. The same crowd might also have gone to "Bagels and Yox," which played six nights at a mainstream theater, the Shubert. Just going to one of the 134 movie houses that year meant hearing a full range of music, either by taking the kids to *The Ten Commandments*," with Elmer Bernstein's Bible-tinged score, or sneaking in to see Elvis Presley in "Jailhouse Rock" for a blast of rock 'n' roll.

Off the main avenues, the *Free Press* also paid attention to very local, focused music groups. In 1947, the paper told the sad story of members of American Legion Post no. 272 in Ecorse, who were "mourning the death of their piano. The poor old box just up and collapsed because of advanced age, leaving the men music-less. If you have one you'd like to give, contact Giles Reeve at AT 0489." In the same year, there's a milestone moment for another private music circle, the budding early music move-ment. It seems the Oratorio Society, missing a harpsichord, just like the American Legion and its piano, got the idea of driving thumbtacks into the felt of piano hammers to get an antique sound. Snidely linking old music to the upper crust, the newspaper explains that "an authentic piece of Bach music without a harpsichord is to a musician about the same as baked beans without pork would be to a Back Bay citizen." The paper points out that the eminent harpsichord builder John Challis would shortly be moving to Detroit to fill in this gap in the city's musical life.

It is this tone of somewhat amused tolerance of any and all kinds of music that makes the *Free Press* coverage stand out in a period marked by high interracial tensions; the decline of the city's only real economic base, the auto industry; and the shift of population from the city center to the suburbs. None of that appears on the entertainment page, which seems to be holding the place together in a common urge to produce and consume music, from the home, to the music club, to the ethnic group, and to the citywide live music locations.

While the *Free Press* listings make Detroit look distinctive, the paper went onto the front porches of just one of the Midwestern cities that shared a common culture. As kids, we waited all week for the Sunday "funnies," the only colorful section in a sea of black-and-white print. One feature that circulated widely was called *Right Around Home*. Dudley Wilson's strip (1938–51) "achieved a perfect blend of whole-some, energetic fun and masterful compositions. It remains an endearing snapshot of a moment in time, modestly asserting no superiority to preceding or subsequent times; a warm, Midwestern affirmation of humanity" that permeated other strips of the day. One Sunday installment of the saga of the family next door (January 26, 1947) zeroed in on musical taste and behavior.

The musical activist is Mrs. Smaltz, with a comic Central European name that would fit anywhere in the Midwest. "Schmaltz"—chicken fat—was a term for over-emotional music, "schmaltzy" being an insult. She is identified as one of those music club ladies whose activities fill the social pages. As such, she is elitist, and is pushing some kind of too-far-out music on the household, a concerto in (nonexistent) Z minor by the imaginary, clearly Central European composer Kpfpntrsznt. One lady chides her grumpy husband, reminding him that Beethoven didn't keep his hands in his pockets, but the rest of the crowd is restless. "You don't understand good music" is countered with "But I understand Mrs. Smaltz," shorthand for the burdens that "good music" supporters lay on their nearest and dearest. Another controlling wife tells her husband not to say what he thinks.

As the reader scans the strip, the focus of attention shifts to young Slug, who only likes music with drums, a clear pointer to the dominance of big-band jazz, with its Buddy Rich and Gene Krupa heroics. The second act of the strip, on the right side, brings the other Maltz sister to the rescue, playing "what the customers want," a frank concession to the commercial values of mainstream American music. Her shift of focus gets the young couple to stay and Slug to rush off for his saxophone.

FIG. 6.11. *Right Around Home*, comic strip by Dudley Wilson, *Detroit Free Press*, January 26, 1947.

It's an all-white scene that doesn't include the powerful African American musical contribution, an angle accentuated by the white barbershop-quartet embrace of the middle-aged men at the back. The whole setup echoes the Hollywood musical, which already in the 1930s started to hammer home the superiority of homemade American youth pop to the stilted European opera-symphonic tradition. The movies even set the scene in living rooms like the Smaltzes', with spontaneous, dynamic kids like Judy Garland and Mickey Rooney, "America's Sweethearts," back in 1939's *Babes in Arms*.

Records of 1947, the year of the family music strip, supported the industry's changeover to youth taste, such as a disc my family bought, the striking Vogue Picture Record, "Tear It Down." It shows romping, sexy youngsters smashing the musical world. But the music itself carries an older white-jazz, 1930s sound that would have been acceptable in the Smaltz household to both old and young. It was before rhythm and blues began to change the tone in Detroit's rec rooms and garage bands. Vogue records produced just seventy-four discs in 1946–47 before going bust, but its sound was at the level of Detroit's high technical standards: "Vogue picture records were of a very high quality, with little surface noise. The records were produced using a complicated process. Engineers spent several months working out the bugs."

FIG. 6.12. Vogue Picture Record, 1949, jazzing up the last days of the 78 rpm record. Author collection.

"Tear it Down" featured Clyde McCoy, a standby artist of Chicago's hotel circuit. Detroit turned to its bigger neighbor as a source and as a destination when local musicians outgrew the city's smaller market. Big Maceo Merriwether, an influential bluesman, was an early émigré, already leaving for Chicago in 1941. Groups shuttled back and forth. A rhythm and blues band like the Fresandos, admired by Otis Williams of the Temptations, used Fortune Records for a raw, local rhythm and blues song ("I Mean Really") that jeers at a girl "from Detroittown," but they also went to Chicago to press a record with Chess, for a Latin-tinged ballad, "Your Last Goodbye." The hero of Al Young's evocative Detroit novel *Snakes* dreams of leaving the city for New York even before he has his moment as a local rhythm and blues band member: "In this daydream, some noted musician, from New York, say, was forever urging me to wind up my affairs in this big country town and sign with him to play the top spots in the country." In fact, the novel ends with the hero MC heading for Manhattan.

The city linked into an interstate highway system of music, extending into the vastness of the country that lies beyond the suburbs. Detroit's people felt a nagging sense of provincialism, despite the bountiful newspaper listings. In a 1952 survey of their self-image, some saw themselves as living in a second-class entertainment city: "Wonder why Detroit doesn't attract the entertainment that you see and hear about on radio and television like New York and Chicago do. Why don't they come to Detroit?" "Detroit is a movie town—not a music or theater town." "The reasons for that of course are the factories and that Detroit is an overgrown small town rather than a large city." This remark points to the problem of Detroit as a sprawling stretch of newcomers trying to create communal culture at a time when most people's minds were on jobs and race relations.

The musicians themselves might see it differently. In the African American community, the rising generation of the 1940s felt they were at the cutting edge. Speaking for her crowd—Kenny Burrell, Tommy Flanagan, Barry Harris—Betty Carter says: "Detroit was one of the first cities in the Midwest to accept bebop. Chicago had not kept with bebop like Detroit had. We were *on* it, and we loved it." And they learned in-town, from all the greats that came to the city, from the big bands to Miles Davis's sojourn in the early 1950s. Staying in the city or moving on to bigger audiences, these local musicians absorbed the best of outside music even as they changed the direction of the musical traffic, in-town, regionally, nationally, and internationally.

Detroit magnetically mobilized the muscle power of a massive workforce from America and beyond with the promise of steady labor and decent wages. It was a provincial powerhouse that punched above its weight for a time. The large talent pool that arrived with the economic migrants added an expressive supplement: creativity and "soul," mainly in music. It all started in the mind and spirit of individuals before merging into the shared lanes just described.

The Merge in the Mind

The city's mobility of sound and the intense inner life of subcultures meant that no one musical source dominated. People tended to bring it all together in their minds—and hearts. As Dwight Andrews puts it, "No one has connected the dots about Detroit's musical story. Labor, public gatherings, public education—all the different strands, helped people to be [musically] multilingual." Musicians all say that this very attitude of openness is what marked Detroit as a special space. Everyone testifies to a kind of aural generosity that made a difference in their lives. I don't know if Detroiters on the whole actually *were* more willing to listen widely than people in other cities, but that's what people think. Above, I've cited the DJs who deliberately sent mixed signals over the airwaves. Below, I offer a sampler of sentiment about how music rejected the traffic patterns of a deeply divided social space, questioning and changing the rules. Al Young says, "That's the way I grew up—you were supposed to know a little about everything. My dad was a music nut; he didn't care what it was called. He would buy pop and classical stuff. We were brought up to not make these distinctions. He told me there was good music, bad music, ugly music, and pretty music." Geri Allen recalled that this urge to take it all in started early:

Detroit was unusual in its training, compared to other cities—St. Louis, Pittsburgh, other regional scenes. It gave you the flexibility to play in any kind of setting. It was instilled in us that good music is good music and it was important to be as versatile as you could if you were going to sustain longevity in this very fickle business. We had an interaction with classical music, gospel, music of the Caribbean—all of these musics of our culture, African culture dispersed . . . that global language that we as musicians were encouraged to embrace. We played with a lot of Motown musicians, who were always going back and forth between genres, were very fluid at it.

I've mentioned the mentors and role models who were influential as young musicians took their breath through breadth. Marcus Belgrave stressed versatility, noting, "We got to be open. We played bar mitzvahs, weddings, blues clubs." For young musicians, just seeing someone on a bandstand taught the lesson of inclusion. Yusef Lateef was particularly influential, with his extreme openness to new sounds: "There was something magical about seeing him play all those instruments. Lateef said: 'it's not that I'm trying to master an instrument; it's like sitting down to a buffet of different foods, and you want to taste those foods.'" Dwight Andrews continues the nutrition metaphor: "Lateef gave me an appetite for all music. Everyone was so hungry to get the next experience." The lesson of Lateef and Belgrave echoed the ethos of the city, which made it both easy and hard when musicians left for other places: "New York musicians told me to watch out for being so eclectic—they wouldn't be able to label me," says Regina Carter. But she refused to be pigeonholed. "That comes from being out of Detroit. It was all just music, whereas if you didn't have that experience, people might look down their nose at *some* kind of music." Gerri Allen had the same experience: "When I came to NY, my foundation was being open. I didn't find that openness in the scene—there'd be cliques. I'd be moving back and forth between these groups in a very comfortable way. Avant-garde, straight ahead. That kind of openness was a natural."

Pheeroan akLaff agrees about the open-mindedness: "There was a pretty wide base of education for me and other Detroiters. There was compartmentalization. But there was edification at the same time. My family stressed education and international awareness. We knew about the Polish community, though we didn't know anyone except the neighbors next door, maybe Irish. There was a natural tolerance and acceptance of others, even though we knew those other tensions existed." What was true for African American musicians held for musicians from the European immigrant groups. Lillian Ruzich pictured it clearly: "We loved to dance. Every Saturday and Sunday there was some affair going on. We'd go to the Croatian Hall for all the *kolos* [round dances] and singing. We'd go to the Slovenian Hall to do all the polkas and the waltzes. We really liked that um-pah-pah stuff. And for the American stuff we'd go to the ballrooms, where I got to do the jitterbug. So we had such a diverse culture. We learned from each other."

Those who moved to Detroit from restricted places, like George Tysh, really felt the difference: "Detroit was a great place. You had so much stimulation. I couldn't believe it, coming from Passaic. It was vibrant, stuff was happening." "Outsiders" included those who simply took the bus in from nearby suburbs to quench their thirst for variety, like the composer Gordon Mumma: "The diversity of the Detroit cultural area spreads all through the first half of the twentieth century. . . . It was everywhere. Living in Ferndale, I had the Woodward Avenue bus to travel in and out of the (then) thriving Detroit."

Some activists, even from a tight neighborhood music scene, sensed the need for expanded hearing and wider audiences. Eddie Gajec, a Polish musician, used his versatility to ooze into all the available neighborhood and downtown slots. Then he helped to create the interethnic festivals, combining the idea of downtown civic presence and multiculturalism, all the while not giving up his core ethnic affiliation. The drive for diversity survived the city's seismic shifts. Obituaries in 2015 for the influential New York DJ Anita Sarko agree that breadth was key to her success and that her roots had something to do with that: "Ms. Sarko grew up in Detroit, where she discovered her love of music early. Eclecticism was the watchword, and Ms. Sarko's musical knowledge was encyclopedic." "She was always coming up with a steady stream of surprising music that enlarged one's consciousness rather than pandering to the tastes of the moment."

Of course, looking back can be a tricky business—nostalgia is notorious for tinting glasses rosy. But musicians, poets, and artists are rarely simplistic when they reminisce. The closing chapter samples the rearview mirror glance of people who, like me, started out in the Motor City and think back years later about where they came from.

Monk's tune—"Ugly beauty," the Detroit story.

—DWIGHT ANDREWS

I thought it was a great city—it was just vibrant, pulsing with that blue-collar energy.
It was so fantastic.

—LILY TOMLIN

No matter where I roam
Detroit is my home.

—ALBERTA ADAMS, "Queen of the Blues"

There's not a musician on the planet that
Doesn't respect our history.

—JESSICA CARE MOORE, "Arise Detroit"

7 The City in the Rearview Mirror

IN TWO WORDS—UGLY beauty—Dwight Andrews, a musician, composer, and
minister, sums up a universe of creative discourse around his hometown. Thoughtful
artists of the verbal, visual, and musical have been summing up Detroit, seeing it in
their personal rearview mirror while driving their work forward. Often, they shift
into a musical gear. This has been going on a while—at least since the 1960s poetry
of Philip Levine, or in Smokey Robinson's 1962 lyrical gesture, which might as well
be about Detroit as about a girlfriend:

I don't like you, but I love you.
Seems like I'm always thinking of you.
You treat me badly, I love you madly.
You've really got a hold on me.

From the 1990s on, the creative energy of retrospect has accelerated, and it has
stimulated and haunted my own imaginative move into the city of my childhood.

Modernist American artists do not tend toward cozy remembrance of their
hometowns, unlike the sometimes smug pastoral poetry and novels of the nineteenth

century. Detroit is a complicated case. As people survey their ruined city, they mix regret with realism. Even the word "nostalgia" gets mixed reviews. "I know of no other place that inspires such a fierce and dreadful nostalgia." Or: "I have never lived anywhere so burdened by nostalgia, which is sort of enemy to history." The influential artist Mike Kelley said he was "more interested in the themes of reexamination and reuse than in the production of nostalgia." Simply, creative spirits have realized that growing up in Detroit has made them who they are. At a certain point in life, they meet the city eye to eye in a moment of recognition. This might happen in other cities. New York has provoked some fine look-back literature, art, and music. But I doubt that smaller, more enclosed places like Detroit have evoked this high quality of nuanced retrospect. The restless wind of history fans creative sparks into fire. I will begin with the older, canonical Detroit poet Philip Levine and a group of younger writers before turning to the visual artist Kelley, and will close out with the musicians Geri Allen and Regina Carter.

Philip Levine was born in 1928 into my Jewish community, fifteen years before me. He felt the firsthand experience of the bitterness of the depression, the turmoil of the war, and the idealism of the Spanish Civil War (for which some of my parents' friends volunteered). Unlike the vast majority of Detroit's Jews, Levine was forced for a while into factory work. He was only fourteen. Levine finally left the city and emerged as a writer who would end up with every prize America can offer a poet, including poet laureate. He succeeded mainly through the distinctive voice of his poems on the Detroit working-class experience. The poems have a frank, even brutal tone, infused with empathy and solidarity. It's a rear view: from now to then. Levine strongly felt a drive to draw readers to his memory of fellow workers: "I hope to preserve some image, a verbal image. . . . These people . . . did something, and nobody remembers them, and I see one of my central functions as the person who remembers them and records their qualities."

But this precise recording arises from heartfelt testimony: "I was myself in the company of men and women of enormous sensitivity, delicacy, consideration. I saw us touching each other emotionally and physically, hands upon shoulders, across backs, faces pressed to faces. We spoke to each other out of the deepest centers of our need, and we listened. In those terrible places designed to rob us of our bodies and our spirits, we sustained each other. I guess nothing grandly heroic ever took place there; it was always automobiles, automobiles, hard work, and low pay." The poet vividly describes eastern European Catholics and southern whites and African Americans who were all in a fellowship with his Jewish self. This, despite his acknowledging, "I spent most of my childhood and adolescence fighting with people who, you know, wanted to beat me up because I was Jewish."

Levine's retrospect is resonant. The assembly line allows for both sonic stupefaction and human interaction. Pitting his voice against the machine, he says, "You could recite poems aloud in there. The noise was so stupendous. Some people singing, some people talking to themselves, a lot of communication going on with nothing, no one to hear." But, more poetically, in "Sweet Will," he brings us a voice that overcomes both din and difference:

> Stash, a worker, in 1948
> addressing us by our names and nations—
> "Nigger, Kike, Hunky, River Rat,"
> but he gave it a tune, an old tune,
> like "America the Beautiful."

In the lines that follow, Levine lifts he workers to heaven on wings of song, trashes (literally) the cars that they made, and positions himself as the survivor:

> In truth all those people are dead,
> they have gone up to heaven singing
> "Time on My Hands" or "Begin the Beguine,"
> and the Cadillacs have all gone back
> to earth, and nothing we made
> that night is worth more than me.

Levine knows that his comrades—unlettered, from different neighborhoods— are as all-American as their Cadillacs, as their song choice shows. When it comes to music, his vision blends the patriotic and the commercial seamlessly, stitching together its ethnic threads. It's the same memory of the popular that ties the poet to his grandfather, at moments when they shared car space and a stock of songs: "Zaydee [Grandpa] and I sang songs back and forth to each other, mainly show tunes, which he adored and invariably got wrong. . . . 'If you knew Solly,' he would belt out, 'like I knew Solly, oye, oye, oye, veh, what a girl.'" His grandpa's singing was like my *bobe* (grandmother) trilling, "Oh, What a Beautiful Mornin.'"

Among Detroit's musics, there's one that offered Levine—and also my high school friends—a bridge out of ethnic worlds and across the racial divide: jazz, a sound and sensibility arising from the harsh reality of African American experience. A child of the progressive politics of the Jewish community, he says, "I was awed by them [black Detroiters], and a little bit humiliated, because I wasn't doing as much as I should have done." One response to his discomfort was to speak the common tongue on the assembly line with his friend "Marion, the ex-junkie and novice drop-forge worker" who had once recorded with Coleman Hawkins. Levine was in awe of the musical mastery of jazz, listening firsthand, or at a distance, as a fan. One night outside a Detroit club, he lurked behind the great pianist Art Tatum, overhearing him talk to a bass player about baseball. To make a poem out of that moment is to offer a special kind of tribute, humanizing an idol through the cross-communal communion of sports.

Levine's stalking of Tatum contrasts sharply with writer Al Young's memory of his black friends following around Lionel Hampton: "Even after he'd walked down off the stage and led them all out into the streets and around the block for a musical walk in under the stars, they'd still be so charged and ready it was all I could do to try and restrain them so they wouldn't tear up the theaters." What a distance from Levine's wary worship of jazz artists—but both moments held their power across a lifetime. The passage that jazz allowed Levine is not just across Detroit's bruises and barriers, but over time. Twenty-five years later, he can still see and feel 1956 in his rearview mirror—almost literally—in the poem "And That Night Clifford Died," which registers the shockwaves of trumpeter Clifford Brown's premature passing, felt both then and now, while driving a Detroit car in California:

> The radio
> softly played gave me music—
> my Polish neighbors worked
> days at Plymouth—the music
> I lived for, created by men
> becoming myths . . .
> the FM station fading in
> and out on the car's radio
> that sound never to be forgotten,
> a gift I did nothing to earn.

The mobility of time-spaces is in overdrive in this poem. Levine layers the memory of his friendly Polish neighbors, bound like him to black music, with the passing of Brown from man to myth, the future presence of the sound, and the way his car radio compels recall and recognition of the gift that Detroit gave him freely in his youth.

So it is through *individuals* that Levine finds his voice in the crowded city, and he creates a poetics of personalities that emerged from the noisy space of traffic and labor. In a memoir, he documents a joyous joy ride to New York with jazz great Pepper Adams—but they can never fully leave a city that pulls them back. The poet drives home from Toledo on Route 24, the very road he helped to pave, with the vast, alien Rouge plant looming up at him and Adams. The car has its own logic, even for musicians, and it can make escape illusory. In yet another striking traffic/music poem, Levine imagines himself sharing a bus with a group of new arrivals coming north on the very same Route 24. "An Ordinary Morning" declares that buses—unlike cars—can enclose a space of communal/musical fellowship. Here, Levine offers mass transportation as conversation, solace, and even ritual. It's a somewhat startling vision, coming from a poet who never writes about churches and synagogues:

> A man is singing on the bus
> coming in from Toledo.
> His voice floats over the heads
> that bow and sway with each
> turn, jolt, and sudden slowing.
> A hoarse, quiet voice, it tells
> of love that is true, of love
> that endures a whole weekend.
> The driver answers in a tenor
> frayed from cigarettes, coffee,
> and original curses thrown down from his seat of command.
> . . .
> One by one my near neighbors
> open their watering eyes
> and close their mouths to accept
> this bright sung conversation.

Surely, the passengers, "newly arrived in Detroit, city of dreams, each on his own black throne," will be disillusioned, even destroyed, by the Rouge plant after their migration. But it is their song the poet wants to record.

It's reminiscent of a poignant moment in Harriette Arnow's weighty Detroit novel *The Dollmaker*. As her stoic heroine Gertie is migrating north, along the pathway Levine describes, she has a song-laden interchange with an African American migrant. Gertie did not sing for her daughter on the train, but she sympathizes with the her fellow traveler, who describes how her child longs for southern song: " 'She misses her granma's singen, thas what she misses away off up heah—an I ain't so good at singen.' Gertie nodded. 'Upon the willows in th midst thereof, we hanged our harps, an they that wasted us required of us mirth saying, "Sing us one a th songs a Zion." But how shall we sing th Lord's song in a strange land?' She flushed. She hadn't meant to say that. But it had run in her head so, since early this morning on the other train, when Cassie had wanted her to sing right before a trainful of people."

Both Arnow and Levine spatialize memory precisely, in traffic terms. In Levine's poems, life on the bus and the streetcar is observable, interactive, made tangible. He even references that rare transport the trolley, musically, in a line about "the gnashed jazz / the trolleys carved into the avenues." For him, the radio is more assertive, as he references the urban blues of his day as "the bad-assed / anthems of the airwaves— / of John Lee, Baby Boy and Big Maceo," the great, raw bluesmen of his youth. He had less patience for the more soothing sounds on the airwaves: "The radio went on playing the same violins and voices I didn't listen to each morning." Philip Levine could never escape Detroit and its music. He stayed mentally and creatively near the assembly line, marking moments of relief and camaraderie that song supplied out on the streets, heading toward that bus:

> We got music, we got underpaid work, a cheap lunch
> with more to follow. On the long walk to the bus stop
>
> and the ride home we hear the birds gathering
> in the elms and maples thickening with summer finery,
>
> and no one cares if we sing to the orange sun
> that also seeks its rest, no one cares that our voices
>
> are harsh from cigarettes and our ears worthless,
> our timing off, and we've got the wrong words
>
> in the wrong places.

Even after his move California, Levine looked into his rearview mirror. There's a moment in his memoirs when he's considering a job at the university in Fresno. He can't help reaching for traffic metaphors when the dean tempts him with hiking in the hills: "In Michigan anything taller than a Cadillac is considered a hill. . . . Hiking was what we did in Detroit when the car broke down." For Levine, writing "was an effort to slow down this voracious eating of time of everything that I cared for," and that included his hometown. In his later years he could say, "I grew up in a city, one I liked"—especially its music.

Not that much younger than Philip Levine, Marge Piercy, another child of the Jewish community, also credits the tough city for making her who she is. In 2015, decades from Detroit, Piercy penned a volume titled *Made in Detroit*. She grapples with her hardscrabble childhood in a tough place, without nostalgia: "The night I was born the sky burned red / over Detroit and sirens sharpened their knives."

It was a place where "factory soot / drifted down like ebony snow," reminiscent of Levine's line "There was snow here, too, speckled with cinders, piss-yellowed, tired." But looking back through this clouded rearview mirror, Piercy has to admit that the place forged her toughness: "I suckled detroit's steel tits. When / I escaped to college I carried it with / me, shadow and voice, pressure / that hardened me to coal and flame." Like Levine, Piercy poses her Jewishness as problematic but positive, in a city that allowed for fellowship across the lines:

> Oh my city of origin, city who taught
> me about class and class warfare,
> who informed me how to survive
> on your ashgrey burning streets
> when as a Jew I was not white yet,
> easy among friends of all colors.

Though I was in a generation that had already moved into official whiteness, Piercy speaks to me as a member of the same Jewish subculture, traveling on the streetcar circuit of the 1940s. She talks about hearing extravagant tales of Old Country endurance and survival. She writes about experiences I shared: the importance of a mother baking ("Pies were obedient to her"), the escape from the city—in a car— on a family trip to Yellowstone. My life was way more comfortable and supportive than hers, but I recognize the common need to balance difficulty with delight and achievement in a city of struggle. Strikingly, she ends her bleak look back on a note of hope, so common among these writers of retrospect:

>   out
> of ruins eerie in their torn decay
> where people lived, worked, dreamed
> something yet begins to rise and grow.

Younger twenty-first-century poets who grew up in a Detroit of decline, devastation, and abandonment share this sensibility. They too look back and forge a language to match their city's industrial metaphors. Music on the move keeps emerging in recent anthologies of Detroit writing. Poet-activist Jessica Care Moore performs a long poem by chanting in the city's own voice: "I was the music made from engines, loud, tough, sometimes just a hum, and a handclap sound. When I grew up, they called me Motown." A grown-up local music industry permeates her praise of the hard-working, politically aware fathers of her West Side African American neighborhood: "Blue-collar Michigan men with jazz in their feet and Motown in their rides / Men who knew music was power and dancing slow was an act of love / Politics was the people's conscience and Marvin Gaye was our battle crier." Music is in the driver's seat.

Every aspect of the car-music relationship gets a workout in recent writers' retrospectives. The 2001 anthology *Abandon Automobile* marks the turn into the twenty-first century, away from the industrial city, but still burdened by the weight of earlier times. Just as Levine found Detroit pursuing him years later through his car radio, current poets keep returning to listening on the freeway. The stereo is an invention that can unite or separate drivers, refresh or repel them. On the positive side, Mary Minock looks back with pleasure at the days of street traffic, when Detroit's invention, the three-color stoplight, marked off driving time:

> Here was a time when we almost got it right:
> when the radios played at every stoplight
> and cutting across the privacy of cars
> and separate wanting
> were words we all knew how to sing.
> We bounced at our steering wheels
> in the rhythm and the rocking
> and gave your name to the music.

Jessica Care Moore also celebrates the mobile dial, specifying her own neighborhood: "With the radio up loud enough for the whole west side to listen, and they did." But even in the city's heyday, the car radio might not give the commuter much satisfaction, as the Rolling Stones pointed out. Jonathan Matthew Schwartz imagines his father's discontented listening in a poem about the 1950s. Apparently Mr. Schwartz did not drive to work when the Jewish hour was on the dial:

> On the car radio,
> my father driving,
> smoking a cigar
> he always turned
> the dial away
> from the stations
> with accordion music,
> the polkas from Poland,
> or voices from the South,
> Gospel singers and blues,
> anything that wasn't his,

which in Detroit wasn't much.
The dial never found
what he wanted, and
all the way to work
down Third Avenue,
he smoked his cigar
and flicked
from one station
to the next.

Kristin Palm updates the trope in a recent poem. She missed the golden age, when Detroiters heard the hits before the rest of America, so instead she invokes the desperation of freeway futility, when listening to the old songs becomes just another futile attempt at empowerment amid the isolation:

We curse
congestion, honk
and gesture, punch up all-news,
all-sports, all-
oldies all-the-time, cut
each other off,
whatever we can do
to simulate control.

Past and present merge in the rearview glance, a kind of simultaneity that the devastated city demands. Does a recent poem by Chantay "Legacy" Leonard, whose very name suggests retrospect, describe the aching, visionary city seems timeless.

I live in a strange city.
Here suffering is eloquent.
Joy a sudden trauma . . .
. . . Potholes and behavior patterns
buckled under the stress of living.
. . . Heaven is music rising
from hollow throats, torn paper,
scratch cuts, ancestral beats,
sobbing strings and flaring horns.
Supplicating hands, arched backs
Sweat testaments on dance floors.

The potholes of the present come together with music in still another poem. It's just one of many car-traffic metaphors that mix with Detroit music. For Crystal Williams in a 2015 Detroit-themed anthology, elite music needs the labor of inner city workers:

> We watch the night shift workers outside tar
> potholes for the Orchestra patrons.
> The way from their suburb
> to this intersection is rough.

You might think that in the privacy of the home, with control of personal music listening, the dominance of traffic metaphors might subside. But not in Marc Maurus's tribute poem "Five/Eight Time," with its memory of his father's tastes in jazz:

> my old man slapping sides
> on the turntable,
> vinyl slabs weeping, moaning,
> scatting alongside Ella Fitzgerald.
> The cruel diamond,
> in the groove of petroleum,
> chrome monsters on the streets,
> digging into the pavement,
> jigging and jiving
> up and down Woodward, Telegraph,
> the long, lazy horns
> wailing, wailing
> in syncopation to dashboard jazz.

The poet slyly plays on the fact that vinyl records, made of industrial oil, are dug into by "cruel" diamonds, perhaps referencing the faraway workers who mined them. He shifts from this household image to the sounding streets, grooved by monstrous machines that manage to carry the music across the wide avenues of Detroit on their radios, with the promise of community. For Maurus, the burdened past was redeemed by music. The poem ends with: "Man, that's devout / such holy sounds!"

Peter Markus also insists on the word "automobile" as foundational for the city, and he overcomes his list of gray, grounding nouns with music's redemptive power:

Detroit is . . . a poem that resists rhyme, a poem that is at times too easy to abandon, a poem that is rooted in the nouns—*house, sky, fire, river, mud, automobile, brick*. And for each of these words there is only one verb: to sing. Yes, to sing, sing—this is why we are here—even if no one hears it.

The writers of *Abandon Automobile* pay tribute to artist-ancestors, as in M. L. Liebler's homage "Roy Allen, Detroit Poet." Liebler points indirectly to the prominence of commercial music, which bypassed projects like black avant-garde theater. But, like so many others, he insists on hope as essential to the city's nature:

> Who stood in the concrete fields and alleys of the Cass Corridor
> With hope as wild as weeds in the every day sidewalk cracks
> Of Detroit. Deep pockets filled with poetry and Black Arts
> Theater that could tell the truth of the future beyond our hidden dreams.
> . . . our Detroit where the theater was not respected or welcomed.

Young or older, black, Jewish, or whatever, Detroit artists feel the urge to testify, sometimes almost ecstatically, to the city's deep and abiding influence on their lives. The highly successful Joyce Carol Oates was not born locally but made her career with a desperately dark Detroit novel, *Them*, which appeared in 1969. In her postscript, she talks about being inspired by the real-life tales of her adult night school students. The experience left a permanent mark on her very being: "How like an exiled ghost I continually revisit Detroit, doomed to see—what? . . . *The essence of a place and a time. That magical conjunction of one's self and the larger, communal, mystical, and unknowable soul.*"

Oates was just a short-term resident, but Crystal Williams grew up in the city. Williams joins the much older writers Oates and Piercy in recognizing the city's power to mold creative lives. "Homecoming" closes the collection, inspired by her experience of coming back after some years of not paying attention to Detroit's deep impact. She looks even farther back, to the Alabama roots of her black community, and once again puts music in the mix:

> Hey, hey, girl, ain't no other/ place knows you, loves you like this, knows
>   that when you shine/ out in the big wide, this here is what's sparking
>   your shimmer . . .
> & there was really no escaping/ this dance city, this holy morning empty
>   street city, this dialysis clinic on every other corner city, this be a smart

girl city/ this play the harp on Tuesdays & Thursdays city . . . this Little
Alabama City, this Smokey/Aretha/Florence city/. . . .
This *This* city, this downbeat to the secret, irrational life of your heart.

These lines have a strong musical impulse, and Crystal Williams credits her Detroit childhood for that need to link sound and poetry: "When I first started writing poems, I would hear a line of music and know the meaning, but have to find the words for it. I'd have to excavate the words from the sound. I'd get a line, then chant out the lines. I was having to edit music at the same time I was editing for meaning, thinking about the musicality of the lines."

Visual artists can be just as imprinted by Detroit memories as writers. High on the list is Mike Kelley, a highly influential figure who left the area early for Los Angeles. Kelley's ability to keep his young years fresh has haunted my own sense of the city. In a series of large-scale projects, he raised the lived city to a high level of both painful and playful artwork, making a strength out of his faulty memory and the forgotten detritus of Detroit. *Educational Project* (1996), Kelley says, "is a large architectural model made up of individual models of every school I have ever attended, plus the house in which I grew up." Conjuring memory, he found he could build the exteriors, but could not recall the innards of the buildings in which he spent so much formative time. "These unremembered sections of architecture are left blank, represented as inaccessible, filled-in blocks." The result was a massive stretch of low white units that looked like a white modernist construction, but for Kelley it was "obviously dystopian architecture, reflecting our true, chaotic social conditions, rather than some idealized dream of wholeness."

As part of this Detroit despair at being unable to muster memory, Kelley dredged up pieces of industrial remains from islands in the Detroit River and sculpted them. One pile turned into a distorted version of his white-bread Westland suburban high school's statue of the astronaut hero John Glenn. While he was trying to photograph the river journey, his camera broke down, so "the images are primarily black, with only a small strip of the film frame properly exposed. . . . The effect is akin to falling asleep in a car and awakening on occasion to radically different vistas." Here, the artist melds mobility, from the riverboat to the familiar Detroit auto metaphor. He is trafficking in images. In 2001, Kelley put several of these works together in a huge mixed media installation with a suitably complicated title: *John Glenn Memorial Detroit River Reclamation Project (Including the Local Culture Pictorial Guide, 1968–1972 Wayne/Westland Eagle).* I put the postcard of this artwork on my fridge to remind me of how difficult Detroit can be as a stimulus—or irritant. Kelley's visual work is more eloquent than much of the recent philosophical and historical writing on memory, trauma, and loss. He took seriously the repeated feeling of what he called "my mind's fall into the shaft of memory."

Music mattered deeply to Kelley, and he kept creating and collaborating with musicians most of his life. He figured in a daring performance-art collective called Destroy All Monsters that straddled the Detroit–Ann Arbor cultural nexus.

It was part of a wave of adventurous multimedia artistic groupings that fed off mainstream American culture while expanding the range of creative possibilities.

The music itself wasn't necessarily the point; it was a dissection of the memory of music: "We were not a real band; we couldn't play music; we had no audience. But we knew what a band looked like. We knew how to package ourselves as a band. . . . And so we became art. It wasn't exactly ironic or parodistic; it was analytical." As much as DAM learned from other avant-gardists of the past and the present, a Detroit edge remains, lingering in this quote from Kelley about their sound: "It's good American physical work to do something over and over again, factory style." In a way, this collective was taking the "hellish" sound of the assembly line and foundry in a redemptive direction, in "an activity that provides an instantaneous and powerful cleansing noise." It's perhaps not all that far from how Motown responded to Detroit's industrial imperative. DAM's stance allowed an artist like Kelley to distance himself from the lived urban anxiety of his youth, even while acknowledging the power of

FIG. 7.1. The adventurous performance art collective Destroy All Monsters, mid-1970s. Photo courtesy Mike Kelley estate.

its music. In still another statement of studied anti-nostalgia, he says, "It's not that I'm interested in high school culture. It's one of the few places where you can see photographs of this kind of ritual."

Music is practically the only overlap between his Detroit and mine, so far removed in space and sensibility from my cozy Jewish community. This is in spite of the fact that he said, "I never had any musical training. I grew up in a household where there was really very little interest in music. They didn't teach music in school. I grew up on rock 'n' roll music, and all the musicians I knew were self-taught." That's almost as far from my experience as his house was from mine. But then his house was literally moved, to the Cultural Center near the museum (now called Midtown), where I and so many Detroit musicians spent time as a kid. Kelley wanted to convey his child-hood home to a downtown museum, but the current owner wouldn't sell. A replica was towed to the site. It's another case of the triumph of the automobile, the con-stant partner of both the everyday and the aesthetic in the Motor City. Suitably, in 2014, the Mobile Homestead project wheeled the house again, all the way to Los Angeles, Kelley's later home. I wonder if the radio played Detroit rock 'n' roll all the way as it mirrored Motown's move from the city in 1972. Kelley kept his hand in music for the rest of his celebrated career, often using his suburban Detroit child-hood as a point of orientation.

"Detroit music" is as portable as Mike Kelley's home. Musicians have always moved away without leaving the city behind. Already back in the 1950s, when the place was still looking strong, jazz musicians took off, mostly to New York, in search of a wider audience and a larger scene. They kept running into fellow Detroiters, making albums with them in comfortable ways. It was a kind of retrospective that was creating the future. As Yusuf Lateef said in 1960 upon arriving in the massive metropolis of New York, "It was like old home week there for us." He brought Barry Harris and other hometowners to his early East Coast recording gigs (*Eastern Sounds*, 1961). Already in 1956, Thad Jones, starting out as a leader, titled his album *Detroit–New York Junction*, inviting hometown friends Kenny Burrell and Tommy Flanagan. That same year, Paul Chambers brought Detroit comrades Pepper Adams and Curtis Fuller onto a breakthrough album (*Chambers' Music*) that included writing by Barry Harris. Music producers also relied on Detroit's tech skills. Larry Bongiovi, "who cut his first records in Detroit, recreated that sound in New York; one corner [of his surviving New York studio] features vinyl flooring and cork walls, an almost exact reproduction of Motown's Snake Pit."

Two well-known musicians who left the city, the pianist Geri Allen and the vi-olinist Regina Carter, rooted two recent projects in the soil of Detroit. Allen had an important album with Ron Carter, another Cass Tech alum, back in 1994. She invited Dwight Andrews to a project involving the Cass choral groups, while paying tribute to the deep sacred music traditions of the city. The album's very title, *Timeless Portraits and Dreams*, suggests an openness to the past in the present. The pianist mentions that back at Cass, alum Donald Byrd worked with the chorus, another example of the homecoming motif that marks so many Detroit artists' careers.

In 2013, Geri Allen produced her most explicit tribute to Detroit in *Grand River Crossings: Motown & Motor City Inspirations*, named for one of those core avenues of the city plan. The two-page photo spread for the album took my breath away. There was Grand River, exactly as I remembered it from childhood. I could recognize the corner by its Richman Brothers sign, since we used to frequent that clothing store—a relative got us a discount. Geri Allen and I came from different physical and musical locations along Grand River but shared the sense of the past city as present influence. That scary street defined her sense of space as a child. She starts her liner notes with the traffic itself: "When I was a young girl, crossing a major street alone was one of the first of many rites of passage. Grand River Avenue, an eight-lane street once one of the busiest urban thoroughfares in the world was my first rite." Surviving the hazards of Cass Tech's music curriculum was the next rite, cementing the familiar traffic-music connection. Following in the hometowner tradition, Allen brought David McMurray to the album.

Still along Grand River, another Cass collaborator, Greg Phillinganes, famous for his work with Michael Jackson, writes the liner notes, which detail Geri Allen's link to the Motor City setting. Beyond a shout-out to the high school, his glance back goes prehistoric, as he points out that Grand River's traffic flows along an older current, the original river that gives the street its name. He sees continuity, with Allen's musical ideas "seamlessly flowing into the next." The tracks themselves are vivid personal versions of Motown and Detroit songs, and the pianist adds two reflective "Grand River Crossings," solo interpolations that sound the note of retrospect along the avenue. Once again, Detroit artists look to the past while creating the present and future of music, and, remarkably, feel the need to make those moves transparent, in a heartfelt way. And they reference roads and traffic as a parallel to music.

Violinist Regina Carter positions Detroit in a field of personal and musical mobility. Growing up through the Cass Tech system in a field of wide musical listening, she carved a remarkable career as an African American woman bridging the classical and jazz worlds. But she wanted to dig deeper into the many available traditions, first creating an African-based project, *Reverse Thread*, then turning to her own pre-Detroit roots in *Southern Comfort*:

As I've gotten older, I've been thinking about my family and trying to know more about them. Checked out ancestry.com, did DNA tests, reconnected with family members, seeing relatives I didn't know. What was the music that was happening then? This is my way of understanding, the closest I'm going to get to knowing my grandfather and relatives, by way of the music. I wanted to share that history and the music.

This urge led Carter to search "for music from the coal-mining world of the Appalachians. And whenever I discovered a new fact about my family, I would look for the music of that moment. I listened to a lot of field recordings. . . . Music of the place and time helped me to create pictures of a world possibly familiar to my grandfather." Strikingly, Carter folds the archives into the present in the actual pieces themselves, blending with and riffing on the voices of southern black singers of the past. This pull to the South parallels Crystal Williams's lines, written around the same time, evoking a resonant character named Johnny Dawson whose "voice holds a note / which would be the strong rich song / of a sad, hard field south of here." But Regina Carter is not looking for mythic memory. She balances reconstruction with personal, sensory knowledge. "I had spent several summers as a child at my grandmother's in Alabama. . . . I began to piece together my own memories, reconciling stories I was told." The album itself has a photo gallery labeled "Our Family Tree." On the cover, a photograph of the musician contains a silhouette, in the style of the artist Kara Walker's memory work about the old South. But unlike Walker's images of brutality, Regina Carter leans leniently toward the past, relying on vital signals from children, preachers, and wayfarers to steer through today's cultural traffic. The living violinist contains her hazy but vibrant lineage, just as Detroit folds in Alabama. In *Southern Comfort*, the avenues of Detroit extend far, far into the distance, past Grand River and the Detroit River, down the highway to the home left behind, still audible if you make the effort to hear distant sounds.

Another Detroit artist who pays tribute to his southern roots is Al Young, mentioned earlier as a poet, novelist, essayist, and a kid who hung out in our recreation room. Al began life in the late 1930s in Pachuta, Mississippi, "a place that few people cared about or even knew existed," but one where his grandmother Lillian Campbell sang "old Negro spirituals along the order of 'Steal Away,' 'Meetin' at the Buildin',' 'Didn't My Lord Deliver Daniel,' and 'Pharaoh's Army,'" which she would "half-sing and half-hum . . . morning, noon, and nighttime, from dawn to dark" as she "drew water from the well, washed, milked, cooked, swept, scrubbed, gardened, quilted, sewed, doctored, scolded and wrung the necks of chickens." Young frames this memory by saying, "We didn't have electricity, running water, gas or a car; nor did we have any idea that what we sang or listened to was American folk music." Later, in Detroit and nearby Ann Arbor, Al would become an enthusiastic member of the folk song revival, playing in coffeehouses and even thinking of becoming a full-time musician, the memory of Grandma somewhere in his ears, staying there until it became affectionate retrospect.

The idyllic mode Al Young reaches for when describing black rural life in Mississippi shifts to big-city aesthetics in memories of Detroit childhood, where he positions his mother's fierce fandom for Sarah Vaughan this way: "Consider my mother: lovely and eccentric, a product of the Deep American South, seated by the household piano, the home tape recorder rolling" to catch her as she "tries out her singing voice" to "carry her out of this nasty, sassy world to the portals of the divine." The city has encouraged Mom to record herself, be a star. It's not spirituals that move her to heavenly emotion but jazz, just as my grandmother did not sing Yiddish prayer tunes or folk songs but Rodgers and Hammerstein when she did the chores in Detroit, just a few blocks away.

It's clear that musical retro-flection, then, shifts into different gears to match the travel conditions on memory road. Al knew the black South firsthand, as a small child starting out, while Regina Carter knew it on visits as a Detroiter. She turned that experience into a quest for family roots, relying on early collectors—Lomax and Work—as sources rather than the sound of Grandma. I knew the Old Country as a Detroiter drenched in European memories, so I assimilated the whole range— Yiddish and Russian folk songs through Broadway show tunes—in childhood, just as Al could layer jazz onto spirituals. Mike Kelley, with no immediate immigrant experience to draw on, had only rock 'n' roll and high school band music to pull up for his pieces—a situation of shallow recall unlike the many layers we newer arrivals felt comfortable with: Crystal Williams's "Little Alabama City" as a descriptor for Detroit, or Levine's Anton at the bar, singing "homeland songs" whether anyone wanted to hear them or not.

Writers, artists, and musicians from Detroit see the place differently in their personal rearview mirrors. They're looking back at varied vistas in the sprawling cityscape of memory. But they all bring a partiality, even a passion, that outsiders trying to leverage the site cannot match. In his 2015 Pulitzer Prize–winning book of poems, *Ozone Journal*, Peter Balakian includes one called "Joe Louis's Fist," evoking his drive through Detroit to see the celebrated statue of the mighty black boxer's forearm and fist. He says the city "was a cliché of the image of itself," an odd outsider's comment, but he goes on to endorse that very trope as he drives past "vacant burned-out bungalows, car parts, metal scraps, arson jobs, abandoned homes, barbed wire playgrounds, shacks pummeled along Six Mile Road—derelict since '67." Not very poetic writing. Seeing the sculpture of boxer Joe Louis's fist reminds the poet of his father's memories of Louis's 1930s victory over the German Max Schmeling, overlaid with the riots in Harlem. He's straining to string together Detroit, his family, and black history. It's a rhetorical reach from a non-Detroiter.

By contrast, the singer Sheila Jordan came up with an ultra-personal musical tribute to the city at the request of legendary producer and Detroiter Don Was. Called "Sheila's Blues," the song chronicles her path as a white working-class girl from early years in Detroit, a move to Pennsylvania coal-mining country, and a return to the Motor City in the mid-1950s. It's a shout-out to the city that gave her entry to the world of jazz:

> I was born in Detroit Michigan . . . but my mother, she was only fifteen years
> old and she couldn't raise me, so she sent me to live with my grandparents in
> a small coal mining town in Pennsylvania state. Grew up with the coalminers,
> they would sit around and drink their whisky and sing their songs—"you are
> my sunshine, my only sunshine."

Here Jordan cites a southern white song that became universal in America, very different from the Alabama memories of a Regina Carter or Al Young. It was the very first song she recorded, in a jazz arrangement, and it brought her to attention in the Detroit music community. "Moved back to Detroit when I was about fourteen. We were always chasing Charlie Parker" on his visits to local clubs, like the Sudan, where the underage Jordan dressed up in her mother's clothes and makeup to get in, but couldn't make it past the bouncer: "The man said 'hey little white girl, you better go home and do your homework.' So I went round in the alley and I was sitting on the garbage can. Bird knew we were there, and he opened up the door and he played his heart out for me. What a dream."

This moment of pure revelation shaped the singer's life and rounds out her song:

> If it wasn't for jazz music, I wouldn't be alive today, oh no. because back when
> I was just a little skinny teenager . . . running down John R just to get all those

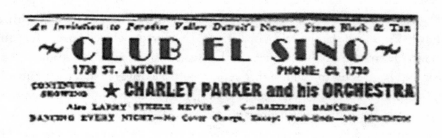

FIG. 7.2. Charley Parker visiting a Detroit club just when Sheila Jordan is looking to hear him. Source: *Detroit Free Press*.

bebop records, I mean the 78 ones, and all because I heard Charlie Parker and got to sing with Skeeter and Mitch all those many years ago—I wouldn't be up here at eighty three and a half years old, and I want to thank Don Was for making my day, as Clint Eastwood would say.

"Sheila's Blues" sums up the intensely personal look back at the "ugly beauty" of this special city, with its garbage-can epiphanies and wide-open ears, the embrace of talent from all of America, and the chance to turn grit into art. The decline of the auto industry tore the social fabric, not just socially and economically; it shredded the common musical sensibility of a great city. Looking back like the other writers and artists quoted here, producer Don Was is both nostalgic and clear-headed: "Everybody had their fate tied to the auto industry. There's a kind of unity in that dependency, a lack of pretentiousness—we're all in the same boat, dependent on the same industrialists. Because of the factories you got this incredible cross section of people who got more exposed to things because of the variety of cultures that migrated there. You actually have a more musically literate group."

After the 1960s, freeways led to a suburbia that separated and atomized an all-city aesthetic. Beyond 8 Mile Road, ears and antennas turned away from the beat of Detroit's sounds. Today's artists are just as excited and conflicted about Detroit as earlier generations, and they keep searching for musical momentum, but it's challenging in such a changed landscape. Shaun Nethercott projects memory forward, toward an endlessly ambivalent, infectious excitement: "You don't ever recover from the Detroit virus. Everywhere else seems pale and innocuous and inhospitable by comparison. We love/hate/need this place. It is a power spot whose vibrations are both thrilling and exhausting." Still, the recent artistic wave privileges visual arts over music. People carry on the heritage traditions of the city, but today's artists have yet to come up with a compelling new Detroit sound that links to the old heyday.

It's less of a problem for entrepreneurs, who love to market the city's past as its future. Shinola, a company invented by out-of-town investors, makes luxury items, including a turntable, which it advertises with the catchphrase: "Have you heard the latest from Detroit?" But they're only selling a shiny product, not some new wave of gritty urban music.

Detroiter Keith Owens warns that the current ebb of musical energy endangers the spirit of the place, using a final, pungent traffic metaphor for today's post–Motor City: "If Detroit music isn't helping to steer the wheel then we're bound to wind up lost."

In an incredibly compressed time frame of just three generations—about 1910–70—Detroit's industrial and musical energy set it off from similar cities.

FIG. 7.3. A Shinola Company ad occupying a wall in New York's SoHo, 2016. Author photo.

Alas, the city's economic and racial setup sowed the seeds of its own decline and the dispersal of both its capital and its talent pool. Seeing the place as it was, as I have tried to do in a limited survey, suggests how in even the most troubled and tentative space, urban music can offer an alternate pattern, a creative opening in the traffic jam that is American society. In a recent illuminating survey of artwork, Marion Jackson points out the difference between the newcomer artists' forward-looking projects and the approach of art workers who are natives: "Longtime Detroiters might see . . . a 'crowded canvas' full of life and energy and the traces of a vibrant past. They sense . . . the traces of Black Bottom, Paradise Valley, thriving factories, elegant neighborhoods, the artistic spirit of the Cass Corridor, and the music of Motown. For them, the city is not an empty canvas, but a rich heritage." For me, a tentative rearview glance at Detroit grew into a series of revelations about my milieu, my city, and American music in the industrial age.

Sources for the City

For a city that was so important and remains a familiar name worldwide, Detroit has not been properly documented, in domains from sociology to music history. Thomas Sugrue's 2005 classic *The Origins of the Urban Crisis: Race and Inequality in Postwar Detroit* (Princeton, NJ: Princeton University Press, 2005) is still somewhat lonely on the shelf, complemented lately by Herb Boyd's *Black Detroit* (Boyd 2017), which offers a quick-paced summary of the long story of the city's African Americans' struggles and achievements. The first comprehensive study of the life of a specific neighborhood, is just being developed, as the Chene Street Project, by Marian Krzyzowski of the University of Michigan. Remarkably, the three main Detroit newspapers remain undigitized.

For music, the anthology *Heaven Was Detroit: From Jazz to Hip-Hop and Beyond* (Liebler 2016) offers a useful jumping-off point for the history of Detroit's spread-out scenes. Its short takes cover a wide variety of topics, many from people who were there at the time. In terms of books I have drawn on liberally, there are a few solid surveys of subsections of the metropolis's musical life. They present the valuable work of journalists, aficionados, and guardians of heritage who have detailed the nitty-gritty of biography, dates, venues, and addresses: Maki and Cady 2013 on country music, Palazzolo 2003b on Polish American music, Carson 2000 on radio, and Bjorn and Gallert 2001 on jazz history. Motown has its own literature, but it is not as thorough and detailed as one would like. Smith 1999 offers a perceptive analysis of the company's context, and there are many useful memoirs and documentary films on individual figures (see Liebler 2016 for a listing), but we still await a major overview of this unique African American corporation. The first article on European immigrant music in Detroit was Nettl and Moravcik 1955, about a handful of songs.

Archival sources are similarly thin. In terms of labor history, there's little on music at the vast Walter Reuther Archives. The Detroit Symphony Orchestra no longer gives access to its materials. On the bright side, Ford and General Motors are generous with supplying materials to researchers. The Jewish community has well-organized archives (http://jewishdetroit.org/jewish-community-archives/), and the *Detroit Jewish News* is digitized and searchable. The Polish community has an archive and an exceptional music historian. In addition to her book *Horn Man* (Palazzolo 2003b), Laurie Gomulka Palazzolo has produced a fine documentary on Polish-American music, *Dom Polski: Dance Hall Days of Detroit's Polonia*, as well as series of vintage polka reissue albums, all available at http://www.hornman-detroit. com. Paula Savaglio's follow-up studies (Savaglio 2004) offer a helpful later look at the Polish story. Ara Topouzian has documented the Armenian music story on film and cd (Topouzian 2015a, 2015b; see also Hagopian 2002). Anne Rasmussen (1997, 2002) did the first writing on the growing Arab-American music of the Detroit area. There is some archival material at the American Folklife Center of the Library of Congress, particularly the Hufford (1982) and Radecki (1981) surveys of southern white music in the upper Midwest. The Detroit and Michigan collecting trip by folklorist/activist Alan Lomax in 1938 is now available online at https://www.loc. gov/collections/alan-lomax-in-michigan/about-this-collection/ and is part of James Leary's valuable survey (Leary 2015), a fine addition to his lifelong series of works on the Upper Midwest's ethnic groups. For African American musical life, no such surveys were done, and there is little to read beyond the blues and jazz sectors of the community's rich musical life, except for references here and there to church music in relation to the Rev. C. L. Franklin and his daughter Aretha or other biographical/autobiographical writings.

Franya Berkman's 2010 study of Alice McLeod Coltrane has a helpful chapter on the musician's early years in Detroit. YouTube currently houses a helpful series of interviews with older African American musicians, some cited above.

Hopefully, the Detroit Sound Conservancy (http://detroitsoundconservancy. org) will secure more archival materials and keep instigating research into the largely uncharted musical life of a great American and world city.

Notes

Page 1   Unless another source is given below, all quotes from Detroiters are from interviews done in 2013–2017.

Page 1   "A place of overlapping borders": Miles

Page 1   "One of them," "My crimes are great": Catlin 1923, 263, 293.

Page 2   "There were a number": Milan 2009.

Page 2   "The belle of the family": Street 1914, 65–66.

Page 4   "In Detroit there were": Cline 1923, 189–94.

Page 4   "I went to Detroit": Nicholas Dawidoff, "The Man Who Saw America," *New York Times*, July 2, 2015, available at http://www.nytimes.com/2015/07/05/magazine/robert-franks-america.html.

Page 4   "Today I saw one of those houses": quoted in Peterson 2013, 174.

Page 6   "Being in a state of continuous flux": Bucci 1993, 47.

Page 6   "I wanted to be in a city": Salvatore 2005, 104.

Page 6   "The car came to stand": Norton 2008.

Page 7   "Detroit is the most important place": Clinton 2014, 352.

Page 9   "If you ride": quote given to me by James Clifford.

Page 10   "Culture is a matter of traffic": Hannerz 1980, 11.

Page 13   "We played all the shoot-em up games": Edmonds 2016, 204.

Page 29   "There's an archived episode": https://www.youtube.com/watch?v=TSQoAyyZaZ8.

Page 31   "I'm from the musical womb of Detroit": Miller 2013, 2.

Page 33   "McKinney was inspired": http://www.mtv.com/artists/harold-mckinney/

Page 35   "The great pop song by Lou Christie": Music 2017, 87.

Page 36   "My mother didn't believe in differences": https://www.youtube.com/watch?v=lfigmx09Dfc. Rest of Regina Carter quote from interview.

Page 36   "We were called factory rats" and "My dad got me a job": Miller 2013, 1.

Page 41   "Major thinkers like Walter Benjamin": Tonkiss 2005, 115, 123, 126.

Page 41   "Ulf Hannerz says": Hannerz 1980, 63.

Page 43   "The boy who blows a horn": Dykema et al. 1941, 9.

Page 44   "It was a mecca for music lovers": This and following quotes on Detroit schools history are from Law 1988.

Page 45   "The function of music in life," "Nothing is more significant" paragraph, and "It is the duty": Dykema and Cundiff 1939.

Page 47   Zerounian biography: http://www.ekfh.net/webcast-archive/2010-2012/7355.

Page 48   "Music in general": Holoman 2012, 16.

Page 48   "In the first half of the twentieth century": Art Lieb.

Page 51   African American population figures: http://www.census.gov/population/www/documentation/twps0076/MItab.pdf.

Page 51   "White parents": Mirel 1993, 188.

Page 52   Clozelle Jones dissertation: Jones 1970.

Page 52   "The aim of instrumental study": Dykema and Gehrkens 1941, 312.

Page 52   "America does not have that racial solidarity": Dykema and Gehrkens 1941, 21.

Page 55   "A monumental achievement": Mirel 1953, 33.

Page 55   "Enviable positions": Begian 1954.

Page 55   Sheila Jordan: Johnson 2014, 9.

Page 56   "Kirk Spry dropped out": Palazzolo 2003b, 75.

Page 56   "When I heard that concert band": Palazzolo 2003b, 196.

Page 58   Quotations on Charlie Burrell's life: Burrell 2014.

Page 57   Quotations from Ron Carter: https://www.youtube.com/watch?v=FKdP1ratv3M; http://forbassplayersonly.com/interview-ron-carter/.

Page 57   Joe Striplin quotation: http://www.democraticunderground.com/discuss/duboard.php?az=view_all&address=439x5131.

Page 58   "At Cass Tech": Allen 2013.

Page 59   "In all my years at Cass": http://www.swans.com/library/art17/saslav28.html.

Page 60   "Cass was often asked" and "People asked me stupid questions": Ouelette 2014.

Page 61   "Begian called him": http://www.banddirector.com/article/michigan_musical_legends_dr_harry_begian.

Page 61   "75% of Begian's band members": Begian 1954.

Page 61   "Begian's groups": https://en.wikipedia.org/wiki/Harry_Begian.

Page 63   "It might have been": Palazzolo 2003b.

Page 63   "In a 1980s study": Lonnert 2014.

Page 64   "He preferred to work," "Alice's confidence": Berkman 2010.

Page 65   Tuesday Musicale information:
           http://www.ksanti.net/tuesdaymusicale/history.html.

Page 66   Bennie Maupin: taken from transcript of his interview for Oral History of American Music, Yale University.

Page 67–8 "Scholars of the Chicago School": Conn 2014, 47.

Page 68   "Robert Sampson argues": Sampson 2012, 361–62.

Page 69   "The idea of showcasing immigrant music": see Lausevic 2005.

Page 69   "Mothballed cultures": Looker 2016, 41.

Page 69   References to Leary here and below are from Leary 2006.

Page 69   "The legendary collector Alan Lomax": Harvey 2013, 17.

Page 70   "Folklorist Albert Friedman": in introduction to Gardner and Chickering 1967.

Page 70   "Leary and others": see Greene 1992; Keil, Keil, and Blau, 1992.

Page 70   "The lusty tradition": Harvey 2013, 17.

Page 70   Thelma James: James 1951. Nettl: interview.

Page 71   "Kasem credited his community":
           http://www.nytimes.com/2014/06/16/business/media/casey-kasem-wholesome-voice-of-pop-radio-dies-at-82.html.

Page 72   Ruzich interview: http://www.slavonicweb.org/oral-histories-ruzich.php.

Page 74   "Exchanging visits with Tamburitzans": http://www.detroittamburitzaorchestra.com/index.php/history-of-dto/english.

Page 74   Vinka Ellesin: http://digital.library.pitt.edu/cgi-bin/f/findaid/findaididx?c=hswpead;rgn=main;view=text;didno=US-QQS-mss758.
           Dan Georgakas: quotes are from Georgakas 2006 and interviews.

Page 77   "Laurie Gomulka Palazzolo's work": quotes are from Palazzolo 2003a and 2003b.

Page 80   "A Serbian played his shepherd's flute for me": Harvey 2013, 20.

Page 84   Charles and Angelika Keil: Keil, Keil, and Blau 1992.

Page 84   "In the 1980s and 1990s": Savaglio 1996 and 2004.

Page 86   "L'Emigrante Disilluso": Leary and March 1993, 281, with annotation by Jennifer Caputo.

Page 87   "Appalachian Circulation": This section relies on Maki and Cady 2013, a comprehensive survey of Detroit's country music scene, and the oral history work in Hufford 1982 and Radecki 1981.

Page 88   "The Brooks Bus Line": Clarkson and Montell 1975, 222.

Page 88   "Dennis Coffey" here and elsewhere: Coffey 2009.

Page 90   Clix Records: Hurtt 2016, 138.

Page 90   "The Michigan Raccoon Club": Bill Lockwood, interview.

Page 90   "Chief Redbird": http://carcitycountry.com/2013/chief-redbird-film/.

Page 92   Michael on Fire's video: https://www.youtube.com/watch?v=KGBdFOLieVQ.

Page 93   "Ed Bryant": Radecki 1981.

Page 94   "Folklorist Mary Hufford": the following section, through "McGurgan's Opera," draws on Hufford 1982.

Page 94   "Everybody loved the Count": Wilson 1998, 126.

Page 97   Leroy Mitchell: Johnson 2014, 20.

Page 97   Parades: Thompson 1999, 48.

Page 98   Paul Berliner: Berliner 1994.

Page 98   Kenn Cox: https://www.youtube.com/watch?v=vy9FEjsBVvY.

Page 98   Bennie Maupin: from transcript of his interview at Oral History of American Music, Yale University.

Page 99   Thomas Kelly on gospel: http://www.freep.com/story/entertainment/music/2017/04/26/thomas-kelly-masters-of-harmony-david-clements/100932358/.

Page 99   "He broke up the convention": Salvatore 2005, 102–3.

Page 99   Betty Carter: https://www.youtube.com/watch?v=j_c-LsI5CaU.

Page 100   "Alice was part of the time-honored tradition": Berkman 2010, 24–25.

Page 103   "Get off the bandstand": Burrell 2014, 86.

Page 100   "Bebop was a West Side thing": quoted in Bauer 2002, 25.

Page 102   James Frazier: http://www.nytimes.com/1975/11/30/archives/a-black-conductor-pushes-the-cause-of-music.html.

Page 102   On Chicago: Absher 2014.

Page 102   Kenn Cox: http://www.nytimes.com/1975/11/30/archives/a-black-conductor-pushes-the-cause-of-music.html.

Page 105   "City space": Berman 2014, 4.

Page 105   "Different voices": Bolkosky 1991, 181.

Page 105   This chapter draws on the *Detroit Jewish News*, the voice of the community.

Page 106   "In 1867": Katz 1964, 11.

Page 106   "The Jews affiliated heavily by family"; "sentiment rather than coercion": Sklare 1971.

Page 106   "The Michigan Legion": Bolkosky 1991, 174.

Page 106   "This encircling pressure": Prell 2007.

Page 106   "Anthropologist Sherry Ortner": Ortner 2003, 56–57.

Page 107   "Urban roots and city smarts": Moore 2014, 83.

Page 107   "Only one study": Netsky 2014.

Page 109   "Dugschitzer": Kazin 1951, 41.

Page 110   "Newer pathways to self-fulfillment": see Summit 2003, 2016.

Page 111   "Littman's Yiddish People's Theater": flourished 1927–58; see Miller 1967.

Page 113   "Significant innovator": Rossen 2014, 33.

Page 115   "A trio of faiths": popularized in Herberg 1955.

Page 116   "Jews were particularly strong supporters": Miller 2011, 3.

Page 119   "The Purple Gang" and "The Little Symphony": Barnett-Goldstein 2006, 7.

Page 120   "Only a great city": Louis Cook, *Detroit Free* Press, October 5, 1957.

Page 121   "As always": Katie Norman, "Detroit's Symphony of Beauty," *Free Press*, November 1, 1957.

Page 122   "Marjorie Fisher": http://www.nytimes.com/2016/07/16/arts/music/a-direct-bequest-to-each-member-of-the-detroit-symphony-orchestra.html.

Page 123   "Mr. and Mrs. Yenovk Kavafian": *Detroit Free Press*, January 6, 1957.

Page 123   "Female-only orchestras": Handy 1981: 27.

Page 124   "Charles Burrell": quotes are from Burrell 2014.

Page 124   "A respected cello soloist": Handy 1981, 69.

Page 125   "His colleagues in Chicago": Absher 2014, 78.

Page 125   "The effect of the violin": Kazin 1951, 63.

Page 126   "A troika of pianists": Heiles 2006.

Page 126   Data on Kottler from Barolo 2013.

Page 127   "Karl Haas": http://www.nytimes.com/2005/02/08/arts/music/karl-haas-radio-ambassador-of-classical-music-dies-at-91.html?_r=0.

Page 127   Information on Fred Butzel is from Bice 2008.

Page 127   "Julius Chajes": http://www.milkenarchive.org/people/view/all/529/Chajes%2C+Julius.

Page 128   "Built on students and amateurs": Heiles 2006.

Page 129   "Six communities": *Detroit Free Press*, May 4, 1952.

Page 130   "A style that would also be Jewish": see Goldblatt 2012.

Page 130   Chajes quotes are from Goldblatt 2012 and a cache of Chajes's writings generously loaned by Yossi Chajes.

Page 133   Chajes on YouTube: "Psalm 142" at https://www.youtube.com/watch?v=VD3lSk Htaf4,

Page 134   "Israeli Melodies" at https://www.youtube.com/watch?v=DAbw7rk2QG0.

Page 135   "I felt I had something to do there": http://archives.savethemusic.com/bin/archives.cgi?q=bio&id=Emma+Schaver.

Page 135   "Partizaner lid" on YouTube: https://www.youtube.com/watch?v=1bFyayuDlkY.

Page 135   "The interpretation of these songs": Schaver 1948.

Page 137   Information on Seymour Simons from Goldstone 1986.

Page 137   "For Buenos Aires": Palomino 2016, 37.

Page 137   "Lila Corwin Berman": Berman 2015, 22, 8.

Page 140   Ford Motor Company and General Motors materials come from the corporations' respective archives, for which I'm grateful to --------.

Page 140   "Hudson Carolers": *Detroit Free Press*, December 1, 1957.

Page 140   "The store sent its bands": Palazzolo 2003b, 108.

Page 143   "A story that's been well-described": Gifford 2010.

Page 143   Ford and square dance: Jamison 2018, 106.

Page 144   "The advisor was": Farkas 2011:26.

Page 146   "Each member was credited": Bryce 1982.

Page 146   "St. Andrews Society": *Detroit Free Press*, January 25, 1947.

Page 147   Mark Norton quote: Miller 2013, 2.

Page 148   "Fife and drum corps": Clark 2011, 74.

Page 148   "Songbook of UAW local": Walter Reuther archives.

Page 149   Jewish peddlers: see Diner 2015 for a thorough account, worldwide.

Page 149   Maurice Sugar: biographical details and some song texts from Johnson 1988.

Page 149   "Bear and Wolf": Leary and March 1993, 264.

Page 151   "Remembering the song": Sugar 1965.

Page 151   "Sit Down" song on YouTube: https://www.youtube.com/watch?v=kVrxruRTtDA.

Page 152   "George Williamson": Hufford 1982.

Page 152   "Maurice Sugar's summary": Sugar 1965.

Page 152   DRUM: Smith 1999, 4, has a description of the demonstration; for DRUM in detail,
            see Georgakas and Surkin 1998 and the film *Finally Got the News* (https://www.you-
            tube.com/watch?v=gw2Wr-odBJg), which features the song by Ford worker Lil Joe
            Carter "Detroit, I Do Mind Dying."

Page 152   "The people in the shop": Hufford 1982.

Page 153   Material from Sid Brown comes from his unpublished memoir (ca. 2005) and Brown
            2002.

Page 155   "We felt we were in a backwater": Arnie Kessler, interview.

Page 158   "African American musicians": Sinclair 2016.

Page 158   Melba Boyd: Boyd 2003:192.

Page 158   Charles McPherson: interview at https://www.youtube.com/watch?v=mQrvQI
            UNe8E.

Page 158   *Guitar Army* quote: Sinclair 1979, 44, 46.

Page 160   Herman Daldin: Daldin 2016, 417.

Page 162   Ed Wolfrum material: http://www.detroitschoolofrockandpop.com/tag/ed-wolfrum.

Page 162   Quotes from Dennis Coffey here and below are from Coffey 2009.

Page 163   Gordy on the assembly line: Maraniss 2015, 51.

Page 164   African-American industrial workforce: Thompson 1999, 9.

Page 171   Bruce Springsteen: Springsteen 2017:70.

Page 164   George Clinton quotes are from Clinton 2014.

Page 165   "Nifty riff": Bjorn and Gallert 2016, 24.

Page 165   Bowles quote: https://www.youtube.cm/watch?v=wfhY8rNmVzQ.

Page 166   Worrell quote: http://www.nytimes.com/2016/06/25/arts/music/bernie-worrell-
            whose-keyboards-left-an-imprint-on-funk-and-hip-hop-dies-at-72.html.

Page 166   Arnoldi: https://wayne.edu/newsroom/release/2002/03/28/wayne-state-university-
            department-of-music-remembers-the-life-and-legacy-of-professor-emeritus-harold-
            arnoldi-713.

Page 167   Cornelius Grant: https://www.youtube.com/watch?v=5iyU2fvfTM8.

Page 167   Material on *Strung Out* comes from an interview with Paul Riser and the extensive liner notes on the reissue, Galloway 2009.

Page 171   American Girl doll: https://www.theguardian.com/lifeandstyle/2016/aug/26/new-american-girl-doll-african-american-1960s-detroit.

Page 171   Wayne Kramer and following quote: Miller 2013.

Page 171   "Dave Marsh: https://www-rocksbackpages-com.ezproxy.wesleyan.edu/Library/Article/mc5-back-on-shakin-street"

Page 172   Material on Detroit radio drawn from Carson 2000.

Page 173   Dorothy Ashby: Handy 1981, 96.

Page 173   "Sat up nights," "favorite disk jockey": Young 1970, 96.

Page 173   DJ Electrifying Mojo: Bredow 2004.

Page 175   Betty Carter: Bauer 2002, 20.

Page 175   CKLW: Clinton 2014, 55.

Page 176   Happy Hank: http://carcitycountry.com/2016/when-cowboys-ranged-detroit- radio-happy-hank/.

Page 176   Quotes from Montell and Clarkson 1975.

Page 176   *Dollmaker* quotes: Arnow 1954.

Page 177   "I remember my mother": Tucker-Sullivan 2017.

Page 178   "Music was dumped on you": Al Young, interview and 1981, 121.

Page 178   John Hartigan: Hartigan 1999, 95.

Page 179   "The Cedars": this set of listings is from 1962.

Page 182   "Dudley Wilson": Heintjes 2012.

Page 184   "Vogue Records": http://www.voguepicturerecords.org/records.html.

Page 185   "In this daydream": Young 1981.

Page 186   Geri Allen: https://www.youtube.com/watch?v=7nbXJjBDwsM, https://www.youtube.com/watch?v=7nbXJjBDwsM.

Page 187   "Some activists": Palazzolo 2003b.

Page 188   Anita Sarko: Michaelangelo Matos, "Reflecting on Anita Sarko, Influential D.J. of the New York Club Scene," *New York Times*, October 26, 2015, http://www.nytimes.com/2015/10/27/arts/music/reflecting-on-anita-sarko-influential-dj-of-the-new-york-club-scene.html?ribbon-ad-idx=116&rref=todayspaper&module=Ribbon&version=origin&region=Header&action=click&contentCollection=Today%E2%80%99s%20Paper&pgtype=article and http://www.villagevoice.com/music/michael-musto-mourns-the-loss-of-nyc-nightlife-maven-anita-sarko-she-enlarged-ones-consciousness-7832007.

Page 189   Jessica Care Moore: https://www.youtube.com/watch?v=KdvveTHkDgs.

Page 190   "I know of no other place": Griffoen 2014, 251.

Page 190   "I have never lived anywhere": Herron 1994, 207.

Page 190   "More interested in the themes of reexamination": Kelley 1998, 99.

Page 190   "I hope to preserve some image": Levine 1981, 62.

Page 190   "I was myself in the company": Levine 1994, 89.

Page 190   "I spent most of my childhood": Levine 1981, 93.

Page 191   "You could recite poems aloud in there": http://www.theparisreview.org/interviews/2512/the-art-of-poetry-no-39-philip-levine.

Page 191   "Stash, a worker": Levine 2000, 242–43.

Page 191   "Zaydee and I sang songs": Levine 1981, 274.

Page 191   "I was awed by them": Levine 2013.

Page 192   "Lionel Hampton": Young 1981, 177.

Page 193   "A man is singing on the bus": Levine 2000, 252.

Page 193   *The Dollmaker:* Arnow 1954, 133.

Page 194   "Trolleys," "Big Maceo," "the radio": Levine 2016, 50, 76.

Page 194   "We got music": Levine 2016, 19–20.

Page 194   "In Michigan": Levine 1981, 205, 250.

Page 194   "An effort to slow down"; "I grew up in a city": Levine 1981, 62; 1994, 78.

Page 195   "It was a place": Piercy 2015, 3–4.

Page 195   "There was snow": Levine 2010, 23–24.

Page 195   "I suckled": Piercy 2015, 3–4.

Page 195   "Out of ruins": Piercy 2015, 21–22.

Page 196   "Here was a time": Minock 2001, 251.

Page 196   "With the radio up loud enough": https://www.youtube.com/watch?time_ continue=3&v=aVOTyNatUF8.

Page 196   "On the car radio": Schwartz, personal communication.

Page 197   "We curse": Palm 2001, 275.

Page 197   "I live in a strange city": Leonard 2014, 221.

Page 198   "We watch": Williams 2015, 44.

Page 198   "My old man slapping slides": Maurus 2001, 234.

Page 199   "Detroit is a poem": Markus 2014, 119–20.

Page 199   "Who stood in a concrete field": Lieber 2014, 109.

Page 199   "How like an exiled ghost": Oates 2000, 540.

Page 199   "Hey, hey, girl": Williams 2015, 44.

Page 200   Kelley: Kelley 2008, 21–22; see http://whitney.org/WatchAndListen?play_id=437.

Page 200   "The images are primarily blank": Kelley 2008, 280; see http://www.dia.org/exhibitions/artiststake/projects/kelley.html#.

Page 201   "My mind's fall": quoted by John Welchman in https://frieze.com/article/mike-kelley-1954-2012-ten-tributes.

Page 201   "We were not a real band": Kelley 1998.

Page 202   "It's not that I'm interested": https://www.youtube.com/watch?v=2-vooVkdMdo.

Page 202   "I never had any musical training": https://www.youtube.com/watch?v= Ji9GDu QwiUs,

Page 202   "It was like old home week": Lateef and Boyd 2006, 83.

Page 202   Larry   Bongiovi: http://www.nytimes.com/2015/09/29/nyregion/as-hit-factory-fades-chrome-faucets-may-supplant-gold-records.html.

Page 203   Gerri Allen on Grand River: Allen 2013.

Page 203   Greg Phillinganes on Grand River: Phillinganes 2013.

Page 204   "This urge led Carter" and "I had spent several summers": Carter 2014.

Page 204   "Johnny Dawson": Williams 2015, 42.

Page 204   Al Young on Mississippi: Young 1981, 16, 56, 64, 67.

Page 206   "Sheila's Blues" quotes: https://www.youtube.com/watch?v=oSfwPb_m1Cw.

Page 205   "Joe Louis's Fist": Balakian 2015, 14.

Page 207   Shaun Nethercott: Nethercott 2012, 217.

Page 207   "If Detroit music isn't steering the wheel": Owens 2014, 165.

Page 208   "Longtime Detroiters": Jackson 2014, 7.

References

Absher, Amy. 2014.*The Black Musician and the White City: Race and Music in Chicago, 1900–1967*. Ann Arbor: University of Michigan Press.

Allen, Gerri. 2013. Liner notes to *Grand River Crossings*. Motema 233768.

Arnow, Harriette. 1954. *The Dollmaker*. New York: Macmillan

Balakian, Peter. 2015. *Ozone Journal*. Chicago: University of Chicago Press.

Barnett-Goldstein, Carolyn. 2006. "Changing Times: Barney Rosen and the Little Symphony of Detroit." *Michigan Jewish History* 46 (Fall): 4–16.

Bauer, William R. 2002.*Open the Door: The Life and Music of Betty Carter*. Ann Arbor: University of Michigan Press.

Begian, Harry. 1954. "Music at Cass Technical High School." Program for the 1954 meeting of the Midwest National Band Clinic, 8.

Berkman, Franya. 2010. *Monument Eternal: The Music of Alice Coltrane*. Middletown, CT: Wesleyan University Press.

Berliner, Paul. 1994. *Thinking in Jazz: The Infinite Art of Improvisation*. Chicago: University of Chicago Press.

Berman, Lila Corwin. 2015. *Metropolitan Jews: Politics, Race, and Religion in Postwar Detroit*. Chicago: University of Chicago Press.

Bice, Wendy. 2008. "Fred Butzel: The Man Behind the Name." *Michigan Jewish History* 48:4–15.

Bjorn, Lars. 2016. "Teddy Harris: A Jazz Man in Motown." In Liebler 2016, 20–25.

Bjorn, Lars, with Jim Gallert. 2001. *Before Motown: A History of Jazz in Detroit, 1920–1960*. Ann Arbor: University of Michigan Press.

Bolkosky, Sidney. 1991. *Harmony and Dissonance: Voices of Jewish Identity in Detroit, 1914–1967*. Detroit: Wayne State University Press.

Borolo, Cynthia. 2013. "Mischa Kottler: Distinguished Musician and Michigan Legend." *Michigan Jewish History* 53 (Fall): 52–57.

"Bosses and Judges, Lis'n to Me." 1938. *Daily Worker,* July 8.

Boyd, Herb. 2017. *Black Detroit: A People's History of Self-Determination.* New York: Harper Collins.

Boyd, Melba Joyce, *Wrestling with the Muse: Dudley Randall and the Broadside Press.* NY: Columbia University Press, 2003.

Boyd, Melba Joyce, and M. L. Liebler. 2001. *Abandon Automobile: Detroit City Poetry, 2001.* Detroit: Wayne State University Press.

Bredow, Garry. 2004. *"High-Tech Soul": The Creation of Techno Music.* Documentary film.

Brown, Sid. 2002. Liner notes to *Spike-Drivers: Folkrocking Psychedelic Innovation from the Motor City in the Mid 60s.* RD Records, Switzerland.

———. ca. 2005. *Still Wobbly After All These Years, or 45 Years and Still Wobblin'.* Unpublished manuscript.

Burrell, Charlie, and Mitch Handelsman. 2014. *The Life of Charlie Burrell: Breaking the Color Barrier in Classical Music.* Parker, CO: Books to Believe In.

Carson, David. 2000. *Rockin' Down the Dial: The Detroit Sound of Radio from Jack the Bellboy to the Big 8.* Troy, MI: Momentum

Carter, Regina. 2014. Liner notes to *Southern Comfort.* Sony Masterworks 88843 005005 2.

Catlin, George B. 1923. *The Story of Detroit.* Detroit: Detroit News.

Clark, James. 2011. *Connecticut's Fife and Drum Tradition.* Middletown, CT: Wesleyan University Press.

Clarkson, Atelia, and W. Lynwood Montell. 1975. "Letters to a Bluegrass DJ: Social Documents of Southern White Migrants in Southeastern Michigan 1964–74." *Southern Folklore Quarterly* 39:219–232.

Cline, Leonard Lanson. 1923. "The Fordizing of a Pleasant Peninsula." In *These United States: A Symposium,* edited by Ernest Gruening, 185–98. New York.: Boni & Liveright.

Clinton, George, with Ben Greeman. 2014. *Brothas Be, Yo Like George, Ain't That Funkin' Kinda Hard on You?* New York: Atria.

Coffey, Dennis. 2009. *Guitars, Bars, and Motown Superstars.* Ann Arbor: University of Michigan Press.

Conn, Steven. 2014. *Americans against the City: Anti-Urbanism in the Twentieth Century.* New York: Oxford University Press.

Cornhusker, Arthur. 1952. *Detroit as the People See It: A Survey of Attitudes in an Industrial City.* Detroit: Wayne State University Press.

Daldin, Herman. 2016. "Grande Haze, Bubble Puppies, and Suburban Hippie Rock." In Liebler 2016, 417–20.

Dykema, Peter W., and Hannah M. Cundiff. 1939. *New School Music Handbook.* Boston: C .C. Birchard.

Diner, Hasia. 2015. *Roads Taken: The Great Jewish Migrations to the New World and the Peddlers Who Forged the Way.* New Haven, CT: Yale University Press.

Edmonds, Ben. 2016. "Excerpt from *What's Going On: Marvin Gaye and the Last Days of the Motown Sound.*" In Liebler 2016, 201–8.

Farkas, E. J. 2011. *The Reminiscences of Mr. E. J. Farkas.* Dearborn, Mi: Benson Ford Research Center.

Feather, Leonard. 1956. Liner notes to *Detroit-New York Junction: Thad Jones.* Blue Note BLP 1513.

Gabriel, Larry. 2016. "Rebirth of Tribe." In Liebler 2016, 27–38.

Galloway, A. Scott. Liner notes to *Strung Out: Gordon Staples and the String Thing.* Motown Records MS 722, released by Reel Music.

Gardner, Emelyn Elizabeth, and Geraldine Jencks Chickering. 1967. *Ballads and Songs of Southern Michigan.* Hatboro PA: Folklore Associates.

Georgakas, Dan. 2006. *My Detroit: Growing up Greek and American in Motor City.* New York: Pella.

———, and Marvin Surkin. 1998. *Detroit: I Do Mind Dying.* Cambridge, MA: South End.

Gifford, Paul. n.d. "Jasper E. 'Jep Bisbie: Old-Time Michigan Dance Fiddler." http://www.oldtimeherald.org/archive/back_issues/volume-9/9-6/jasper-bisbee.html

Goldstone, George H. 1986. "Seymour Simons: The Engineer Who Became a Composer," *Michigan Jewish History* 26:26–29.

Ford, Henry and Ford, Clara. 1926. *Good Morning: After a Sleep of Twenty-Five Years, Old-Fashioned Dancing Is Being Revived by Mr. and Mrs. Henry Ford.* Dearborn MI: Dearborn Publishing Co.

Greene, Victor. 1992. *A Passion for Polka.* Urbana: University of Illinois Press.

Griffoen, James D. 2014. "The Fauxtopias of Detroit's Suburbs." In Anna Clark, ed., *A Detroit Anthology.* Cleveland: Rust Belt Chic Press, 2014, 136–153.

Hagopian, Richard, prod. 2002. *Kef Time Detroit.* CD, Traditional Crossroads 80702-4312.

Handy, D. Antoinette. 1981. *Black Women in American Bands and Orchestras.* Metuchen, NJ: Scarecrow.

Hartigan, John, Jr. 1999. *Racial Situations: Class Predicaments of Whiteness in Detroit.* Princeton, NJ: Princeton University Press.

Harvey, Todd. 2013. *Michigan I-O: Alan Lomax and the 1938 Library of Congress Folk-Song Expedition.* Atlanta: Dust to Digital.

Heiles, Anne Mischakoff. 2006. *Mischa Mischakoff: Journeys of A Concertmaster.* Sterling Heights, MI: Harmonie Park.

Heintjes, Tom. 2012. "The View from On High: Dudley Fisher's 'Right Around Home.'" *Cartoonician,* http://cartoonician.com/the-view-from-on-high-dudley-fishers-right-around-home/.

Herron, Jerry. 1994. *AfterCulture: Detroit and the Humiliation of History.* Wayne State University Press.

Holoman, D. Kern. 2012. *The Orchestra: A Very Short Introduction.* New York: Oxford University Press.

Hufford, Mary. 1982. *"The Mountains Stay with Us": Southern Upland Folk Life in the Midwest.* Detroit: Great Lakes Arts Alliance..

Hurtt, Michael. "Nine Times out of Ten: The Clix Records Story," in Boyd and Liebler 2016, 132-41.

Jackson, Marion. 2014. "Introduction." In *Canvas Detroit,* edited by Julie Incus and Nichole Christian, 1–7. Detroit: Wayne State University Press.

James, Thelma, ed. 1951. *Ethnic Groups in Detroit: 1951.* Unpublished document, Wayne University Department of Sociology and Anthropology.

Jamison, Phil. 2018. Review of *Hoedowns, Reels, and Frolics—Roots and Branches of Southern Appalachian Dance. Journal of the Society for American Music* 12/1, 104–6.

Johnson, Christopher H. 1988. *Maurice Sugar: Law, Labor, and the Left in Detroit, 1912–1950.* Detroit: Wayne State University Press.

Johnson, Ellen. 2014. *Jazz Child: A Portrait of Sheila Jordan.* Lanham, MD: Rowan & Littlefield.

Katz, Irving. 1964. "Detroit's Jewish Community in 1867." *Michigan Jewish History* 4, no. 2 (May): 11–13.

Kazin, Alfred. 1951. *A Walker in the City.* New York: Harcourt.

Keil, Charles, Angelika Keil, and Dick Blau, 1992. *Polka Happiness.* Philadelphia: Temple University Press.

Kelley, Mike. 1998. Talk at "I Rip You, You Rip Me," June 9, 1998, cited in Branden Joseph, "The Hippie Apocalypse." In *Hungry for Death: Destroy All Monsters*, edited by Cary Loren, n.p. Boston: Boston University Art Gallery, 2011.

Law, Arlene Sandra. 1988. "From Morality to Patriotism: The Role of School Music in Nineteenth Century Detroit." Ed.D. diss., University of Michigan.

Lateef, Yusuf, with Herb Boyd. 2006. *The Gentle Giant: The Autobiography of Yusuf Lateef.* Irvington, NJ: Morton.

Leary, James P. 2006. *Polka Billy: How the Goose Island Ramblers Redefined American Folk Music.* New York: Oxford University Press.

———. 2015. *Folksongs of Another America: Field Recordings from the Upper Midwest, 1937–46.* Madison: University of Wisconsin Press.

Leary, James P, and Richard March, 1993. "Farm, Forest, and Factory: Songs of Midwestern Labor." In *Songs about Work*, edited by Archie Green, 253–86. Special Publications of the Folklore Institute 3. Bloomington: Folklore Institute, Indiana University.

Leonard, Chantey "Legacy." 2014. "Strange City." In Clark 2014, 211.

Liebler, M. L., ed. 2016. *Heaven Was Detroit: From Jazz to Hip-Hop and Beyond.* Detroit: Wayne State University Press.

Loner, Lia 2014. "On Professional Female Harpists: 'The Delicate Fingers of the Ladies.'" *IAWM Journal* 20, no. 1: 5–9.

Maki, Craig, with Keith Cady. 2013. *Detroit Country Music: Mountaineers, Cowboys, and Rockabillies.* Ann Arbor: University of Michigan Press.

Maurus, Marc. 2001. "Five/Eight Time." In Boyd and Liebler 2001, 234–35.

Milan, Jon. 2009. *Detroit: Ragtime and the Jazz Age.* Charleston, SC: Arcadia.

Miles, Tiya. *The Dawn of Detroit: A Chronicle of Slavery and Freedom in the City of the Straits.* New York: The New Press, 2017

Miller, Leta E. 2011. *Music and Politics in San Francisco: From the 1906 Quake to the Second World War.* Berkeley: University of California Press.

Miller, Steve. 2013. *Detroit Rock City: The Uncensored History of Rock 'n' Roll in America's Loudest City.* Boston: Da Capo.

Moore, Deborah Dash. 2014. *Urban Origins of American Judaism.* Athens, GA: University of Georgia Press.

Morton, Chris. 2016. "Freeform Radio Master: Dave Dixon on WABX." In. Liebler 2016, 406–7.

Nethercott, Shaun S. 2014. "The Detroit Virus." In Clark 2014, 214–17.

Nettl, Bruno, and Ivo Moravcik. 1955. "Czech and Slovak Songs Collected in Detroit." *Midwest Folklore* 5, no. 1 (Spring): 37–49

Norton, Peter D. 2008. *Fighting Traffic: The Dawn of the Motor Age in the American City.* Cambridge MA: MIT Press.

Oates, Joyce Carol. 1969. *Them*. New York: Random House.

Ortner, Sherry. 2003. *New Jersey Dreaming*. Durham, NC: Duke University Press.

Owens, Keith A. 2014. "Music as the Missing Link." In Clark 2014, 164–65.

Palazzolo, Laurie A. Gomulka. 2003a. *Dom Polski: Dance Hall Days of Detroit's Polonia*, video.

———. 2003b. *Horn Man: The Polish-American Musician in Twentieth-Century Detroit*. Detroit: American-Polish Music Society.

Palm, Kristin. 2001. "Motor City Trilogy." In Boyd and Liebler 2001, 271–76.

Pablo Palomino, 2016. "The Musical Worlds of Jewish Buenos Aires, 1910–1940." In *Mazal Tov, Amigos! Jews and Popular Music in the Americas*, edited by Amalia Ran and Moshe Morad, 25–43. Leiden: Brill, 25–43.

Peterson, Susan Jo. 2013. *Planning the Home Front: Building Bombers and Communities at Willow Run*. Chicago: University of Chicago Press.

Phillinganes, Greg. 2013. Liner notes to *Grand River Crossings*. Motema 233768.

Piercy, Marge. 2015. *Made in Detroit*. New York: Knopf.

Prell, Riv-Ellen. 2007. "Community and the Discourse of Elegy: The Postwar Suburban Debate." In *Imagining the American Jewish Community*, edited by Jack Wertheimer, 67–90. Waltham, MA: Brandeis University Press.

Radecki, Patricia. 1981. *Southern Whites in Detroit: Final Report for Great Lakes Arts Alliance*. Detroit: Great Lakes Arts Alliance.

Rasmussen, Anne. 1997. "The Music of Arab Detroit: A Musical Mecca in the Midwest." In *Musics of Multicultural America: A Study of Twelve Musical Communities*, edited by Kip Lornell and Anne K. Rasmussen, 73–100. New York: Schirmer.

———. 2002. "Popular Music of Arab Detroit." In *The Garland Encyclopedia of World Music*, vol. 6, *The Middle East*, edited by Virginia Danielson, Scott Marcus, and Dwight Reynolds, 279–88. New York: Garland.

Rossen, Rebecca. 2014. *Dancing Jewish: Jewish Identity in American Modern and Postmodern Dance*. New York: Oxford University Press.

Salvatore, Nick. 2005. *Singing in a Strange Land: C. L. Franklin, the Black Church, and the Transformation of America*. New York: Little, Brown.

Sampson, Robert J. 2012. *Great American City: Chicago and the Enduring Neighborhood Effect*. Chicago: University of Chicago Press.

Savaglio, Paula. 1996. "Polka Bands and Choral Groups: The Musical Self-Representation of Polish-Americans in Detroit." *Ethnomusicology* 40, no. 1 (Winter): 35–47.

———. 2004. *Negotiating Ethnic Boundaries: Polish American Music in Detroit*. Detroit: Detroit Monographs in Musicology.

Schaver, Emma. 1948. *Songs of the Concentration Camps from the Repertoire of Emma Schaver, Arranged by Lazar Weiner*. Philadelphia: Itzchok-Hendele Foundation and Lazar Weiner.

Sinclair, John. *Guitar Army*. 2007. Los Angeles: Process.

———. 2016. "Strata Records." In Liebler 2016, 39–46.

Sklare, Marshall. 1971. *America's Jews*. New York: Random House.

Smith, Suzanne E. 1999. *Dancing in the Street: Motown and the Cultural Politics of Detroit*. Cambridge, MA: Harvard University Press.

Springsteen, Bruce. 2017. *Born to Run*. New York: Simon & Schuster.

Sugar, Maurice. 1965. Letter to R. Serge Denisoff, December 10. Walter Reuther Archives, Maurice Sugar Collection, Accession No. 232, Box 14, Folder 14.

Sugrue, Thomas. 2005. *The Origins of the Urban Crisis: Race and Inequality in Postwar Detroit*. Princeton, NJ: Princeton University Press.

Summit, Jeffrey. 2003. *The Lord's Song in a Strange Land*. New York: Oxford University Press.

———. 2016. *Singing God's Words*. New York: Oxford University Press.

Julius E. Thompson. 1999. *Dudley Randall, Broadside Press, and the Black Arts Movement in Detroit, 1960-1995*. Jefferson NC and London: McFarland.

Topouzian, Ara. 2015a. *Guardians of Music: Armenian Music in Detroit*. Documentary film.

———. 2015b. *Homage: A Tribute to Detroit Armenian Musicians*. Ara Topouzian Quartet. CD, American Recording Productions.

Tucker-Sullivan, Lori. 2017. "Bused in and Bused Out: How Judicial Rulings Changed Warrendale." In *The Detroit Neighborhood Guidebook*, edited by Aaron Foley. Cleveland: Belt.

Walden, Joshua S. 2014. *Sounding Authentic: The Rural Miniature and Musical Modernism*. New York: Oxford University Press.

WestSiders. 1997. *Remembering Detroit's Old Westside: 1920–1950*. Detroit: The WestSiders.

Wilson, Sunnie, with John Cohassey. 1998. *Toast of the Town: The Life and Times of Sunnie Wilson*. Detroit: Wayne State University Press.

Young, Al. 1981a. *Drowning in the Sea of Love: Musical Memoirs*. Hopewell NJ: Ecco.

———. 1981b. *Snakes*. Berkeley, CA: Creative Arts Book Company.

———. 2016. "A Top-Down Motown Bebop Prepubescence: Twelve Takes." In Liebler 2016, 3–7.

Index